Now *That's* Funny!

Now *That's* Funny!

Conversations
with
Comedy Writers

David Bradbury
and Joe McGrath

Drawings by Joe McGrath

METHUEN

First published in the United Kingdom in 1998 by
Methuen Publishing Limited
20 Vauxhall Bridge Road, London SW1V 2SA

1 3 5 7 9 10 8 6 4 2

Random House Australia (Pty) Limited
20 Alfred Street, Milsons Point, Sydney, New South Wales 2061, Australia
Random House New Zealand Limited
18 Poland Road, Glenfield, Auckland 10, New Zealand
Random House South Africa (Pty) Limited
Endulini, 5a Jubilee Road, Parktown 2193, South Africa

Methuen Publishing Limited Reg. No. 3543167

A CIP catalogue record for this book
is available from the British Library

ISBN 0 413 72520 0

Typeset by SX Composing DTP, Rayleigh, Essex
Printed and bound in Great Britain by
The Bath Press, Bath

From Joe for P. J. McGrath,
also known as Jimmy Jay, Principal Comedian

From David to Jane

Contents

Contents

Introduction

The men and women interviewed in this book are among the most distinguished and original creators of comedy in Britain during the past half-century. Not only have they kept this nation – and others – laughing with their inventions: many of them have also created characters and catch-phrases which have become part of our culture and language. Yet in comparison with their creations they are in many cases hardly known to the public, whose attention is first on the characters, then on the performers who bring them to life and only after that on the writers who imagined them in the first place. We think of Alf Garnett, then Warren Mitchell, then Johnny Speight; of Del Trotter, then David Jason, then John Sullivan. Some viewers, seeing Eric Morecambe and Ernie Wise once more greet André Previn, may not be aware that the scene was written at all, let alone that it was painstakingly conceived and typed by a Liverpudlian called Eddie Braben. Only in comparatively recent years have the professions of writer and performer largely merged into one, and the originators of the fun been able to share in the applause.

We hope these conversations with master craftsmen and craftswomen will help to enlighten readers about an extraordinarily demanding and difficult trade, much of it carried on alone and in a virtual vacuum as the writer faces the frightening question: Is this funny? The test comes later, usually at a read-through or rehearsal, when the material is first seen by the performers. This is not often an occasion for unrestrained hilarity but for serious, sober professional assessment. Eric Morecambe used to signal his highest praise for a line or an idea not by breaking into laughter but by peering solemnly over his spectacles and declaring firmly: 'Now *that's* funny! We can use that.'

Very small numbers of people, in the scores rather than the hundreds, earn their livings by creating jokes – so small that the scarcity value of comedy writers means that their livings are good ones – but even so there are too many of them to fit inside this book. So this selection is our personal choice, though most people will agree with a great deal of it. We were not able to speak to all the writers we would have liked to interview, and there will certainly be writers emerging into the business whose names we have not heard. We hope that we have spoken to a selection which, although it cannot be representative in a profession made up of such individualists, nevertheless shows their remarkable variety.

This book concentrates on the performing arts, which are at present dominated by television, so that is largely the medium under discussion, and all the people in this book have written for it. But many of them have also written films, novels, journalism, songs, plays, stand-up comedy and performance pieces, commercials and promotions, and radio – still a medium where ideas can be developed at little financial risk.

Radio and cinema were the dominant media when our writers pick up the story: *Take It From Here*, written by Frank Muir and Denis Norden, started its first series in 1948. The transition to television may have been easier than it now looks: one pioneer, Eric Sykes, advised Galton and Simpson on the essential difference between radio and TV. On radio, he said, you use the line: 'Pick up that bucket!' On TV the line is: 'Pick that up!'

Audiences have not always been ready for innovation: *The Goon Show*, in particular, divided families, in those days when a typical home contained one Bakelite-cased three-waveband five-valve superheterodyne mains receiver, because it was incomprehensible to anyone aged over thirty. And there will be those today who are baffled or even shocked by the ideas of the *TFI Friday* writers – Chris Evans, Danny Baker and Will Macdonald – on what constitutes comedy.

The growth of television seems now to have been predictable: why stand in a cinema queue in the rain to buy a ticket and a choc-ice when you can sit on your own sofa with a knife-and-fork supper on your lap, or at least a pot noodle in your mitt? But surely nobody could have foreseen the revival of the stand-up comic, who had apparently been buried under the rubble of the Metropolitan, Edgware Road, and the Ardwick Empire, but popped up again in Soho at the Comedy Store twenty years ago? So there is no attempt in these pages to see far into the future.

Our interviews were informal; although we had a basic list of questions, we did not ask them of every writer and their main purpose was to serve as prompts in case a writer's train of thought should run into the buffers. We wanted to hear what the writers themselves wanted to talk about, given the opportunity, rather than make points ourselves. Nevertheless, we did speak up from time to time, rather more often than would appear from this book; in editing the transcript of our tapes we have assumed that the reader will be more eager to learn the writers' opinion than ours. The interviews have been edited to remove the usual hesitations and false starts of unrehearsed conversation, and to bring more coherence to discussions which leaped freely from subject to subject; we have often altered the sequence in which subjects were raised.

Throughout we have had the pleasure of meeting people who were variously friends, heroes, legends, stars and complete strangers. They were unfailingly polite and generous with their time, and a nicer bunch of people you could not hope to meet. We left every interview uplifted by an encounter with talent.

Although all the writers in the book take comedy seriously, that does not mean that they are solemn. Nobody tries to build a mausoleum of theory about how comedy works, perhaps warned off by the famous story about Frank Muir and Denis Norden, appointed Advisers and Consultants on Comedy to the BBC Television Light Entertainment Department. On a talent-hunting visit to New York in the Fifties, they were introduced in their exalted roles to Mel Brooks, who gazed at them in awe and breathed: 'You mean you *know*?'

David Bradbury and Joe McGrath
June 1998

Two notes and some acknowledgements

Practitioners make a distinction between film and tape in the production of sketch shows and sitcoms. Typically, exterior scenes used to be photographed on 16 mm or 35 mm film, using one camera, with the actors repeating the scene if it needed to be photographed from a second or third angle. The same technique is still used, though generally with videotape and a lightweight portable video camera. People nevertheless refer to this as 'filming'. Studio sequences are as a rule recorded on videotape through a number of TV cameras, which are generally heavy devices mounted on wheels – 'Daleks' was Victoria Wood's name for them. The studio has to be lit from above for all cameras operating simultaneously: the result of this top-lighting is usually a flat, characterless picture. The director chooses shots for recording on tape by watching a group of monitors and 'mixing' from one camera to another; in effect, he edits the performance while it is in progress. Any 'filmed' inserts are screened at their appropriate places in the show for the studio audience to watch (and their laughter to be recorded). Most writers dislike being at the mercy of the speed at which the director or his vision-mixer can think, and some shows, such as *Roger Roger* in Britain and *The Larry Sanders Show* in the United States, are now being made in the studio with a single camera and without a studio audience. For others, such as *TFI Friday*, the bulky studio cameras have been supplemented by hand-held video cameras which provide flexibility at the cost of a less stable picture than that of the pedestal-mounted models.

There are several references in the interviews to Dennis Main Wilson, a name which is familiar to comedy people but is less well known to the general public. Wilson was the most influential and rebellious BBC producer-director in a particularly creative period which began in radio after he was demobbed in 1945. For the BBC Home Service he produced the first series of *The Goon Show*. For television he produced and directed *Till Death Us Do Part*, *Citizen Smith* and *Only Fools and Horses*. After retiring he claimed to be writing his autobiography, to be titled *Incest with Auntie*. Sadly, it was unfinished at his death in 1997.

We owe a debt of gratitude to Samantha Hill, who transcribed the great bulk of the interviews, painstakingly listening to hour after hour of tape, much of it interrupted by laughter. Any errors in the final version are, of course, due to us, not to her. We are also deeply indebted, for his support and encouragement, to our publisher at Methuen, Michael Earley, and his team, particularly David Salmo and Judy Collins.

Among the many people who assisted in the making of this book we wish particularly to acknowledge the help of Jack Bell, Lisa Clark, Melanie Coupland, Norma Farnes, Roger Hancock, Christopher Kenworthy, Tessa Le Bars, Daniel McGrath, Peter McKay, Tim Mack, Ann Miles, Shelagh Milligan, Mike Molloy, Jan Murphy, John Pilger, Piers Pottinger, the late Dennis Selinger, and Nick Storey and his staff at the Savile Club. Our thanks to them and to those who also helped but prefer to be anonymous. Our apologies to anyone we have inadvertently left out.

Denis Norden

Always have one secret

From the loose-limbed way Denis Norden lopes around his flat and office in Soho it is hard to believe that half a century has passed since he and Frank Muir began to write one of the funniest and best-remembered comedy shows on radio, *Take It From Here*. When *ITMA*, which had cheered Britain up throughout the war, ended in 1949 with the death of its star, Tommy Handley, *TIFH* took its place at the centre of comedy broadcasting with an appeal to listeners that did not halt at class barriers. In 1950 Muir and Norden launched the show's most enduring element, a weekly situation comedy about a prototype dysfunctional family, the Glums: the disreputable Mr Glum, played by Jimmy Edwards, his moronic son Ron, played by Dick Bentley, Ron's genteel fiancée, Eth, played by June Whitfield, and the disembodied howling of Mrs Glum, provided by the show's singer, Alma Cogan.

Muir and Norden moved into television with *Whack-O!* starring Edwards as a beer-guzzling headmaster with a predilection for caning small boys, a character which Nineties writers might find difficult to fit into a comedy. When the partnership ended amicably – its working methods are described in Muir's autobiography, *A Kentish Lad* – Norden concentrated on film scripts and also forged a new career as a writer-presenter of compilations such as *Looks Familiar* and *It'll Be Alright on the Night*, while appearing alongside Muir in the panel games *My Word!* and *My Music. My Word!* exploited their mastery of the extended pun, in which they are rivalled only by Myles na Gopaleen and his tales of Keats and Chapman. Out of sight of the general public, Denis Norden also writes scripts for sales conferences in association with Europe's largest company in the field of 'industrial theatre'. He had this conversation with us a few weeks before Frank Muir's death: at Denis's request we have kept references to Frank as he made them, in the present tense. After making coffee in the kitchen, Denis seated us around a big desk in a work-room lined with books, files and playbills.

DENIS NORDEN: What's the most difficult part of writing comedy? Two things, I suppose. One is beginning. Always beginning: Fred Allen, who was a great American comedian, used to say: 'Dirty the paper.' In other words, while that paper is white, it's virgin and it's in charge. Once you've dirtied it, you've taken its virginity and you're in charge of the paper. So I would always say, begin. And the other difficult thing, when you're writing a series, is that you have to get into a frame of mind where there's something working at the back of your head the whole time. For example, when I do an *Alright on the Night* it takes seven months to prepare it, to find the material, to look through literally thousands upon thousands of clips, of which at least ninety-nine per cent are just boring crap, but you get a gleam of gold somewhere.

So at the back of your mind, all day and all night for the seven months, you want something, thinking: Suppose I did a compilation about old ladies? or, Suppose I did a compilation about timing? and it's churning the whole time. You then write the script, do the show; and then the difficult part is to change that frame of reference you've set up in your mind, so that you don't go to the next job thinking in the same way.

Other than that, the difficult thing about writing comedy is toothache. Toothache's difficult. That's the great part about collaboration: it lets you have toothache in comfort and luxury; it makes toothache a pleasure when you've got somebody else there.

This desk here is the one that Frank and I used to write at, way back in the Fifties. It's what they call a partners' desk, in that it has knee-holes both sides and drawers both sides, and it was scruffy when we bought it. After working at it for about five years we decided things were going well enough that we could get a new desk. So we went down New Oxford Street, which was then the street for office furniture, and we went into showroom after showroom and they didn't have a partner's desk with the drawers both sides and knee-holes. We finally ended up at some place way down by the British Museum where we described it and the guy said: 'Yes, you won't, you won't get one. That partner's desk,' he said, 'they don't make them any more – because, you see, there aren't the number of partners today. There just isn't the trust about.' And that became a kind of little private code between Frank and me: There just isn't the trust about.

As for equipment, I work on a word processor . . . Is this the kind of thing you want?

DB: Well, it's interesting to people who are trying to write.

DENIS NORDEN: We used to write in longhand and then push the pages in to the secretary, who then typed them out – which was very good, because the script takes on a sort of different character when it's typed. And then Frank and I split, and it's very difficult, after eleven years of writing in tandem, to write on your own. When you're collaborating, if two of you think a line or a set-up or a situation is funny, then the odds are somebody else will. When you write by yourself, you're suddenly faced with the situation that you may be the only person in the world who thinks that's funny. So I used to do all sorts of terribly shameful things for reassurance. Like I would take the hand-written pages in to the secretary and leave them with her and then I would lurk outside the door. If I heard a snigger I would rush in and say: 'What was that? Which line was that?' Or if she wasn't there I would read it to the lift man.

But then of course along came the word processor, which has just changed my way of life – it's one of those great life-changing gadgets. I distrusted it until I had a particular job to do, a script which had to be handed in at midday on a Tuesday, and I left it on the Monday evening. It needed to be twelve pages. I'd done ten and a half pages and I came in here in the morning to do the last one and a half pages. I knew where I was going, but at about ten o'clock suddenly all the lights went out and there was an electrician working outside. I said: 'What have you done?' He said: 'I don't know. I just threw the mains switch . . .' I said: 'You couldn't . . .' and I went to the screen and it was blank. And I thought: It's gone. Everything's gone. And I have two options: I can cry and have hysterics, or I can try to remember. It's about half past ten, I've got an hour and a half . . . I'll try to remember as much of it as I can. I remembered the first sentence. And so I typed in the first sentence, and suddenly a little message came on the bottom of the screen, and it said: 'This exists in back-up. Do you want it?' And I typed 'Y' for yes, and it leapt on the screen and involuntarily I threw my arms around the computer and I said: 'You beauty!' And I suddenly realised: I'm alone in an office and I'm embracing a machine . . . But that did it, that cemented our relationship.

So now, no secretary, I work on my own, and always in this room. I've always believed in a parachute descent between work and home, office and home. I keep office hours, and I work five days a week, or, when we're on a project, six or seven days a week. I set myself a target to finish and I work on until half past five. But if I haven't hit the target, I stay until I get there, and then – well, the best advice ever was Hemingway's: 'Always stop, knowing what your first sentence is going to be next day.' So after I finish the target, I work out the next sentence, then pack it in.

JMcG: Do you prefer to work alone or with a partner?
DENIS NORDEN: When I was working with a partner I liked working with a partner. We split not through any rancour or anything: we split because we accepted a spell as consultants and advisers to the BBC Television Light Entertainment Department, and I hated that. I felt trapped within an organisation. I'm a kind of congenital freelance and I wasn't very good at being an executive. Frank (a) liked it, (b) was excellent at it. So it came to a point where we said: What do we do? Frank wanted to carry on, I couldn't wait to get out, so the sensible thing was to part. And everybody thinks, if people split up, then there's some ill will, and they treat it like a divorce, and they say, 'Well, who's doing your laundry?' But it wasn't in any way like that and in fact we speak to each other at least three times a week, and, if anything, we're sort of closer now.

Collaboration is a funny thing, actually. We used to sit across this desk, as I say, and two human beings weren't really meant to gaze at each other for that number of hours across such a small space. I worked with Melvin Frank for two years and he had a long collaboration with Norman Panama – they wrote some of the Bob Hope-Bing Crosby *Road* films – and he said that collaboration in some cases bears the seeds of its own destruction, and that we were wise to go our ways before rottenness set in. Frank's my closest friend and I'm his, and, you know, you should be able to collaborate and you should be able to work on your own. Alan Simpson and Ray Galton are wonderful at it, but like Frank and me they don't see a lot of each other outside their work. You find that people who are in each other's pockets don't tend to last as long.

Frank and I, really we only met when we were here in an office, and because we're two entirely different people – you know, it's terrible, this interview, it's like being in a health farm. The whole purpose of a health farm is that it allows you to go up to strangers and say: 'I lost three pounds today and I'm feeling a lot better.' It's a licence to talk about yourself non-stop – just like this kind of book.

Anyway, Frank and I had entirely different ideas about what comedy is. It's probably a reflection of the people we are: Frank thinks all the best comedy is essentially kindly; I think all comedy, all jokes, all laughter is a way of saying 'Thank God that wasn't me'. In other words, it's essentially selfish. So who is right? You can't lay down the law, but those are the two poles.

People laugh at different things. I've always been attracted to comedians who are untrustworthy, who play characters who are treacherous. I mean people like W. C. Fields, Larry Sanders, Groucho, Tony Hancock: you could never trust them, could you? As distinct from the lovables, the adorables.

A lot of people say that it must have been very difficult, writing comedy for radio, where you weren't allowed to mention sex, religion or politics, which are the very stuff of what comedy consists of today. And my answer is: 'Yes, but think how many things we could talk about that you can't talk about today,' meaning that our audience then was homogeneous – they all had the same references, the same allusions, the same kind of education. We could do jokes about specific poems, about Picasso, ballet . . . and everybody, while they may not have been experts, knew – you could rely on their knowing – what our references and allusions were about. There was a sort of common popular culture.

Nowadays, everything is much more fragmented. It may not be as compartmentalised by class, but the laddish group and the non-laddish group are just as wide apart as any 'classes' were, and there's no cultural cement that binds the football and lager-drinking jokers to the non. The country is divided, it's multi-cultural. Whereas in the past we could make references to names, to attitudes, that people shared. To films, for instance. We did so much about movies: every *Take It From Here* had a pastiche of a movie at the end of it. They have television today, but nothing in television is as much an event as a big Hollywood movie used to be. Everybody in the nation knew about it, they'd been to it, or they were going, whereas some of today's people will never watch BBC 2; there are even some who will never watch BBC at all – their set is jammed on ITV.

That kind of thing used to bind a whole community together, you see. It's subdivided so much now. So we didn't miss not writing about sex; in fact, we *did* write about it, but you had to do it ingeniously. The great one was Spike Milligan – what he got away with, with his allusions. But those ingenuity muscles that he had to exercise stood him in good stead; he then had them developed for the rest of his life.

I think most comedy needs a framework of common references and allusions. Comedy works very well when there are agreed social conventions and prohibitions it can butt its head against. Many great novels and plays are based on adultery and people doing the morally wrong thing. Most farces work on a common agreement that it would be just awful if, for instance, this guy's wife finds out he's spending the afternoon with a young lady at a hotel. Well, now that it's no longer the wrong thing, how can you be really funny about it? You can use words, words such as 'bonk' and 'fuck', but they don't replace the 'heavy', the authority figure: the policeman knocking at the door who's going to find out that the maid is in bed with the master. And because you haven't got those powerful figures any more, it's difficult for the comedian to register fright, dismay, the very stuff of comedy.

The Glums? What they were about to a great extent was that at that time engaged couples didn't do it. So Ron and Eth being engaged allowed us to make all sorts of comparisons, such as: 'It's like driving a car with one foot on the accelerator and another foot on the brake' or 'It's like being given a Christmas present but you mustn't open it until Easter' – those kind of things. People have forgotten that convention, that engaged people didn't do it, they waited uncomfortably until they were married. And as this was in the Fifties going on the Sixties, when change was in the air, Eth had all those passions boiling within which she couldn't articulate, she didn't even know what they were . . . And that was our 'secret' about her.

That's another good thing we learned, and I forget who we learned it from: 'Always have one secret about your sitcom characters that you never reveal to the audience in so many words'. Never utter it, but if you keep it in your mind you can make a sitcom character behave in ways that are not completely predictable – which is the bane of sitcom. For example, in *Whack-O!*, Pettigrew, the assistant master, loved Jimmy Edwards; he was in love with Jimmy physically – true homosexual love. That was our secret; we knew it, but we never revealed it in any way. But it motivated him, that physical devotion to Jimmy. And it always helped us.

JMcG: **What about Eth? What was her secret?**

DENIS NORDEN: Well, her secret was that she was boiling to do it. Without realising it, she was, as they say today, 'gagging for it', but she couldn't say it in so many words. Whereas Ron, he was a lump, he had no fires aflame down there. If you know that's what's happening in their heads, but you don't say it in words (not that the words existed back in those days), then you can kindle some humour. That 'Oh, Ron' was really, she was as horny as . . . But it was unsaid. The audience catch something of it, but they can't be sure, so it just becomes different. That's all.

DB: **What are you working on at present?**

DENIS NORDEN: They're just negotiating another contract with LWT for a further two years, and at this stage I'm looking at clips. Every show that I do, I inspect every clip that comes into the office. Then I do other things – conference work, for example, and that's great because it has an immediacy like television has. Films, as you know, can break your heart: it's hope deferred the whole time; you get paid, but you write things that don't get made. Whereas in television what you do gets made and with conferences you've even got a 'box office' because you have a client. And the client says: 'Yes, we liked that and we did business,' or, 'No, we'll never use you again,' or, 'We won't pay.' And not only does conference work put you in touch with a different group of people, the sketches you write get cast up to the top level. You get a top star cast, you get music, Gillian Lynne used to do the choreography, and you pick for yourself the ones where you end up in Rio de Janeiro or the South of France.

When we did these conferences, the sketches I'd write were often about some new product they were launching. One I remember was a food product to go into all the supermarkets, and the head of the company was watching the rehearsal of a sketch and I was standing about nearby. And he came up and said: 'Are you sure this is funny?' I said: 'If I was sure that anything was funny, you would be working for me, not me for you.' There is no way comedy can ever be anything but a risk venture, you can never know for sure. Noel Coward said: 'Write what pleases you. When it ceases to please an audience, get out of show business.' So all you do is you hope that if you find it funny, other people will.

It's impossible to convince anybody else, particularly somebody in authority over you, that a thing is funny if he thinks it isn't. There is no rationale, no logic you can use. What you've got to learn to do is cut it, and write something else, or hope that someday you'll get to a position where you can say to him: 'Listen mate, it's funny, and we do it.' But in most cases you should never waste energy and stress up the situation by trying to convince somebody who doesn't think it's funny that it really is. Particularly if it's a comedian who tells you: 'I don't like that line.' If he doesn't like it, he won't do it right, so give it away. Write another one.

DB: **Do you keep them and use them again?**

DENIS NORDEN: Oh, yes. They never notice. No, never throw anything away. We were into conservation long before the Government hit on the idea.

DB: **Are there any rules for comedy?**

DENIS NORDEN: Robert Benchley said: 'We must understand that all sentences that begin with a W are funny.' In *The Sunshine Boys*, one of the characters says: 'Words that have a K in them are funny.' Now, because there are no rules for comedy, those two rules are as good as any.

The only other rule that I found is that audiences don't laugh when it's hot. A cold audience, they'll sit there shivering and they'll warm themselves with laughter. But if it's hot, something physiological happens. It's like sex, I guess: it's easier to be horny when you're very cold than when it's 'Too Darn Hot', as Cole Porter said.

I do think there's a case for saying that there's too much comedy around, that one advantage we had back then was that there wasn't a lot of comedy to be had, whereas today every bloody thing is funny. You pick up a matchbox, it's got something funny on it. You go to a greetings card shop, you can get a funny condolence card, or Best of Luck With Your Gangrene. And so there's a certain laughter overload, or laughter exhaustion. Years ago, comedy was an event. There was only BBC on television, so if something like *Whack-O!* came on, they had no choice. They watched it and they were hungry for a laugh.

JMCG: **Is there anybody you rate highly now?**

DENIS NORDEN: Oh, lots of people. Paul Merton. Strange, complex sort of performer. I think he'd make any writer's mouth water because there's something there yet to be brought out – that quality that emerges when he's ad-libbing, and you think: How can you trap that? Josie Lawrence is another one who I think is a magnificent comedienne, really one of the great comediennes.

I think with this new stand-up thing – as a kind of generalisation – that their material is better than they are. They are essentially writers, they don't have the 'fun' quality. When you think of a Jimmy James, or a Sid Field or a Ken Dodd, they are funny people. I'm not talking about the comic actors but the real comedians, the performers who brought funniness along with them. Stand-ups are as good as their material, and their material is very good, but, on the whole, they don't add very much to it by their performance.

JMCG: **Which writers do you admire?**

DENIS NORDEN: Alan and Ray, I think, are head and shoulders above every writer who was around back then. Now that Harold Pinter's plays are set for O levels and A levels, I think they'd do as well setting Galton and Simpson's scripts, because they show the same grasp of the rhythms and the poetry of ordinary speech. And their pauses are equally as powerful. Today there's John Sullivan, who I think is a tremendous writer. He has all the old-fashioned virtues, creates a world that is completely true to itself all the time. Paul Whitehouse, I think, is a good good-ideas man, and full of quirkiness.

Victoria Wood stands head and shoulders above other solo comediennes. She ploughs her own furrow. The brand-name thing that she does has never been handled better by anybody. She does what Cole Porter did with lyrics.

Now that's another thing with writing. The amount of time that you waste on details like names, particularly in a collaboration. You'd say: 'We'll call him Paul.' 'I don't like that. I don't see him as a Paul.' It doesn't matter, but you spend hours . . . When Frank wrote his autobiography, the first thing I said to him was: 'At least you'll have no trouble finding a name for the principal character.'

JMcG: **Is there something that you really want to do now?**

DENIS NORDEN: In my line of country, if you really want to do something it comes out somehow in what you're working on. When I did *Looks Familiar*, the actual topic I was pursuing was 'middle age'. I was older than middle age at that time, but 'middle-aged' was as funny to me as 'engaged' had been. It's practically the same, in a way. You've got all the 'want to', but not so much of the 'can do'. So I did loads and loads of stuff about that. These days 'old' is fruitful. I had to do a radio programme for the Queen's seventieth birthday, and as I'd just gone seventy myself, I took a line about the 'consolations' of being that old. One is that you need only four hours' sleep. Trouble is, you need it about three times a day. I suddenly thought, Right, now there's another area, and it's now what that engine at the back of the head is dedicated to. It goes into the scripts that I write now; the jokes about the absurdity of old age emerge willy-nilly.

I'm not a writer, though. To my mind, a writer is somebody who creates a novel, or who writes a play. I'm more like a journalist with his own special subjects. You feel you're a writer, though, when you start earning your living by putting words down, and that began fairly early on after I left the RAF and started writing monologues for comedians on radio – *Workers' Playtime*, *Variety Bandbox*, that kind of thing. They all used to finish with a song for which they were given plug money by the publishers and that was the cash they gave me for writing their scripts. Which meant that if I wrote for Issy Bonn, who was what they'd call a 'big plug' – in other words, if he sang a song it would sell umpteen sheet-music copies – I earned

more money than if I wrote for Harold Berens, who was not considered much of a plug by the publishers. I had to write for a hell of
a lot of comics. One of them was Bill Waddington – Percy Sugden
in *Coronation Street*. He used to be a North-country comic – well,
he is still North-country, but in those days he was a very fast-talking
comedian. And a hard taskmaster.

The purpose of comedy? Well, other people may have different
views on it, but I think it is simply to cheer people up. That's all anybody has to do, in spite of all the claims made for satire, or for the
way comedy can change the course of history. Which it never has
done, incidentally . . .

One quintessential writers' story? I was chairman of the Writers'
Guild for a time, and there was an agent called Charles Tucker, an
American, who lived over here for something like twenty-five years
and drove a big car. But if he was ever stopped by the police for
speeding, he would say: 'Is that right, officer? I've just arrived in
your beautiful country.' He was almost a caricature of an agent.
Well, somebody once got in touch with him and said: 'Our local
Scouts put on a show twice a year in the Scout hut, which is so funny
and it's written by a fellow who's a railway clerk in Clapham
Junction, and I really think you should see these shows because the
writing is very, very good.' So Charlie Tucker went along to one of
these Scout shows, and it was excellent, all about a Cockney family
called the Larkins.

So he went round and found that the writer was a man called Fred
Robinson who, sure enough, worked as a railway clerk, in the ticket
office, and he said to him: 'Could I have a look at as many of those
scripts as you've written?' So Fred gave him, I think it was eight, and
he read them that night, took them to the BBC next morning and
said: 'I have a great series for you.' They came straight back to him
and said: 'Yes, certainly, we'll do these.' And they cast David
Kossoff, and so on, and offered £125 per script – the going price in
those days. Whereupon Charlie Tucker goes back to Fred Robinson
and says: 'I've read your stuff and I don't know. But, look, I'm a
gambling man and I'm prepared to take a chance on you. What I'll
do, I'll pay you £75 for each of these episodes. If I can sell 'em, I keep
what I sell 'em for; if I can't, all right, I'm a gambler, I'll lose.' And,
remember, he's already sold them. So not only did he make fifty
quid on each episode, but he charged Fred £7.50 commission on each
£75.

Now, the Writers' Guild got to hear about it, and I rang Fred up
and I said: 'Have you got a moment, because there's something I'd
like to tell you about.' This, incidentally, was when Frank and I had

an office in Conduit Street. So he came up – nice, ordinary-looking guy – and we explained: 'You're being taken for a ride. But the Writers' Guild will go to bat for you, because you're entitled to the *whole* £125. All right, pay him £12.50 commission, but that's all.' And he said: 'But I don't want it all. I'm already getting more money than I've ever had in my life. I don't even know how to spend £67.50 a week.' So that was that.

They then booked a second series and in the middle of it we get a phone call from Fred Robinson: 'Could I come up and see you?' Comes up, and he's wearing a camel-hair overcoat, with the belt – you know, one of those long belts – and he says: 'I'd like to take you out to lunch.' I said: 'Oh, that's very nice.' He said: 'I've booked a table at Verrey's' – remember Verrey's in Regent Street? – 'because there's something I'd like to discuss with you.' So I said: 'All right, it's only round the corner.' So Frank and I go down with him in the lift and as we're walking there he says: 'What are you going to eat? I know what I'm going to have.' I say: 'What's that?' He says: 'Scampi.' Now in those days, you see, scampi was the big luxury. He says: 'I have it all the time.' When we sat down he said: 'Now, remember you kindly offered to intervene for me with Charlie Tucker? Well, it would be a help now. The money doesn't seem to be going as far, and I wonder if you could get me up to the £125.' So we said: 'Certainly, Fred, no problem,' had a word with Charlie Tucker and he said: 'Oh, all right.' And he paid the money.

The lesson we drew from that, Frank and I privately, was that when you hear talk about people who have tasted of the tree of knowledge and were corrupted, the tree of knowledge at that time was scampi. We worked out that there was a scampi line. Beneath it were the people who had never eaten scampi and above it were the people who had it all the time. And once you'd got into that group, that was it for evermore. He died, Fred Robinson, soon afterwards . . .

Spike Milligan

A finger of God somewhere

The anarchic tendency in British comedy was represented in the Fifties by *The Goon Show*. It drew a generation into a fantasy world which excluded parents, schoolteachers and older workmates, to whom the cult – as it would be called now – was incomprehensible and irritating, particularly when whole classrooms of adolescents combined in mass mimicry of Bluebottle. Spike Milligan was the Goons' chief author, co-ordinating the apparent chaos generated by himself, Harry Secombe, Peter Sellers and, initially, Michael Bentine. Part of the delight which young rebels took in the Goons was in their irreverence towards the most respected institutions of the post-war era and such idolised figures as Churchill, Montgomery and Auntie BBC. Spike's scripts even subverted the announcer – for most of the show's run the pompous-sounding Wallace Greenslade – into reading out spurious credits such as: 'Script by Spike Milligan and Hugh Jampton.' The Goons eventually fragmented, Sellers's multiple talents taking him towards Hollywood and Secombe finding a series of niches for his ebullient personality and blowtorch tenor voice.

Milligan took on television with *A Show Called Fred,* and the Q series which followed it, the fearless innovations of which were watched attentively by the fledgeling writers who later combined to create *Monty Python's Flying Circus*. Alongside his writing Milligan developed a career as a performer of other writers' work, including a major West End success in *Son of Oblomov* which benefited from his own improvisatory powers, and appearances as William McGonagall, Poet and Tragedian. He also established himself as a best-selling author with a novel, *Puckoon*, several volumes of verse, and a hilarious series of wartime memoirs beginning with *Adolf Hitler: My Part in His Downfall*. Harry

Edgington, mentioned in the interview, was a comrade in the Royal Artillery.

Spike and his wife, Shelagh, have their home in East Sussex, where he is a living local treasure: mentioning just the name of his village at a shop in the nearest town brought the question: 'Are you going to see Spike, then?' On a wintry day the stone walls of the house gave it a grim, grey look. But Spike let us in and ushered us through to a warm, comfortable sitting-room at the rear of the house with a panoramic view of the Channel and the shipping. He started by talking about his earliest influences.

SPIKE MILLIGAN: My early influences were Edward Lear, Beachcomber, the Marx Brothers and W. C. Fields. They were the start. I used to laugh at them. I suppose the joke that set me off was in a Marx Brothers film. Groucho was in a room with Margaret Dumont, singing 'I love you, my dear', when suddenly there's a knock at the door. And she says: 'Oh, it's my husband!' Groucho says: 'What'll I do?' She said: 'Duck behind the couch.' So he went behind the couch and the husband came in and Groucho stood up and said: 'There's no duck behind this couch!' I thought that was marvellous. That set me off on abstract comedy.

After that time my first sort of intimation of writing funny was in the army. Harry Edgington and I used to be on signals duty and we'd write sort of Beachcomber stuff. Then we went overseas and it stopped. I wrote one comic limerick, the first of my poems. There was a chap in our regiment called Edser. It went:

> There was a young man called Edser,
> When wanted was always in bed, sir,
> One day at one,
> They fired the gun,
> And Edser, in bed, sir, was dead, sir.

That was the first comic verse I ever wrote . . .

I stayed neutral then until about 1947 when I heard a comic called Michael Howard. He never made me laugh, except one joke. He said there was an old woman who'd never seen the sea. So he took her there and she watched it and she said, 'Is that all it does?' I thought that was wonderful. So I started to write for him. And it must have been terrible stuff I wrote, because he paid me but then he borrowed £5. With interest, that's now about £110. Alas, he's dead. Well, they buried him, so he must have been.

Then there was a very early crazy show, no audience, that influenced me. *Men at Work,* it was called, and that used to make me laugh. I think Max Kester used to write some of it. Then I left the musical trio I was playing with because they weren't doing anything different – the same thing every night. So I decided to leave and the violinist said: 'Yew'll nevah fahkin' work agin.' Well, he was wrong. I went to work as a barman at Jimmy Grafton's pub. He was currently writing for the world's unfunniest comedian, Derek . . . what was his name now?

DB: **Derek Roy?**
SPIKE MILLIGAN: Derek Roy: he was on radio, *Variety Bandbox,* and when he came to the punch line he put a funny wig on to get a laugh.

JMcG: **On radio?**
SPIKE MILLIGAN: Yeah. I wrote a show with Jimmy Grafton and I realised Jimmy really wasn't, he was not really funny. I put some of my jokes in, which Derek Roy delivered, so they were certain death and I didn't think I was funny at all. Then I met up with Harry Secombe again and Peter Sellers and Bentine. We used to clown about and come up with these abstract jokes. Peter Sellers had an in at the BBC – it was Pat Dixon, he was a very avant-garde producer, he did *Breakfast with Braden.* I had somehow written a script and he took a chance and said: 'Yes, we'll do a show,' and the BBC, masters of the obvious, called it *Crazy People.* That meant they didn't think it was funny. They still don't. Anyhow, they broadcast *Crazy People,* which made the band laugh – thank God – and one of the jokes, which was Harry's, was: 'I've played the Palladium!' and Peter said: 'I've never heard it played better!' That was *one* of the jokes. So we went on. Eventually we had an audience that were tuned in to this type of humour. Larry Stephens, who wasn't really a funny writer, who was writing it with me, he died in my arms in a restaurant. So I was obliged to write it myself.

JMcG: **He died?**
SPIKE MILLIGAN: Well, he had high blood pressure and he used to take these blood-pressure pills in a glass of brandy. I said to him: 'You'll be the first to go, you know' . . . and I remember him looking at me, a horrible stare.
So I started to write on my own and I started to write full-length stories which I can only say were inspirational . . . I don't know where it came from. I had to get away from my little daughter, who

would come in and stop me, so I got an office with Eric Sykes. I felt I could get better, and I did improve all the time. I used to take a long time to write them. That was the worst part of it. I used to go and get on a train about nine o'clock, the Tube, and go to Shepherd's Bush, and I'd work, maybe till midnight, and sometimes there was no transport and I had to phone Peter Sellers to pick me up to take me home. So it was a hard slog and then I had this nervous breakdown and the AA towed me away. So I don't know, Joe, where it came from. No more than Van Gogh knew where his paintings came from. There's a finger of God in there . . . somewhere . . . The hundred and what-ty odd shows I wrote, I cannot tell you, Joe, how. I have no idea. It was inspiration, but I know not from where. I suppose it's me really, but I can't take credit for it . . . Where the ideas came from, I don't know.

JMcG: **You invented a complete world.**

SPIKE MILLIGAN: Do you know, to my amazement, I'd forgotten about it. I've never been very good at praise. I haven't a very big ego, but when my son was twelve he said: 'What's all these *Goon Shows*?' So I said: 'Well, I've got some on a reel here.' So Saturday morning in this hut at the bottom of my garden, he used to get all his mates, and I heard this howling laughter of schoolboys. He said: 'That's very, very funny, Dad.' It reoriented my thinking about it and now apparently I get two or three hundred pounds a year from these tapes released – I don't know whether they're released by or they escape from – the BBC. They're going to put six on near Christmas. I don't know why they're so fucking stupid. It's one of the funniest shows ever and they've got it sitting on a shelf. And they won't repeat *Q*, which was the most . . .

JMcG: **Which we did together.**

SPIKE MILLIGAN: It was a breakthrough in comedy. And *Monty Python* copied it. Mind you, I had some very talented performers in *The Goon Show*, Peter especially. Bentine, yes, we had him playing a part as Osric Pureheart, the inventor of the lead violin and the permanently submergible submarine, which was active until the crew died. And the Giant Bombardon – it's a huge tuba – which could fire a cannonball . . .

And then . . . very disappointing – not many people know this . . . then Michael Bentine said to Peter Sellers – and Peter recounted exactly what he said – he said: 'Look, we don't need Spike. He's not funny.' And that has stuck in my mind ever since.

JMCG: You were one of the very few people that I ever knew who could give Peter Sellers a reading of a line, and he would take it.

SPIKE MILLIGAN: He used to do it wrong sometimes. I had to correct him. Well, he was a very close friend. But the Clouseau films . . . except for 'zee aksant'. He only did previous stunts from comedy films. He was much funnier in *The Goon Show*. As for Bentine . . . Harry thinks he's wonderful. I went to his memorial service, and they all eulogised this bastard – whereas, he only bluffed his way. I went off him when he told me that his mother, sitting at a table, had levitated in a chair, and gone across the table and gone down on the other side. I just couldn't take that.

I was a very good friend of his; I used to adulate him and I publicised him, being brilliant with that funny look. He was not a comic or a clown, he was that extraordinary thing called a droll . . . He went on mixing up his act with spiritualism and jokes.

When I first saw Harry Secombe, in Italy, he used to speak at 100 miles an hour. Very young, and a Welsh accent. I honestly thought he was a Polish count. He was the greatest straight man in comedy. He played Neddy Seagoon superbly. He was perfect for it; that cutting voice.

JMCG: And you did some characters, like Little Jim.

SPIKE MILLIGAN: That line came from my father – 'He's fallen in the water!' We were on a liner coming back from India and the crew had rigged up a canvas swimming pool. My brother, who was about six or seven, couldn't swim. But there was a rope which he used to swing across, dangle his feet in the pool and go to the other side. One time he missed and he went under and this little girl said to somebody: 'He's fallen in the water!' and my dad came and pulled him out.

DB: Do you have a work routine?

SPIKE MILLIGAN: I get up in the morning, and I start to write and I work until the afternoon. Then I come down and have dinner. Watch some telly. Then I go to bed. Pretty routine, author's routine.

DB: Do you decide that you're going to do, say, a thousand words?

SPIKE MILLIGAN: No, I don't anticipate. I do as many as I can. I'm struggling to make *Treasure Island* funny, but there really is no room for putting in the comedy. It's all difficult to me, all very difficult to write funny. What I do is, I bowdlerise great classics like *Wuthering Heights* and my current book is *Frankenstein* and the next one is *The Homosexual Hound of the Baskervilles.* Owoooooooh, wow, woof, woof! They wouldn't accept it, because it was too short. Well, the original story is very short by Conan Doyle and it's the worst bloody story he's ever written; not plausible. Finally, my manager said: 'Look, just sell it cheaper.' 'Oh, that's a good idea,' said they. So instead of selling it for nine ninety-nine, they sold it for seven ninety-nine. Thank God they accepted it. Jack Hobbs used to write books with me. He would egg me on and laugh at what I'd written.

DB: **Is that how collaborators are helpful to you?**
SPIKE MILLIGAN: Yes, yes, yes. I would be inspired by his laughter . . . Yes, we wrote, I forget, *McGonagall meets Gershwin*, or something.

JMcG: **You must tell David the story about when Jack Hobbs was going back in the train . . .**
SPIKE MILLIGAN: Yeah. Actually, he went to Cyprus for a holiday and he got the squits when he was out there, and when he came back home from his holiday he still had the squits, but he went to work and, suddenly, in the middle of the afternoon, these fucking things come on again, and he says: 'Christ, I can't go on the train like this.' So he went to a shop in Queensway and he said to the man at the counter: 'Could I have a pair of trousers, 34 waist, and a pair of jockey pants?' The chap said: 'Right, sir.' He was getting a bit strong, so he went outside and walked about a bit. Then he went back in, chap gave him a plastic bag with the things in and he got to King's Cross, but, alas, the rush hour had started. He thought, I can't sit in a carriage like this – I'll go to the toilet, and he locked the door, and then he took off these terrible trousers and the underpants and threw them out of the window. Think of the poor blokes on the line! *Blonge!* So he opened the bag and all that was in it was a lady's pink cardigan. So he . . . he had no option . . . he started to put his legs through the arms and he pulled them up his body, like this, and forgot where the neck was, and all his lunch was hanging out. So he got his trilby hat and he tucked it all around the insides, so it looked like a giant hernia. Now when he got off, typical of the English, they don't comment on the obvious. They all went past him, never said a word. Except the ticket collector: he said, 'Ah, you've been on holiday, Mr Hobbs.'

JMcG: **That is Jack Hobbs in a nutshell. If anything was going to go wrong . . .**

SPIKE MILLIGAN: Yeah. But it didn't happen to him. It happened to his friend, who was with him.

DB: Do you see yourself as different people doing different things as a writer for radio, for TV or for books or poetry?
SPIKE MILLIGAN: I suppose basically I'm very talented, but I'm not personally aware of that. No, but that's what I am. I'm very glad that I can do it. I wrote a funny poem last week. I'll do it now.

> *I've got a three-legged dog,*
> *His name is Rover.*
> *Whenever he barks*
> *He falls over.*

The first 'I say, I say' joke I heard was: I said, 'I want to join the Navy.' 'You go to the bos'n at the British Museum at three o'clock on Saturday.' I went there. I said, 'I want to join the Navy.' He said, 'Can you swim?' I said, 'Why? Haven't you got ships?' It's very funny, isn't it?

I like Irish jokes, because they just aren't factual. My favourite (I used it in my act on the stage) is: An Irishman goes to a fish-and-chip shop, says, 'Fish and chips twice.' The guy says, 'I heard you the first time!'

Irishman goes to an optician. 'What's wrong?' 'Can't see.' 'Can't see?' 'No!' 'Right. Come outside in the garden. Look up.' 'Yes, yes.' 'Ah now, can you see the sun?' 'Yes!' 'How bloody far do you want to see?' There's a sort of abstraction about it.

Another abstract one: A drunk goes to a Dublin pub; the barman sees he's got this wonderful coloured parrot on his shoulder, says, 'Jaysus! Where did you get that?' And the bloke says: 'Ah, the trees are full of them.' Fucking marvellous jokes! Aren't they wonderful? Just abstract.

There's an Irish diver on a wreck at the bottom of the sea. Voice from the ship says: 'Are you down there, Mick?' 'Yes.' 'Come up right away!' 'Why?' 'The ship's sinking!'

JMcG: You used to go to Twickenham when Ireland were playing.
SPIKE MILLIGAN: Ireland always lose. There's a lovely Irish story about when they were very good about six years ago. They won the Triple Crown and decided to give the team a new captain, Ciaran Fitzgerald, an army officer. He called a meeting of the team and they said: 'Aw Jeez, Ciaran, come in. Have a jar.' He said: 'No, lads. First things first'. So he opened an Adidas bag and he took out a ball:

'Now, this thing here is a Rugby ball.' And a voice said: 'Jaysus. You're going too fast for us.' Isn't that marvellous? Only the Irish.

My father was Irish. He used to do an act. He was a bloody good clown. He told me about when he was a boy in Sligo. Very poor. The whole area was poverty-stricken. They'd go to church on a Sunday and the plate would go round and they'd give it to the priest, Father' McCartney. He'd say: 'Jaysus! The number of buttons in this plate, it's a wonder your clothes aren't droppin' off!' True story.

My father woke me up at three o'clock one morning and said: 'Son, I've never shot a tiger.' 'Oh, why do you have to tell me?' He said: 'I've got to tell *somebody*.' Maybe that's where it started.

Johnny Speight

Treading on everyone's toes

Johnny Speight brought to the television screen a contemporary comic character to rank with Mr Pooter and Lord Emsworth, though without their sweet-tempered natures. Alf Garnett, as brilliantly brought to life by Warren Mitchell, was so accurate, if exaggerated, a personification of the dark side of the British character that some people just could not see the joke; many of them took him to be their spokesman. The result was that every episode of *Till Death Us Do Part* seemed to leap on to the front page as the self-appointed advocates of various brands of self-righteousness whipped themselves up into a public rage over some sentiment Alf had expressed or the words he had used to express it. A brilliant cast, with Mitchell backed up, or, rather, challenged, by Dandy Nichols, Una Stubbs and Tony Booth, was skilfully directed by Dennis Main Wilson into intense comedy: Alf's frustrated rages were like thunderstorms in an armchair. The idea was exported to the United States for a sentimentalised version, *All in the Family*, with Carroll O'Connor as Archie Bunker. Johnny continued Alf's saga with *In Sickness and in Health*, and collaborated on other sitcoms: with Ray Galton on *Spooner's Patch*, about a police station, and with Eric Sykes on *The 19th Hole*, about a golf club (he was a member of several). Sadly, Johnny died while this book was in preparation. A few months earlier, he came from his home in Hertfordshire to meet us in the West End – in a private room at the Savile Club.

JMcG: **Tell us something about the problems of writing for a half-hour slot.**

JOHNNY SPEIGHT: You haven't got time for anything except getting down to the bones of it. It's not a half-hour, even, more like twenty-seven minutes on the BBC, and if it's a good one and you get 'spread' – where the audience laugh their heads off – you might have to cut some of the dialogue. We had eight minutes cut out of one show at the Beeb because it spread. Don't cut the dialogue, cut the laughs – otherwise the listeners don't know what the studio audience are laughing at.

Years and years and years ago I was writing a Frankie Howerd show for radio and for some reason during the recording Gladys Morgan, the comedienne on the show, came out dressed up in some funny clothes, which made the audience laugh. Immediately Billy Ternant, the bandleader, rolled up his trousers and put something like a model battleship on his head. Then Frank came on and couldn't resist: he started to arse about too. Now we went for about seven minutes of radio without a word being spoken – it was all this pantomime. I thought, Well, the producer, Alistair Scott Johnson, will obviously cut the seven minutes out for the broadcast. But when I heard it broadcast, it was all there: no dialogue, but screams of hysterical laughter! Monday morning I get a phone call from Jimmy Davidson, who was head of radio variety in those days – used to wear a green visor and his shirt-sleeves rolled up like an old-fashioned city editor – and he called me up to see him, and I thought, Well, I'm not taking the blame for it. I mean, I'm not going to be the fall guy on this, I'm going to put the blame where it belongs; it belongs to the producer: he should have cut it out. So I walked into his office and he looked at me and he said: 'You're a genius.' I said: 'What, Jim?' He said: 'You made radio history. You're a genius and that's all I want to say, Johnny. Keep it up!' I walked out, thinking: I'm in a madhouse.

After that I put in one script: 'Minute of silence. Suggest this could be recorded.' Got a phone call from Alistair Scott Johnson, saying: 'This minute of silence . . .' and I thought he'd seen the joke, but he said: 'It's very difficult to record.' I said: 'Is it?' He said: 'Yes, because we're getting atmospherics.' I said: 'What kind of tape are you using?' Pause. Then he said: 'I've just had a brilliant idea. I'll throw this idea at you, Johnny. What I suggest we do is: no one speaks for a minute; that will give you the silence you need.' I said: 'Brilliant. That's great. That is it.' When we came to do the show, Frank said: 'What's this bloody minute of silence?' And that was the end of that.

The way we're going on, with increasing repeats and more channels, we'll end up with a lot of television shows made by people who are long dead, and the audience that were laughing will be long dead. I've heard some of our laughter on other shows. It's distinctive laughter; you'll be able to say: 'That's Auntie Elsie laughing, that is – laughing on a show that she would never laugh at, or never got to see, and they're using her laughter unpaid.'

I'm sure that some of the shows now have no audience at all. You can hear canned laughter: it cuts off. Real laughter dies out . . . it doesn't stop dead. You have to speak the next line and you have to be careful you don't tread on a laugh; you have to really manoeuvre around the laughter. Treading on a laugh has always been a crime in comedy – I mean speaking the line while they're still laughing. Half-hour comedy shows are live. You record them but they are live, because you've got an audience there and once they've heard the joke or seen the scene they're never going to laugh the second time like they did the first time and if you go for a third time the spontaneity goes out of it completely. I always say that if the scene is going well, if the rhythm's going well, even if the actors are making little mistakes, unless it's a complete disaster you play the scene right through and then patch up afterwards. But immature directors say, 'Oops, stop, cut and start again'; it throws the actors and they worry that they'll never get the same laugh again and so that makes them less real than they would have been.

All the work is done in the rehearsal room and one of the big dangers is leaving the show in the rehearsal room. A good director will know exactly when to say, 'Let's leave it, let's go.' I always go to rehearsals; Warren Mitchell wouldn't work unless I was there. The script you take in is really a blueprint. Even the greatest play in the world is a blueprint until it gets to the actors and then it's still a blueprint when it goes to the audience, because a play is never a play until it meets an audience. Then you can test it out on various audiences to find out how a scene goes. You can find out very fast with an audience reaction. I mean, if it's nothing, you can't say, 'Well, they're thick up in Macclesfield,' you have to find out why they didn't laugh. Because they're the same in Macclesfield as they are in bloody London: if it's funny, they know it's funny. As long as it's in the same language, it's got to play anywhere where people are living under the same conditions. A very funny Neil Simon play set in New York will work in London, because people are living in roughly the same conditions, in a block of flats, all the same things happen . . . the plumbing goes wrong . . . all those things happen and they are recognisable as sufferings of people.

JMCG: **You wrote a lot for Peter Sellers in the early days of ITV, didn't you?**

JOHNNY SPEIGHT: It was for ATV, as it was then, and, God, when

I think about it now, it was thirty-odd shows on the trot, live, one after the other. It started with *The Winifred Atwell Show*, starring Morecambe and Wise, and that was followed by *The Dickie Valentine Show*, starring Peter Sellers, because Sellers had seen what I'd done with Eric and Ernie and asked if I'd write for him. By the end of that he was going on with his own show, called *The Peter Sellers Show*, and I wrote that as well. It's horrifying, isn't it, when you think of doing that now?

Peter was a very intelligent person and people were after him just for himself. They weren't concerned about the script or anything else – get Peter Sellers and you'd got a film – and he was left to worry about the script. Films have always been like that: not by the script but by the stars. Unfortunately it makes a lot of sense because the public are like that.

DB: **Are there any special subjects for comedy?**

JOHNNY SPEIGHT: Great comedy is about the sufferings of people, and the audience recognise them as their own sufferings, and you show the funny side of it and they laugh at it. The great writers have always written for the masses. I'll give you an example: my father had never read Bernard Shaw or seen a Shaw play, he'd just heard me talk about him. One day I went to the place where he was living in east London and he said: 'I saw that mate of yours you're always talking about, Bernard Shaw. One of his plays was on the box the other night. Very funny; liked it.' He would never go to see a Bernard Shaw play in the theatre. Wild horses wouldn't have dragged him there. Max Wall he'd go and see at a theatre.

Art should be able to go out into the marketplace and earn its keep. If it's art it should affect the whole people. Shakespeare did it properly, in front of real people. All the emotions in Shakespeare would affect everyone; the only thing that would be off-putting to some people is the fact that it's in blank verse. Modern people haven't acclimatised their ears to it. It doesn't make complete sense to them immediately, but the thoughts are great. The myth is that Shakespeare is only correct when it is spoken in the upper-middle-class English voice. Why did they snigger when Brando did Shakespeare? Brando is a great actor. The reason why he wrote all those soliloquies, Shakespeare, was to give the groundlings a chance to take aim with the orange peel.

DB: **Are you still using a typewriter?**

JOHNNY SPEIGHT: I use a computer now, because it gets rid of the longest walk of the day to the typewriter and the blank sheet of paper. You know that cliché you get in films: the writer puts the sheet of paper in the typewriter, then tears it out and crumples it up and throws it into the wastepaper basket ... Well, with a computer you don't have that, because you can just start writing knowing that if you don't like it you can wipe it off or remodel it.

Writing, and observing people, fortunately I get paid for it as well; it's a fascination and a hobby that I can't stay away from for long. All the other hobbies bore me after a while. The English language is a fascination and I'm still learning it. People ask me have I ever learnt any other language. I say it takes me all my time to learn English.

I don't go anywhere else where they don't speak it. If they haven't got the energy or the brains to learn English I don't want to know about them. It's all right taking the short cut and using these cheap and inferior languages, but the greatest language in the world is the English language and it dominates the world now.

JMcG: **Before Alf, you wrote *The Arthur Haynes Show* ...**
JOHNNY SPEIGHT: I had a Silver Dawn Rolls-Royce that I was very proud of and I was driving it to the BBC. At Hanger Lane then there was no underpass, just traffic lights, and I stopped at the lights and the door of the Rolls opened and some old tramp got in, and the lights changed to green and I had to move forward. I looked at him and after quite a time he said to me: 'Rolls-Royce, innit, Guv'nor?' I said Yeah and he said, 'I prefer them. You get a better class of people entirely in these.' He said: 'I've had a couple of cars go by, but I thought, No, I'll wait for something decent, and you come along.' And he started telling me his life story and about going to Southend to see his wife. We were getting down towards the BBC. He said: 'Now, keep straight on,' and I said: 'No, I'm going right here.' He said: 'No, keep straight. I'm going to Southend.' I said: 'I'm not taking you to Southend.' He said: 'Well, a pound, eh? How would that go?' So I said: 'Oh, all right.' I dropped him off and gave him the quid, and as soon as I got to the phone I rang up Arthur and I said: 'I've found this most marvellous character.'

The Arthur Haynes tramp character wore a lot of medals, but he had nothing to do with military service. I mean, I don't think a tramp would want to go into military service. I wouldn't think the Army would necessarily want him either, one of those people who would spend all their time in the glasshouse. There's a strange morality about tramps, they're a kind of outsider, which always fascinated me.

There's one saying, you want to get in jail for Christmas because of the hard weather: out on the streets in summer, but come cold

January, like, you're better off inside. It's always, you know, all my Christmas cards'll be in there, my Christmas pudding and my Christmas dinner is in there. And it's a fear you have a long time. The prison system is unfair in that it's a worse punishment for a middle-class person to go into prison than it is for someone further down the scale. For a middle-class person the actual fact of being in there is terrible punishment and what he has left outside, but certain people go in there and it's just a part of their lives.

I've got medals like Arthur's: I had to go to France in the end, but I went on D-Day plus, Thomas Cook were there when I got there. Alf Garnett was in a reserved occupation, on the docks, but talked about the war as if he'd been in it. He talked about it more than the ones that did go, in general. His get-out was No, Winston Churchill says I've got to stay here. I'm more important here, behind the lines, than I'd be at the front.

I grew up with Alf and people like him. They were all round me in the East End of London. Still are. In all the golf clubs and every-where you go, you find all the sods, wearing different suits and dif-ferent accents, you know. In fact years ago Robert Morley wanted me to write a sort of upper-class Alf and he wanted to play it. But people would have believed it more, accepted it more convention-ally, with the upper class talking that way and it would have been more respectable. The rhythms of the language are very important, and with a character like Alf Garnett you have to capture the rhythm of the way he would speak, the kind of words he would use, and if he used certain words he wouldn't use them correctly. I don't use phonetics: Warren Mitchell knows the voice and he knows how to say them. It's the way people talk, even the upper classes, they do not speak in complete sentences.

Dandy Nichols was marvellous – I mean a marvellous woman – she was great, and for the show so was Anthony Booth; and so was Una Stubbs: she really played that suffering daughter marvellously, you know. But Alf can stand on his own really, because he convicts him-self out of his own mouth; he doesn't really need people around him.

JMcG: **Why did you make Alf Garnett a Tory?**

JOHNNY SPEIGHT: It was because he lived among the working class all his life and knew there wasn't much they could do, so he went for the ones who had money, and he didn't realise they knew no better either. H. G. Wells said that he was fortunate that his mother was a domestic help in a big house so he lived below stairs and realised from a very early age that above stairs weren't very bright. So he got rid of all that thing very early, this reverence – like being brought up to respect your betters, this reverence for people above you – which carried this country, or muddled it along for a long time.

In the war we were made aware that other people's mistakes could cost you a lot, and it made you very wary, and you lost reverence for leaders and realised that they were making some bloody awful mistakes, and some of them should not have been anywhere near leadership. You were in the hands of idiots. One of the worst things about it was having an idiot corporal, just made up, telling you things you knew were stupid and you had to say, 'Yes, corporal,' and do it. From the very beginning the officer class that descended upon us knew damn all. In politics today, you see the big mistakes they're making, they're like doctors, they bury their mistakes.

JMcG: **Can you tell us about your latest screenplay about Alf?**
JOHNNY SPEIGHT: The question is: What happened to Alf's grandchild? Well, the daughter and her husband, they left, they couldn't stand living with Alf any longer, and he persuaded her to go back to Liverpool with him. After a few years he left her and the last time we observe him he's teaching Marxism to the Aborigines.

So the son, the grandchild, grows up in a single-parent family, because she can't go back, she can't stand Alf and his ways. He goes to school, he's quite good, she helps him, grammar school and all that; he passes his exams and his A levels or whatever. He goes to Cambridge, and up there he joins the Labour party because of his background – his mother struggling, Liverpool, that kind of thing. He's full of ideas, and he comes down from Cambridge and becomes an MP, becomes the Labour party leader, all unbeknown to Alf, and the election comes up and he becomes Prime Minister. As the film starts you see the election starting; there's pictures in the paper of the Armani-dressed, champagne-swilling little git from nowhere. Alf hates him.

After the election the unions have started to attack the leader on the grounds that he has no real working-class roots, and he's talking to the spin doctors and saying, 'What are they talking about? I was brought up in a single-parent family'. And they say, 'Well, go on television and talk to the people. Let them know you're one of them.' So he tells one of the TV presenters, Frost or someone: 'My mother and father, they were so poor they couldn't even afford their own home, and they had to share my grandfather's house.' And Frost says, 'Where was that?' And he says, 'Wapping, in Wapping.'

Alf's in the local pub and it's on television while he's drinking with his cronies. Frost says: 'What was the family name?' And he says, 'Garnett. Garnett was the name. Garnett.' It's like in a Western: all the drinks go down, and every eye turns and looks at Alf, who just can't believe it. It's like when the gunman comes in and everyone stops: what's going to happen now?

Some people might see it as an attack on New Labour. It's not; if anything, it's an attack on all politicians. Alf treads on everyone's toes, you know: you think he's on your side for the moment . . . The Liberals thought that at one time, but suddenly found out that he was attacking. What he does is he takes their beliefs to their logical conclusion and they're hoist by their own petard, sort of thing.

DB: **What does Alf think of New Labour?**

JOHNNY SPEIGHT: He would prefer the original, not the copy. I mean, how do they get away with it? We put up with it; we put up with it all the time. I think we should persuade the British public not to vote at all for anyone. It must be a joke around the rest of the world. If elections changed anything, they'd make them illegal. You know what happens in an election: a lot of the public vote Labour, a lot more than vote Tory, and the next day nothing's changed: the same poor people live in the same poor houses, and the rich people live in the same rich houses, and Labour's own MPs get better houses for themselves, better cars, and the rest of us go on the same as we ever did.

The political situation makes it difficult for you to get comedy on. Because they don't like reality, they don't like the truth being pointed out and laughed at. I had a comedy for Eric Sykes, called *The 19th Hole*, about golf clubs, and that was taken off because it wasn't politically correct. How you can write about a golf club in politically correct terms, I'll never know, because they treat their own wives as second-class citizens. It seems to me they don't want anything realistic on the television – especially if you're making jokes, serious jokes, about the people who are supposed to be running the country.

If we all knew we were going to live to 500 years, 600, 700 years old, our plan would be a lot different, but the public now has never been really keen on socialism, or Christianity for that matter, because it means looking after others; and no one really has got much time or inclination to look after others until they've got a lot of time on their hands, and then they'll poke their noses in for the wrong reason, and start looking after you in the way you don't want them to. But if we all knew we'd still be here in 700 years' time, we'd all be much more aware of things happening on our planet because we'd know we'd be here to face the possible results of our own actions.

Ray Galton and Alan Simpson

Two guys who are still friendly

Comedy seems to be haunted by the troubled spirit of Tony Hancock, who was given his special place in the affection of the public by the character so superbly moulded for him by Ray Galton and Alan Simpson: Anthony Aloysius Hancock, unemployable actor and layabout, residing in seedy self-delusion at Railway Cuttings, East Cheam – an instantly ridiculous location which could hardly have suggested itself to anyone but two South Londoners. Galton and Simpson are the first writers in this book too young to have served in the Second World War and, in fact, were not well enough to be conscripted into National Service: they met and began to collaborate at a sanatorium for tuberculosis in Surrey. After taking Hancock to stardom on radio and television, Galton and Simpson were offered *carte blanche* to write half a dozen thirty-minute comedies, effectively as pilots for possible sitcom series, under the title *Comedy Playhouse*. One of them, *The Offer*, gave the first glimpse of the war in the junkyard that was the background to *Steptoe and Son*. The series starred Wilfrid Brambell as the father, cheerfully wallowing in the gutter, and Harry H. Corbett as the son, Harold, wistfully gazing at the stars. Galton and Simpson also worked for the movies – the British film industry was then in one of its periods of non-recession – on such pictures as *The Wrong Arm of the Law*. In private life, they became gourmets and connoisseurs of wine. Alan retired, to become chairman of his local Hampton Football Club – now promoted to the Football League – and take gastronomic journeys to France. Ray continues to write and has lately used his encounter with Alan in the sanatorium as the basis for a sitcom, *Get Well Soon,* in collaboration with John Antrobus. They travelled together from their homes near each other in Surrey to talk with us at the Savile Club.

JMCG: **Didn't you start your career by sending a letter to Frank Muir and Denis Norden when they were writing** *Take It From Here* **?**

ALAN SIMPSON: They wrote back and said: 'The best advice we can give you is to write a script and send it to Gale Pedrick at the BBC script department, who we know are avid for new writers' . . . avid.

RAY GALTON: We had to look that word up, avid.

ALAN SIMPSON: So we wrote to Gale Pedrick and his letter was sent to my house and I immediately got on a bus and went over to Ray's house – we didn't have a phone . . .

RAY GALTON: We had a bus, but we didn't have a phone.

ALAN SIMPSON: I remember running down to his house and waving the letter like Chamberlain did the paper – you know, Look, look, look, look! Because it was British Broadcasting Corporation and it said 'Dear Mr Galton and Mr Simpson' – this is from Gale Pedrick – 'We read your script and we were highly amused by the content. Do not read more into this than appears on the surface but we would like to meet you . . . and make an appointment with my secretary.' And we went out and got pissed.

RAY GALTON: Legless.

ALAN SIMPSON: Because even if we had gone nowhere further we had a letter from the BBC saying that they found it amusing, and it's like winning a medal at the Olympic Games, isn't it? At least when you are trying to pull a bird you can say, ''Ere, look. Read that!'

RAY GALTON: 'I'm not rubbish, you know.'

ALAN SIMPSON: 'You're not dealing with a wanker here; look, I got a letter from the BBC!' We phoned up Gale Pedrick and went up to the meeting at Aeolian Hall and he was charming, a lovely man.

RAY GALTON: In Bond Street, just around the corner from here.

ALAN SIMPSON: He took us under his wing. He told us lovely stories about how in 1930 he got a job with *The Times* earning £20 a week. He had a flat in the West End, dined out at Café Royal every night, you know, on £20 a week.

RAY GALTON: Well, actually, he was getting twelve guineas a week and this was for the BBC before the war and he lived in Mayfair.

ALAN SIMPSON: Anyway, he gave us a lovely interview and took the script we'd written and put it around the department. It was a pirate sketch for *Take It From Here* about Henry Morgan.

RAY GALTON: Captain Henry Morgan.

ALAN SIMPSON: Captain Henry Morgan. Jimmy Edwards played him, and Dick Bentley was . . . I don't know who; Joy Nichols was the girl stowaway or whatever. Jokes like: 'I will drive!' 'No, you can't; you've not driven a boat before.' 'But I insist on driving!' 'See, you've run the ship aground. I told you to practise what you beach!' All puns. The entire script was full of puns.

RAY GALTON: There was one good joke.

ALAN SIMPSON: There was one good joke, which was the only joke that was ever used out of that. I'll let my colleague tell it.

RAY GALTON: It could still be used today! It was about the crew below, playing Jane Russell pontoon. He says: 'Jane Russell pontoon? What is Jane Russell pontoon?' 'It's the same as ordinary pontoon only you need forty-eight to bust!' 'Now look here . . . !'

ALAN SIMPSON: That was the only joke that was ever used. Another was: he says, 'The side of the ship . . .' 'Sides of ships are bulwarks!' 'Bulwarks to you, too!' That one was never used.

RAY GALTON: We still haven't got a better joke than that one, forty-eight to bust. It was Pedrick's job to find new writers.

ALAN SIMPSON: To the day he died, Gale always used to be so proud of Ray and me as really the only ones he ever found. We were the ones who justified his existence. Writers were hardly heard of in those days. There were about a dozen of them in radio. The kings were Frank Muir and Denis Norden – they were the governors – and then you had Sid Colin, Eric Sykes, obviously, with *Educating Archie*, George Wadmore, Spike Milligan . . . Bob Monkhouse and Denis Goodwin. Ray and I sort of got in on the ground floor when we were twenty, twenty-one.

RAY GALTON: George Wadmore was the lead writer on *Ray's a Laugh*. He used to sit in his tiny car behind the Aeolian Hall with his portable typewriter, knocking out the 'wheezes' for *Ray's a Laugh*. You'd say to him: 'How are you going, George?' He'd say: 'I'm knocking out a few wheezes.' Dennis Main Wilson really gave us our first break – he said: 'I want these two to write the show.'

ALAN SIMPSON: It was *Happy Go Lucky*, with Derek Roy. Roy Spear, the producer, had a nervous breakdown and Dennis Main Wilson took over.

RAY GALTON: It was in the basement of the Playhouse Theatre. Jim Davidson, who was the Billy Cotton of Australia, came to the BBC and took over variety and all that crap. He assembled the cast at the Playhouse and delivered a Hollywood speech: 'OK, kids, we've got a turkey on our hands, but you're all troupers and we're going to turn it round.' All their shoulders went back and they did it. We thought: Hey, this is show business. Next week we were summoned to Derek Roy's lounge – we'd never been allowed in before – and we were introduced to Dennis Main Wilson. He said: 'Are you writers? You will write the next series.' The entire show had collapsed. Derek Roy and his wife had a lot of transcriptions of American radio shows sent over from the States and they couldn't see any reason why they shouldn't just use them as they were, whole chunks of them – *Ozzie and Harriet*, *Allen's Alley*. They just didn't work with a British audience.

When we first took *Steptoe and Son* to the States, CBS said they had problems because everyone in it was from a different ethnic background. So we suggested they do it black. When CBS dropped out three years later Norman Lear and Bud Yorkin said could they do it black, and we said yeah, course you can.

ALAN SIMPSON: They cast Redd Foxx, a great comic, a really filthy comic, against a young actor; it didn't have the balance that Wilfrid Brambell and Harry H. Corbett had. So they had to build a group around Redd Foxx and make it a quite different show.

RAY GALTON: Jack Benny wanted to do the show at first, but he decided he was too old: He said: 'I won't last halfway through the first series.'

ALAN SIMPSON: He suggested Mickey Rooney for the Brambell part. Benny kept ringing up to offer ideas.

RAY GALTON: The heart of the BBC was the BBC Club. It was the greatest place in the world. There were people doing everything in different groups in the same room – *Z Cars* over here, *Not Only But Also* over there . . .

ALAN SIMPSON: They wanted Eric Maschwitz – he wrote 'A Nightingale Sang in Berkeley Square' – to take over Light Entertainment, and they took him all round the BBC, and then said: 'Let's talk salary.' And Eric said: 'I don't want any salary. I'll just take the franchise on the BBC Club!'

JMCG: I remember that in the Sixties you were writing films for Peter Sellers, like *The Wrong Arm of the Law*.
RAY GALTON: Peter kept changing his mind about what part he should play. I mean, he was going to be the policeman and then he went back to being Pearly Gates, the crook. Halfway through the first week he just said to Lionel Jeffries: 'I've got the wrong part here, Lionel.' He said: 'It's your film, but I'll do my best for you.'

ALAN SIMPSON: He said: 'This is your film', and he just played to Lionel.

RAY GALTON: When Peter came back from Hollywood with that massive heart attack and was down at Elstead . . .

ALAN SIMPSON: First thing he did was marry Britt Ekland.

RAY GALTON: Bill Wills, who was Peter's money man, he got on to us and said Peter would like to make a film, an English film, a domestic English film, nothing too . . .

ALAN SIMPSON: Strenuous.

RAY GALTON: . . . strenuous. So we said, 'Right.' Well, funnily enough, we were beginning to write a film then and Peter might be ideal for it. It was *The Spy with a Cold Nose*.

ALAN SIMPSON: We finished the screenplay.

RAY GALTON: And we took it down to Peter and he could only read it in sections because he was rolling about on the floor. There he was, just died thirteen times on the operating table, and he was rolling about with hysterical laughter and I thought, Christ, we're going to kill him.

ALAN SIMPSON: Peter said: 'We'll make it ourselves. We don't want to bring in any studio; we'll hire the studio and we'll use your company name.'

RAY GALTON: We said: 'Look, are you sure, Pete, that you are not tied up in any way?'

ALAN SIMPSON: He said: 'I can do what I like, do what I like.'

RAY GALTON: 'No, no, no, I can do exactly what I like.'

ALAN SIMPSON: He said: 'We'll get Lionel to play the policeman. I'll play the vet.'

RAY GALTON: At that moment he just wanted to work.

ALAN SIMPSON: Well, we thought, Hello, here we go! and we were just waiting for the call and suddenly, about three or four weeks later, we got a phone call from Bill Wills: Will we go up to a meeting in Soho to discuss the Peter Sellers movie? So we think: Here we go, now it's starting up. And Peter wasn't there, of course. Anyway, the thing was now, the problem is that Peter is under contract to do a film in Paris called *What's New, Pussycat?* written by Woody Allen, so to cut a long story short he can't do yours, ducky, and that's basically what it is and thank you very much, good night. So we made the film with Larry Harvey and Lionel.

JMcG: **All these years later I can tell you why he couldn't do it: he told me that no company would insure him to do a movie because of his bad health. Then Charlie Feldman, who produced *What's New, Pussycat?*, insured him personally. And after Peter got through that, he became insurable again.**

ALAN SIMPSON: Well, Joe, I wish I'd known that, because for years we've been saying he was totally unreliable. We thought it was another example of Peter's capriciousness and waywardness. I'm glad we came, now.

DB: Tell us about working together again, adapting *Hancock* and *Comedy Playhouse* scripts for Paul Merton.
ALAN SIMPSON: We were very pleased with Paul Merton – working with him, you know, great. The first thing we said was, 'It's your career,' which he thought was quite funny. We warned him right at the beginning that it was dangerous, because of the Hancock fans and people who identify with the show. But everybody went into it with their eyes open and I think in a way it's done Paul good.

One problem is that the shows are for ITV, which means twenty-two minutes of material in each half-hour show. When you do a BBC show it's twenty-seven minutes of material. Now five minutes in half an hour is a long, long time. That's a lot of development, a lot of characterisation, a lot of plot, which you have the luxury of in a BBC half-hour. The biggest problem that Ray and I have in adapting for Paul Merton is the BBC half-hours where you have to take five minutes out. Taking five minutes out of any of the Hancock shows is surgery, major surgery.

DB: Some of the later Hancock shows are disturbing because Hancock's eye-line is all over the place, looking for the cue-cards.
RAY GALTON: When some of the radio stuff was re-created for a record because the BBC realised they had a fortune on their hands, Tony's timing, which was his great asset, was completely gone, and we were ten minutes over.

ALAN SIMPSON: This was in '64 when Tony was really gone, and Ray and I went into the studio and edited the performance down to half an hour by taking out the pauses which shouldn't have been there in the first place. Tony had been the greatest timer ever. That is very sad.

DB: It's interesting that they should revive your shows rather than commission new ones.
ALAN SIMPSON: If Ray and I were writing together now we would stand more chance of getting it on than two unknowns. Because we are Ray Galton and Alan Simpson and they don't want to take chances – you know: it must be good because Galton and Simpson did it.

RAY GALTON: I don't know, there's another thing. In all the years since *Steptoe and Son* finished, the BBC never asked me – and I don't know if they knew Alan had retired – they've never asked me or us jointly whether we would like to write any more, and that's going through all their ups and downs and everything else. Never asked us whether you are alive or dead or whether you would like to write. Nothing, not a word. The only reason I can think of is the same situation exists as existed in the BBC in 1945, '46, '47, when all the people in charge of the BBC were just out of the war and so were all the comedians and writers probably and it was all new, young and new, the broom was sweeping through the corridors. The new generation started, I suppose, with the Footlights at Cambridge, *Beyond the Fringe* and all that, so there weren't just new artists, there were new producers, new directors, and they were employing their own, I suppose.

JMcG: **Ray, you and John Antrobus have now done *Get Well Soon*, a sitcom based on how you and Alan met in a TB sanatorium in 1947. What sort of thing were you and Alan writing at that time?**
RAY GALTON: In the sanatorium I was in a ward, a two-bed ward, and half the room was taken up with engineering equipment that belonged to the other fellow – you've got to bear in mind that people are there for three years, not two weeks; virtually it's your home. Also this guy had an RAF radio receiver out of a Lancaster bomber, a very powerful thing, so he threw an aerial up and connected it to six or seven cubicles so that we could all listen to American Forces Network, great jazz and comedies broadcast from Bavaria. And then the guy, in a dressing gown and pyjamas, and me on absolute rest, not supposed to be doing anything, we covered the whole sanatorium with a secondary radio network, climbing all over the women's quarters and everywhere, and built a radio room in a linen cupboard, where Alan and I first started writing. We wrote half a dozen . . .

ALAN SIMPSON: Supposed to write six and we ran out of ideas, dried up. We contracted for six quarter-of-an-hour shows. For Radio Milford at the sanatorium.

RAY GALTON: I got extra mince at lunchtime. That was the deal, I think.

ALAN SIMPSON: We performed it – never get Ray on a stage now, but in those days he was working away like a good 'un. It was called

Have You Ever Wondered? and it was a satire on sanatorium life about nurses and doctors . . .

RAY GALTON: What they really do when the door shuts.

ALAN SIMPSON: Have you ever wondered what would happen if . . . if the patients ran the sanatorium? That sort of thing. Only Ray and I and a couple of our friends were doing the voices, hand mikes, had a sound-effects man, you know; it was all done very professionally.

RAY GALTON: This is where we started. It was a couple of years later, after we were out, that we wrote to Muir and Norden. I had a job and Ray was on National Assistance.

DB: You shared an office to write in later?
ALAN SIMPSON: I used to do the typing because in between the sanatorium and becoming a writer I was a shipping clerk, so I learned how to type. Ray had no reason to learn.

RAY GALTON: Still no reason to.

ALAN SIMPSON: So we used to work all the time, but he used to look to see what I was typing. If I did dagga, dagga, dagga, dagga on the keys, he'd say: 'What, what, what? What's that?'
   The only reason I packed up is because I thought: I cannot spend the rest of my life doing this. If I didn't have the money I'd still be doing it. My wife died and I suddenly realised I had enough money, with no children, to live the rest of my life. After-dinner speaking, I would do that till the cows come home. You, on the other hand, carry on writing. Ray is different. Ray is prepared to spend the rest of his life doing it because that's what he likes. That's what Ray wants to do with his life and in that case why do anything else?

RAY GALTON: Can't put a shelf up at home, you know, but . . .

ALAN SIMPSON: No, but every three days away from the work on holiday, he feels guilty. When was the last time you went on holiday?

RAY GALTON: I don't know.

ALAN SIMPSON: Twenty years, thirty years and dragged by his wife or his daughter saying, 'You've got to go . . .' But can't wait to get back to working.

RAY GALTON: Alan and I never put a word down that wasn't agreed between us. In the same room. I mean I would come in and say: 'Oh, I had a good idea . . . you know, out with the dogs this morning, you know . . .'

ALAN SIMPSON: When we shared an office I was never angry if Ray wasn't there, because I knew I wouldn't have to work. In the early days he was always first and I was always later. We could go two or three days without talking to each other. We'd never say it was crap, we'd just grunt. If one said something and the other said nothing, then you knew you were wrong. If we were in good nick we'd talk about things, but I can remember going four days without saying anything.

RAY GALTON: Although I love Alan and he loves me there was some hostility – something to do with who said the last thing. It could last for days. I'd say: 'Are you going to say something?'

ALAN SIMPSON: I will always give way to Ray. If he'd said we're not going to do this today, we wouldn't be doing it.

RAY GALTON: I don't know how Alan puts up with me – I thought I wasn't very nice to him. He was always the pussycat, he'd never say: 'Where have you been?'

ALAN SIMPSON: I didn't mind where he'd been. If he wasn't there, I didn't have to work.

RAY GALTON: I'd be waiting for him to say something that would advance the script. So I thought: It's not up to me to say something. I've done my bit. Well, fuck it. I don't know how we survived as two guys who are still friendly. It's a marriage. I was perfectly horrible to you – I don't know how we did it.

ALAN SIMPSON: If I'd behaved to you the same way you'd have thought it was totally indefensible. But as it was, I thought it was great. He'd make some excuse, and he'd be gone. If I'd been late he would have wanted to kill me. I just thought: I don't have to work – lovely!

RAY GALTON: You see, my wife didn't understand that I could go to Christine Keeler's flat and just talk to her.

ALAN SIMPSON: Neither did I.

RAY GALTON: Alan was never interested in the *demi-monde*.

ALAN SIMPSON: I'm not the slightest bit interested in show business as such. The best six years of my life were the ones between 1979 and '85 when I wasn't working and the world was my oyster.

RAY GALTON: Now I see him every Monday. His cleaning lady chucks him out of the house.

ALAN SIMPSON: I found out he was getting upset.

RAY GALTON: He brings his own sandwiches and my daughter makes him meals to take away.

Keith Waterhouse

Living in compartments

Keith Waterhouse became master of the Fleet Street columnist's trade when it was highly competitive and an unwritten agreement restricted popular newspapers to one star each – women, political editors, gossip-writers and sports journalists not counting for the purpose of the treaty. Now, of course, the floodgates have been opened to scour the papers' pages clean of costly news, and Keith is up to his ankles in column-mongers. He smiles with genuine approval on some promising ones; but his oblong, as he once described it, stays impregnable, though not in the same place. He has compared himself to an act on the variety stage: if the Holborn Empire no longer offered the appropriate environment for the act, he would move it to the Palladium. So Maxwellisation brought the transfer from the *Daily Mirror* to the *Daily Mail.* But the column is only one aspect of Waterhouse: there is a steady flow of novels, with *Billy Liar* already a modern classic, and of plays: *Billy Liar* once again, making stars of its first two leads, Albert Finney and Tom Courtney, and *Jeffrey Bernard is Unwell,* which brought Peter O'Toole a West End triumph. And, with or without his long-term collaborator Willis Hall, there have been movies, musicals, television series, and two books which show that Keith is, more than most writers, conscious of his craft and the need to pass on its skills to a new generation of practitioners, *Newspaper English* and *English Our English.* He has described his progress from south Leeds to the West End in two volumes of memoirs, *City Lights* and *Streets Ahead.* Keith is gregarious, making friends wherever he goes, but generally hides from the limelight. We talked at the Savile Club, starting with his daily routine.

KEITH WATERHOUSE: I just start, and I go on until I've done a thousand words and then I stop. That's my routine. And coming to the humorous side of it, if I've drafted a sentence that isn't funny, then I try to make it funny, if it's apposite that it should be. To give you a concrete example, in one column I was talking about privacy, about how Prince William survived with a girl on a Greek island and there were thirty photographers up a tree. Well, originally I'd written 'and the Press are there in force', which doesn't create any kind of image. Thirty photographers up a tree isn't particularly funny, but you get an image of something, don't you? So I alter stuff all along on that basis. I really use humour as a narrative tool more than anything else, just to help the flow, help the words along. Also you can say things humorously that you can't say seriously. It's a kind of anaesthetic, isn't it? You can get away with more if you write humorously. I hate that word, humorously.

The aim isn't comedy. The aim is simply to be read, and the humour, I think, makes it easier to read it, propels it in some way. I'm always conscious that the thing has got to have flow, that it's got to move along, and this method of narration is the best one I know. I don't think I'm capable of writing in any other way. My mentor was Wodehouse. I never laugh very much at other writers; I just look at the technique, at the craft, and from the earliest age I was really studying Wodehouse and how he gets his laughs and the superb craftmanship in those books – how he gets people in and out of doors and whatnot: it's because he was working in the theatre all the time, of course.

DB: **When you worked with Willis Hall, did you test lines on each other?**
KEITH WATERHOUSE: What we always did was speak. I think a lot of duo writers work this way: one of us would sit at the typewriter, the other would pace the room. We'd just dictate to one another and improve each other's lines. We revised as we went along. I've always revised as I go along.

JMCG: **Did you laugh a lot?**
KEITH WATERHOUSE: Not a lot. Chortle, perhaps: we would permit ourselves a chortle. Willis is a craftsman too, and interested in how it's done, rather than the effect it's going to have. You presume the effect, and if you don't know what effect it's going to have you shouldn't be in the business. Which is not to say on stage-work that the expected laugh sometimes doesn't come, as you know . . .

DB: **Do you think that there is some sure-fire way of predicting** 'this will score' ?

KEITH WATERHOUSE: There are situations where, 'Well, if this doesn't get a laugh, I'm just going to go out and hang myself,' but, again, you cannot utterly depend on it.

DB: Do you think that anyone knows? For sure?

KEITH WATERHOUSE: I think that formula gag writers know – those massive teams of American writers, when there are more of them than a bloody Rugby side – they know that the one-liners will work, I suppose because they laugh among themselves anyway, through gritted teeth: 'Oh, you've got a funny line there.'

I spend a lot of time at rehearsals, under the impression that I'm working – I'm just skiving really – but I continue to put odd bits in because you can just remove a word or add a comma and, again, it's flow, and suddenly an unfunny line will become funny or funnier. I follow Kingsley Amis's dictum that the best written English is spoken English – write as you speak.

DB: What are your methods for differentiating between one character and another, to give a different tone? Apart from just thinking about it.

KEITH WATERHOUSE: You do hear voices in your head; in fact, I go around with my lips moving when I'm writing a novel, just short of directing traffic in Tottenham Court Road. I don't like giving people very superficial characteristics, like a stutter, or chain-smoking, or whatever. I think you've just got to hear a voice, you've got to hear a real person. If they're not real you're in big trouble, so I sometimes do use a gimmicky thing. In the book I'm writing now I've got a woman who never finishes her sentences, like a lot of people don't. But in general, wait until you've got a voice for somebody and just let them speak. A book may be written in the third person, but I see the whole narrative through one person's eyes. So I've got to have that person invented before the story's invented.

JMCG: And writing a novel from a woman's point of view, how does that affect you?

KEITH WATERHOUSE: Change of sex, yes, I've done that three times now. Again, it's a matter of getting someone in your head, isn't it? I don't go around watching women or anything like that.

JMCG: Do you mentally put different clothes on?

KEITH WATERHOUSE: Yes, I'm wearing a polka-dot dress at the moment.

DB: **How do you do research?**

KEITH WATERHOUSE: I do a lot of change-jangling and mooching round. I start with some vague idea of what the book is going to be about, or who it's going to be about, where he lives, or where his travels are going to take him. And I like to do my thinking on location, so to speak . . .

Having fixed a venue for an imaginary suburb, I will pick on the real suburb and just go wandering about there. For example, I wrote some years ago a book called *In the Mood*, about adolescence in a small suburb of a small northern town. I couldn't go up North every time I wanted to think about things, so I just fixed on Hornchurch. I used to take the Tube out to Hornchurch, and wander about and come back with whole scenes of the thing. So I need to be able to see something . . .

The present one I've set in leafy south London, and getting to fucking Forest Hill is very, very difficult indeed. It's not too late, I can make this Wimbledon. It's fixed on Forest Hill now.

The people are more or less made up, or they're sometimes based on real people, but you put them through the blender and they become fictitious people.

DB: **What do you find most difficult in writing?**

KEITH WATERHOUSE: Thinking of the storyline. I'm not very interested in stories, I'm far more interested in characters, but I've realised a book has to have a story in it somewhere.

DB: **You seem to imply that even if you're writing a piece of drama, you're thinking of it as a book.**

KEITH WATERHOUSE: No, it's the other way round: if I'm writing a book I may be thinking of it as a drama. The one I've just done, *Good Grief*: I thought of it as a play right from the start, but wrote it first as a novel, and then I've written it as a play.

DB: **That's the one you were doing simultaneously, is it?**

KEITH WATERHOUSE: Yes, except I didn't. I started to do, but one obviously takes over – the novel. I did the novel and then I wrote the play, but that mode of thinking, that you're thinking in one character, is of course very useful for the stage, because you find you've written a stonking good part for somebody.

DB: **Do you find you have written not such good parts for everybody else?**

KEITH WATERHOUSE: No, because I go with the Wodehouse dictum which is in his memoirs somewhere, when he says that you've got to think of a book as a musical, or as a stage production. It's no use giving the Earl of Uxbridge a jolly good scene in Chapter One, and then you don't see him again, because what's he doing? He's sitting in his dressing room, he's being paid, he's got to work. So I try to give all except the most subsidiary characters good parts in the book.

DB: You can separate the novel from the play?

KEITH WATERHOUSE: Yes. I live in compartments anyway, because I write the column one day, the book the next. It's a matter of waking up saying: 'Who am I?' Most people say 'Where am I?', but I say 'Who am I?' If it's Wednesday or Sunday, it's column morning, so I put the columnist's head on, I think as a columnist, put everything else out of my mind until that's done; and the next day I've my novelist's head on, or some other head on, but it is literally a matter of deciding which compartment I'm going to live out of on that particular day. It's a very crafty substitute for work avoidance – what every writer wants to do and that's put off the work that's got to be done – so that in putting it off you do some other piece of work, so it's constructive work avoidance, I suppose.

DB: Are you still going to sit down at the typewriter, whatever you do, about the same time?

KEITH WATERHOUSE: At the same time. Morning, which I call prime time, when I don't answer the phone, don't read letters, and work until lunchtime. I used to start about seven, but I'm at the machine by about nine these days, and I work until one. Then I have my bath. I'm unshaven and filthy: I'm more like a bloody tramp all morning. One o'clock, I wash it all off and I go for lunch.

DB: Presumably you didn't work like that when you were working in a partnership.

KEITH WATERHOUSE: Yes, we used to work until lunchtime, and go out and get pissed, or not work until lunchtime, as the case may be. Play Scrabble until lunchtime.

DB: Do you miss working in a partnership? Or are you happier on your own?

KEITH WATERHOUSE: You get more done not working in a partnership. If we'd broken up as many partnerships do, like marriages do, then I think I would miss it, but I talk to Willis nearly every day and we chew the fat, and ring one another up for, we wouldn't presume to call it advice, but 'to pick your brains' is the phrase we've always used.

He lives in Ilkley now and in Malta and I'm in London and in Bath. We've always done our own work separately, and it's a hell of a slog working in tandem, as you know: it's much slower, everything's got to be argued out. Not that we've ever had real arguments. We used to argue about the most stupid things. One will say: 'He goes out through the door,' and the other one will say: 'Of course he goes out through the fucking door. He doesn't go out through the window.' 'Well, I've put it down.' ' Well, take it out.' And it goes out. That kind of discussion. Meaningful.

DB: **You've worked with other people consistently, as well.**
KEITH WATERHOUSE: On the stage I always work with Ned Sherrin. I wouldn't feel comfortable with anybody else by now. I think friendship is very important, I would find it impossible to work with someone I didn't like. I think it's got to start with respect.

JMcG: **Tell us how you go about getting the words on to the stage with Ned as director.**
KEITH WATERHOUSE: Well, I write the thing, and then we have what we call the Jackson Frères session. Jackson Frères is Mr Pooter's champagne, and when I wrote *Mr and Mrs Nobody* by splicing *The Diary of a Nobody* and *Mrs Pooter's Diary* I had some champagne bottles made up with a label which I had printed, of 'Jackson Frères, Female Penitentiary Road, Holloway, N, Runner-Up, Gold Medal' – all that kind of nonsense. The play was far too long, so Ned and I had to cut it between us, and it took three bottles of champagne before we were satisfied. Ever since then, we've always said, when I present Ned with a play, 'Oh, this looks like a three-bottle problem.' We get on the Jackson Frères, and it's very much testing lines, and I will insist on some lines remaining, and let other lines go.

Ned always creatively adds something of great value. On *Jeffrey Bernard is Unwell,* the idea of a pissed set was his, having it at a drunken angle – marvellous bloody idea actually, and a great contribution to the success of the thing. And also having that laughing shutter, where people do one-liners. I'd thought of it as a six-hander, and he wanted to do it as a four-hander, so that people were dashing around madly round the bloody set, coming on putting hats on and this kind of thing, and that freneticism really worked. So, he's a very creative director, but won't touch the words. That's the kind of director I like. By request I will touch the words, if I think they need doing. I can be very touchy, if I find actors have just altered my lines without a by-your-leave, but if anyone has a better line, and puts it to me, I will say: ' Yes, mark it.'

JMcG: **What's the discipline like on Ned's set, in rehearsal with you?**

KEITH WATERHOUSE: It appears to be very relaxed, he always starts the morning by telling half a dozen anecdotes, telling us what he saw last night. You begin to think: 'Oh, fuck it, come on, Ned, get on with it.' But in his own good time he does get on with it and you find you're rehearsing and the thing is moving along at quite a rate. He's very experienced, Ned, and he never loses his cool, ever. I was with him in Australia when we were doing *Jeffrey Bernard* in Perth, and he was doing his *Loose Ends* live from there. At the final dress rehearsal there was some trouble with the curtain, and just hoisting the bloody thing up and getting it down took about five minutes. Ned finally glanced at his watch and said: 'I hope we get this right soon. I'm on air in seven minutes.' He had a car waiting. He said: 'You'd better stop by the wine shop. Mr Waterhouse can't be expected to sit through my programme with a dry mouth.' As we got in to the studio and he thrust the bottle into my hand, he said: 'I do apologise, you'll have to open the bottle yourself. I'm on in one minute.' He goes in, he puts the muffs on, he picks up a script he'd never seen in his life before, and he starts the show.

JMcG: **You've written movies; do you see any difference between writing for a movie, the stage, or whatever?**

KEITH WATERHOUSE: The substantial difference is that in movies the director and the producer are in charge. It's their production, you're only the hired help as a writer. I think the only satisfactory way to work on a movie is to direct it. We've done some very successful movies, but it's a different world. By the time you've written the scenes in a movie, there's no going back. I've felt waves of trepidation when there's a ten-line scene, and you see men hammering a set of a pub together; it's costing thousands of pounds, and you're thinking to yourself: Actually, this scene isn't necessary at all.

You've got more control of your own work on television. These days I only write for my shelf in the BBC. I've thought of offering them rent because they've got so much of my work there. It's remarkable that with so much television now, it's harder and harder to get the bloody product on, particularly in the BBC.

People complain about writers' conditions in Britain, but conditions in America are terrible. I once worked with CBS, who were doing an American version of a series I did called *The Upchat File* with John Alderton, and it was meetings, everything was meetings. We were sitting at a long table, and my Los Angeles agent was there, and there was the producer and the chap that in the unlikely event that the series was ever made, which of course it wasn't, would have been the director, and there was a humourless young man right at the end of the table, and we asked who he was and word came back that he was a 'Humour Consultant Trainee' and he was sitting-in learning humour. That's what he was doing at this script conference – you can imagine it, can't you? He's probably giving the thumbs-down to series himself by now.

DB: **When did you feel that you had been accepted as a writer?**
KEITH WATERHOUSE: When I started writing, which is now, bloody hell, forty years ago since my first book was published, I was working on the *Daily Mirror* and, life being snootier then, they found it peculiar that anyone who worked for a tabloid could write a half-decent novel. But I think *Billy Liar* battered the buggers down. There comes a point when you're just accepted as what you are and what you do.

DB: **When were you able to dictate terms and walk out if you didn't like projects?**
KEITH WATERHOUSE: Well, I think it was in the Sixties, when I started working with Willis, when there was so much work around that you could sell film rights in a bus ticket. The heady Sixties; we had a film industry, we had a television industry and everything. The emerging writer now would go about things a different way; he would turn himself into a production company and he would make his own stuff. We were just too early for that. It's what we should have done, in retrospect.

JMcG: **Is there something that you still really want to write?**
KEITH WATERHOUSE: I would love to write a successful musical. Willis and I wrote the book for *The Card*, which was done with Jim Dale, and it was revived in the Regent's Park Open Air Theatre a couple of years ago. But I'm talking crash hit here . . . I'm talking about running seven years in Japan . . .

JMcG: **You're not going to tell us what it is – or perhaps you don't have an idea?**
KEITH WATERHOUSE: Yes, I do. But as you say, I'm not going to tell you.

Barry Cryer

A performer's temperament

Barry Cryer is the king of the one-liners and has written for the royalty of international show business: his jokes have been used by Jack Benny, Bob Hope, George Burns, Phil Silvers, Phyllis Diller, Richard Pryor, Tommy Cooper, Stanley Baxter, Morecambe and Wise, Dick Emery, Dave Allen, Frankie Howerd, Les Dawson, the Two Ronnies, Mike Yarwood, Bruce Forsyth, Billy Connolly, Russ Abbot, Bobby Davro, Rory Bremner, Jasper Carrott, Les Dennis and Clive Anderson. He dispenses gags in person at awards ceremonies and other semi-public occasions as well as on television and the long-running radio panel game *I'm Sorry I Haven't a Clue.* William Rushton, his fellow-panellist and stage partner in the touring show *Two Old Farts in the Night,* had died a few months before our conversation. Barry told us how he left his native Leeds under the guidance of David Nixon, the magician whose trademarks were a hesitant manner and a bald head, and eventually found a niche in television writing with David Frost, which brought him eventually into a writing partnership with Graham Chapman. They collaborated on TV sitcoms for Barry's former cabaret colleague, Ronnie Corbett (one of them with Eric Idle as co-writer), and Barry used his own material on television in the quick-fire gag show *Jokers Wild* and the impersonation series *Who Do You Do?* Barry asked us round to his workroom overlooking the Grand Union Canal in north London.

BARRY CRYER: I hardly ever write alone, I write in partnerships – that's what I enjoy. But it is bloody hard work, we all know that, and I'm not saying performing isn't, but I prefer performing, because I started as a performer and I've got a performer's temperament rather than a writer's temperament. I always felt a bit of a fraud, which I was, I was a performer fallen into writing by lucky accident, whereas with David Nobbs, my old partner, who's a novelist and everything, I thought, Ah, that's a real writer. I was always quite good at dialogue and lines, whereas I wasn't very good at plot and structure, so ideally I liked to work with a partner who was good at construction. But once you got the characters into a situation I was quite good at writing for them. I liked working with somebody like Peter Vincent I've written with for years. Graham Chapman and I wrote over fifty sitcoms together; I wrote more with him than anybody else outside *Python*. We wrote sitcoms for Ronnie Corbett and all sorts of things. Graham was rather good.

I was the writer and Graham would pace about, light his pipe and twiddle with his sideburns and gaze out of the window and say: 'Oooh, they're open!' in the quaint old days when you waited for the pub to open. 'Oooh, shall we have an early one?' Graham used to say, and I'd think: Oh, boy, there goes the day.

It was saddening in the finish. I mean, I love the pub as much as anyone else, but the joy of a pub is when you've done a solid belt of work, and you go to unwind. So I gradually became used to this pattern, and it saddened me, because I loved the man. He'd 'Oooh' about noon – 'Oooh, ooh, let's make it an early one,' that was his catch-phrase, and you'd say: 'Yeah, an early one' – day gone, and you'd still be in the pub. And then of course he stopped drinking, very bravely, because he knew he was killing himself. He had a complete seizure or something one day, and he never had another drink, to anyone's knowledge; he was wonderful. But he still loved pubs. We would go to the Angel in Highgate. Graham liked the ambience of pubs, and he'd drink his Tab or whatever. Willy Rushton, God rest him, didn't drink for the last ten years of his life. But Willy would come in a pub with you: he enjoyed the company. Diet Coke, Will, always. I said: 'How do you drink that all day long?' He said: 'You get used to it.' That was so quick, when Willy went. It was all over in three days.

JMcG: **When you work with somebody, is it great fun?**
BARRY CRYER: John Cleese and I just laughed and laughed, because we tried working together and it wouldn't work at all, but it was so funny. We wrote, tried to write, a sketch. Now my attitude to a sketch is, you take a run at it in a white heat, and then you screw it up and throw it in the bin and start again. But, oh no, not John. John wants to start at Page One, and start going line by line, word by word, and I said, 'Come on, let's write this bugger' – and, very

amiably and amicably, we never wrote together again. We couldn't, because we were two different worlds. John is fastidious (and quite right too), and bloody good at it, and I'm, Oh, it's the idea that matters, we'll sort the lines out, we'll go back on it, but let's write the sketch, in a burst of fire, and it'll be a mess, but hopefully we'll get the good tag or whatever, and then we'll go back over it, then we'll tidy it up. I like to take a run at it.

JMCG: **If you're working with somebody that you're in sympathy with, if you do come up with a funny line you can laugh for twenty minutes.**

BARRY CRYER: Oh yes. And you do the great unusables as well, if it's a dreary afternoon. Graham and I used to write, 'It's morning. We discover Ronnie wanking,' and we'd laugh for about half an hour at the idea. Unfortunately John Cleese and Sheila Staefel was not a marriage made in heaven on *The Frost Report*; they did not hit it off at all. So John Cleese and Graham Chapman wrote a sketch that had John and Sheila in, but the heading of their original version was 'The Sketch in which John in No Way Kisses Sheila' and they thought, Oh, nobody'll print that up . . . And it's printed up. We sat down for the read-through: imagine Sheila Staefel's face. Graham and I used the runnning theme in one of Ronnie Corbett's series, script-wise, of 'The Goat Has Just Left'. 'We see that some of the sandwiches have been nibbled by The Goat.' 'The Goat is obviously outside in the garden.' Solemn direction in the script. And we turned up for the last recording and there was The Goat on the set: they'd got a stuffed goat. It's just to keep yourself going and have a laugh. We used to write things like 'It is obviously Friday'.

I was really proud when John Junkin and I were writing for Morecambe and Wise: we followed Eddie Braben – he was the man, a great original, he was wonderful. And before him Sid Green and Dick Hills, who became forgotten, but they'd really done great stuff for them at ATV. Junkin and I were talking about Eric looking at the camera, and we did a thing about the dawn patrol, the Royal Flying Corps in the First World War. Eric was on first – which was unusual: we changed the format a bit – Eric was on with Pete Murray or somebody, and they're waiting for this new recruit. And Ernie entered wearing the lot – the leather helmet, everything – and Eric turned into the camera and said: 'They're sending us kids!' I was very proud of that. And the other line I was very proud of in that: 'Where's Fanshawe?' 'He's outside, servicing the Camel.' We had carefully mentioned the plane earlier on.

DB: How much are you involved in the process of getting the
words on to the screen or the stage? Do you follow it through
rehearsals?

BARRY CRYER: My life's gone full circle now: I'm almost retired as
a scriptwriter *per se*, because the young 'uns write their own, or they
have their self-contained groups, like *Python* was. So the phone's
stopped ringing. The tide went out. But having been a performer,
you have a different attitude as a writer. A lot of writers would say:
'That idiot's paid to do this. He's supposed to be an actor.' They had
no understanding. And I would say things like, 'Well, the door
opens the other way,' and they'd say: 'Oh, please, are we dealing
with children?' and I'd say, 'No, *you* walk through that door and try
and do that line when you've got to turn the other way.' I had a sort
of . . . bit of compassion for these nerks.

   Sometimes, of course, performers can do it differently from the
way you wrote it and it's funny: you can say, 'No, that's better.'
Ronnie Corbett was terrific on intonation and things. He'd come up
with something a bit quirky, or one of his hesitations in the middle
of a line which seemed to break the rule: he made the line much funnier by choking off in the middle of it for some reason, as if he was
too nervous, or whatever: it was called acting, really. Very good
actor, Ronnie – full of nuances. Well, the *two* Ronnies, I mean: just
immaculate. You knew your stuff was going to get good treatment
with those two. Very relaxed.

JMcG: You worked with them at the club, at Danny La Rue's . . .
BARRY CRYER: Well, not Ronnie Barker; Ronnie Corbett was in
Winston's – it wasn't Danny's own club – off Bond Street, in
Clifford Street. That's where we met up. And then Danny had his
own club in Hanover Square. That was an amazing period.

JMcG: David Frost used to go in there all the time.
BARRY CRYER: That's how I started on television really, Joe. I've
been so lucky with the accidents: I wrote a couple of revues for the
Fortune Theatre, older-style revues, and Danny came in to see one
and invited me to write his night-club shows. The first time I met
Denis Norden, he came to the club, and afterwards he came over and
shook my hand and said: 'I didn't know there were so many cock
jokes in all the world.' I had prided myself on the wording: there was
no effing, there was no language in any Danny La Rue show. It was
full of jokes like: 'What do you think of Michael Foot?' 'A wild
exaggeration!' 'Let's talk about Edward Heath, and people do, you
know!' I would shout: 'Oh, he's coming from the rooftops! That's a

clever trick if you can do it!' You know, all that rubbish. I always like the words to be innocuous, but the jokes were incredibly dirty: 'Something here inside says I love you,' and Danny would look straight down the crutch and say: 'It speaks!' All that . . . I like there to be a slight bit of dirty elegance. Julian Clary's doing jokes that Danny was doing thirty years ago.

My wife said: 'You're getting a hang-up that you're a blue writer.' That was my living then: I was in the show, I wrote it, and I thought: Oh, this is what I'll do for the rest of my life probably, writing rude jokes for night-clubs. Then Frostie came in and asked me to write on television and my wife said: 'There you are! David Frost thinks you can write other stuff, not just in a night-club.' It was a great school, it was a wonderful experience.

Frostie invited me – this was after *That Was The Week That Was* and *Not So Much a Programme* – to work on a one-off called *A Degree of Frost*. And then David invited me on to *The Frost Report* and I was off and running. And then if you were a Frost writer, that started opening doors; as you remember, the whole of *Python*, before *Python*, were on the writing roster on *The Frost Report*. That's where I met them all. Frostie put me and Graham, and initially Eric Idle, together to write a sitcom for Ronnie Corbett. And then Eric left after the first series, got something else, so Graham and I wrote all the remainder of the Ronnie Corbett sit-coms. Frostie's great strength was as the entrepreneur, the fixer: he brings people together. I mean, Graham and I got on from the moment we met, but you'd not necessarily have said we could write together, because we seemed to be from two different worlds of writing. I was jokey, gag, show-bizzy man and he was fey and a doctor, who had a weird sense of humour, but we hit it off and it was a joy to write with him, until, as I say, the days began to be truncated. We finished up on about an hour's writing a day, and it broke my heart.

JMcG: **And Marty Feldman? Did you ever work with Marty?**
BARRY CRYER: Marty was officially script editor on *The Frost Report*. And the big joke at the time was, we will do a different theme every week. So at the first meeting we said, 'What are we going to do?' and Marty said, 'Holidays,' and disappeared on holiday. But he was a joy, Marty, he was a lovely guy. Of course, he was a performer, you see – he'd been in 'Maurice, Marty and Mitch' in variety, it was wacky and zany and a lot of props and hitting each other. Then he turned to scriptwriting, and then he came back, in *At Last, the 1948 Show*, as a performer. John and the others said: 'He's

funny. Let's have him in the show,' and he hadn't performed for years.

JMCG: **Writing to order very quickly as you did for Danny La Rue, what's that like?**

BARRY CRYER: I prefer it. I prefer the deadline, the white heat; the adrenalin gets going. You know the old saying, 'We don't want it good, we want it Monday,' and you hope it's good *and* Monday. I like the pressure. Eric Morecambe used to say: 'It's all done on fear, you know.' Eric liked the world where you got the scripts on a Monday morning, sat round a table, and it was pressure, pressure, and then on Friday you went for it. That really affected his health terribly, but what can you do? There's a temperament in the man. But when John Junkin and I were writing for Eric and Ernie at Thames, he had three months, so of course they could go off stuff, they would discard a whole show, piece by piece. You'd have to write the whole show again. Eric had too much time, he didn't really like that leisure. He had to do something to fill the time, which was suddenly to go off the script he'd liked before.

DB: **What was it that got you into comedy?**

BARRY CRYER: BA Eng. Lit. failed at Leeds University. I went to university with the idea of being a journalist and of course immediately I discovered girls and booze, and we all wrote and performed shows, and I got a real taste for it; but I'd got no showbiz ambitions. I just thought: I'm enjoying this. Then I got my first-year results, and they were not good. A guy came up to Leeds to see somebody else in a student show, and he saw me in our *Rag Review* in the old Empire Theatre in Leeds, and offered me work. And I thought: This is fate. I'm obviously not going down the groves of academe. And I went off and did six weeks as a comic in strip shows, *Strip, Strip, Hooray* or *Nudes of the World* or whatever it was called, and that was a false start. Crawled back to Leeds, back to the Empire Theatre, and got a job as a stage-hand. And I used to empty and fill three bars in the morning. Ever done that? Empties are heavy, I tell you: they're as heavy as fulls, for some strange reason. Then I'd go home and have a kip, and then at night I would work as a stage-hand, fly-gallery and everything.

Then David Nixon arrived to do a pantomime, which is a horror story in itself. Pre-M1 he and his then wife, Paula Marshall, drove up the A1 to Leeds in separate cars, with all the gear for the pantomime, and she had a heart attack at the wheel and crashed off the road. She was dead. David actually drove past the crash, not realising. He arrived in Leeds, they told him his wife was dead, and he collapsed. But he said: 'I'm going on with the pantomime. She would have wanted it,' and another woman came up from London to replace her and they started rehearsals.

The manager of the theatre was called Leo Lion, I swear – military sort, moustache and a carnation and all that. I was regarded as a bit of an eccentric, this one who'd been kicked out of Leeds University, working as a stage-hand. He called me 'Toff'. Anyway, he called me to his office and said: 'Do you want to look after Mr Nixon? Be his dresser and assistant?' The guy was in an awful state, taking pills and sleeping between shows, and we became friends then. And he said: 'You've got to get out of Leeds. Go to London.' I took him at his word; got a night train from Leeds immediately after the end of the pantomime. He took me out to dinner, and introduced me to agents, and invited me to his radio shows, TV shows.

So that's how it all started, and then I got the job in the musical, *Expresso Bongo*. I played Beast, the leader of the skiffle group. I had a scene with Paul Schofield, who had never done a musical, he's a great classical Shakespearean actor. Burt Rhodes, the musical director, said, 'He's practically got perfect pitch for singing, but no sense of timing,' which is strange for an actor, and he would get one and a half bars ahead of the band, and Burt used to cut the whole band and the pianist would find where Paul was – oh, it was brilliant to watch – and Burt would give a beat, and the whole band would be: 'Where the fuck are we? Oh, right, we're back!' It was wonderful. And then I was off and running, I was quite smug.

JMcG: How do you write? In longhand?
BARRY CRYER: I'm an old scribbler. I'm getting left behind now, you know – you do really feel a dinosaur, because I can work a processor, but I don't *enjoy* working at a processor. I don't trust the words I see on the screen: I think they look too neat and beautiful, and I think it's probably a load of crap. I can only think with a pen. I just scrawl and scrawl, and I daren't leave my writing for more than about twenty-four hours before I type it up, because I've got my own form of speed writing, and after a gap it's completely illegible to me . . .

JMcG: Do you know what's funny?
BARRY CRYER: Joe, how long have we both been around? *Nobody* knows. I've never, ever said to an actor, or actress or a comic: 'This is funny.' I've said: 'We like this.'

Eddie Braben

Chipping granite with a spoon

For Merseysiders and Mancunians the equivalent of the French Riviera is North Wales, and that is where Eddie Braben has settled, halfway up a mountain, in a house none too easy to find in the dark. A tall, bespectacled man with a gentle manner, he, more than anyone, created our memories of Morecambe and Wise, the most universally loved of all post-war comedians. When he took over writing Eric and Ernie's show from Sid Green and Dick Hills, Eddie adjusted the characters they played to give a new dimension to the classic double act. His flights of imagination gave their work a unique and irreplaceable flavour, and a quite different one from the quality Eddie had provided in a long association with Ken Dodd. He created still another fantasy world for the radio series *The Worst Show on the Wireless*, on which he had a speaking part. As we discovered as we sat and talked over tea and sandwiches provided by his wife, Deirdre, there is a performer lurking inside Eddie: his warm, quiet voice falls naturally and unaffectedly into uncannily evocative impersonations of the people he is quoting: Dave Morris, Ken Dodd, Eric Morecambe, Ernie Wise – even Jerry Lewis.

DB: **We're trying to discover what writers think about comedy.**
EDDIE BRABEN: What I think now is, 'Thank God it's all over,' because I never liked it. No, I never ever enjoyed writing; it's so hard. If anybody said, 'I'm going to spend this day writing comedy. I am looking forward to it,' I'd think, Well, there's an idiot. It's the hardest job I've ever done, and I've done a few. All the manual labour: I've been a brickie's mate, loaded crates of cigarettes in Ogden's; I was a dishwasher in the RAF when I was doing my National Service – it's true, I was . . . I *wanted* to be a dishwasher.

Because I knew that by virtue of being in the cookhouse and doing the dishes I was excused all duties, because it soaked right through my overalls, everything, my boots, the lot; it was caked in grease, it was rotten, I stank. So nobody wanted me to go on parade: no guard duty, no fire drills, nothing.

I've done a variety of jobs. I was in the police for forty-five minutes. There's a big police school in Liverpool: you have to go there to do so many weeks before you're a policeman. I went into this room, and it was a lecture that lasted about twenty minutes, all standing up at attention. I thought: What's this? Left right, left right, left right, down the corridor, left right, left right, left right . . . I thought: Hello. Left right, left right, into this room for twenty minutes. 'Stand upright!' Left right, left right, left right. I thought: Oh, I don't like this one little bit. Left right, left right, left right. Right turn! I went left turn! hup two . . . and went home.

But writing, that is the most difficult job in the world. It's like chipping granite with a spoon, it really is.

JMcG: **You said once that you drew a television screen on the wall and watched it?**
EDDIE BRABEN: Yeah. I just did the square on the wall, and I could act it out on that square. I thought: That looks good. My wife was delighted to be seeing me drawing a square on the wallpaper, she was thrilled to bits. I said: 'You start to worry when I do it in Cinerama.' It was in my head, and I'd just visualise it on this screen, this little square. I could see it, and I'd go: 'No, that's not going to work.' Sometimes it just looked good, and I thought: Yes, that will work.

JMcG: **Depends who's directing it.**
EDDIE BRABEN: You put your life in your hands, because other people take over, don't they? But I got to the stage where I'd say: 'There it is, I've written it. You can do what the hell you like with that now.' I got to that stage where I wasn't bothered, because it was so hard. But then if it was easy, everybody would be doing it, wouldn't they?

DB: **How do you know when it's funny?**
EDDIE BRABEN: They send you a cheque. When the cheques stop coming, it's not funny any more. I was, like, at the sharp end of comedy: doing twelve years with Ken Dodd, you're at the sharp end because we used to work on about six gags a minute. He went bang, bang, bang, bang: 'He's got three children, one of each . . .' They were like that. I can't remember them until I hear somebody else do

them now. I heard one the other night. Doddy was on – it was a clip
– and he said: 'I was at medical school. I was a PhD: Prepares Hot
Dinners . . . PLJ: Puts Lumps on Judies . . . Well, I'll talk to you, sir;
you look sensible. He *is* sensible: he's fast asleep . . .' Bang, bang,
bang, and it never stopped, at *that* rate, and that wore me out.

The Ken Dodd shows were quite successful on radio, doing two a
week, Sunday and Wednesday, and with Ken Dodd you don't start
the next one. You do one on Sunday . . . never mind the one you're
doing on Wednesday, let's get this Sunday one right. We used to
come back on the train at midnight, get back to Liverpool at four
o'clock in the morning, and I'd be straight home and straight to the
typewriter, because it was Monday morning by then and it had to be
in by Tuesday morning. I used to write it in eight hours.

But I was able to write gags. You watch a situation comedy, as I
do now, and I'm going: 'It's been on now five minutes, and there
hasn't been a funny line yet.' 'It's been on seven minutes, there
hasn't been a funny line yet.' I know the machine's laughing, but
nobody else is. They can't write a funny line. They get a funny idea
and this carries them through thirty minutes. I'll exclude things like
Only Fools and Horses – John Sullivan, who's probably the pick of
the bunch. Now, John's a very, very fine writer. I think John is the
best at the moment. And where are the stand-up comics? They're
there, but are we going to see them on television? We're not, because
there's no Light Entertainment any more.

You take something like *The Morecambe and Wise Show*, where
you'd got to have an opening stand-up, two-hander, which is the old
variety thing, two men being funny. Then a quickie, then a five-
minute sketch, then something that'll last a minute, then something
that'll last six minutes, then something that'll last one minute, then
the sketch at the end . . . So we were doing about nine, ten, separate
comedy items in every programme. That's the sharp end of comedy,
and it was exhausting, mentally.

From the top, the story is that Bill Cotton rang and said to me –
I'd left Ken Dodd – 'Do you want to write for Morecambe and
Wise? I would like you to write for Morecambe and Wise.' I said: 'I
can't do it.' He said: 'Why?' I said: 'Because I'm not good enough.'
He said: 'Well, I think you are.' I thought a lot of Bill: he's a nice
man. He said: 'Well, would you come down this week and meet the
boys?' – it was always 'the boys'. I went down and met them, we got
on well together from the word go, and I said: 'Look, I couldn't
write the way you've been working all your lives, and the way I've
seen you on television. It will have to be the way I write. I can't copy
anybody else, because I wouldn't be able to write anybody else's

style, only my own.' So Bill said: 'Well, come back next week and let's see what you've got.' I was very prolific, I used to write quick, so I went down with about twenty, twenty-five, maybe thirty pages and the first thing Eric said was: 'Christ! It's got Eric a line, Ernie a line, me a line, Ernie a line . . .' and he said: 'All these pages, we've got lines, it goes right through to the end!' I said: 'Yeah – what's wrong?' He said: 'Well, we've never worked like that!' I said: 'How have you worked in the past?' He said: 'Well, we've just got ideas on a piece of paper. We all sit down and work on them.' I said: 'Oh, I didn't know you could get away with it like that. I wish I'd known.'

Anyway, they read it, and Eric said: 'Oh, gosh, it's very funny. We could never do this.' I said: 'Well, it's the only way I can write.' He said: 'Look, there's a sketch here, with two of us in a flat. It's like a feature-length film. We couldn't do this.' Bill said, because he liked it as well: 'This is the new Morecambe and Wise we have never seen before. I think it will work. Let's do two or three on BBC 2. Only a million or two million people will see it. You won't destroy your-selves completely.' So they did that and you know the rest . . .

JMCG: **You changed their characters so that Eric became the smart guy, not the idiot comedian, and Ernie became the idiot.**
EDDIE BRABEN: That's true to a certain degree. But also they could be two funny men, or Eric could be a straight man at some times, because he let Ernie have funny lines, the difference being that Ernie didn't realise he was saying something funny. Like, they'd be in bed, and Ernie'd be trying to write, and he said – how did the gag go? It was a good line – Ernie said: 'I could be another George Bernard Priestley.' Eric said: 'Shaw.' Ernie said: 'Positive.'

Eric said: 'You're from Yorkshire, weren't the Brontë sisters?' Ernie – he's supposed to be the writer, you see – said: 'Don't Sit Under the Apple Tree with Anyone Else but Me,' that was one of their best. Ernie would say something funny without realising it.

I remembered one the other day, it came from a bed sketch. Eric was getting into bed, Ernie was writing, and a police car went past and Eric said: 'He's not going to sell much ice-cream going at that speed.' I had to fight for the bed sketches, because they didn't want to do it. For obvious reasons: didn't want the public to think they were a couple of homosexuals. Eric said: 'They're very funny, but I don't like the idea of two men in pyjamas in bed.' This was pro-tracted: it went on over a couple of hours. In the end I said: 'Well, if it's good enough for Laurel and Hardy, it's good enough for you.' And Eric said: 'That'll do me.'

So what he did, when they were in the bed, to try and point up the fact that he was masculine, he was male, he had the pipe, in bed. And he might be reading the *Dandy*. Ernie'd be reading the plot of his play. I think it was something about 'Hank Somebody, Private Eye, flew into Roma airport and it was his first visit to Amsterdam'. And Eric just went: 'Twenty-four, Ern.' 'Twenty-four?' 'Cow pies. Desperate Dan today.' And everybody loved it.

I've always said it was a childish humour; I've probably undermined my own writing, but it was a childish humour. There was never anything mucky. The nearest we got was the way Eric would say: 'Pardon?' Ernie would say: 'I'll go in the kitchen and have a look at it now,' and Eric would say: 'Pardon?' 'The dinner.' But we'd get a big laugh on 'Pardon?' If we'd left it alone, it wouldn't have got a laugh: 'I'll take it out and have a look at it.' 'Pardon?' 'I'll take it out: the meal.' 'Oh . . .' We didn't have to paint lurid pictures.

But the pressures have always been there. That's why I say I never enjoyed it, never. I enjoyed the end product. The very first gag about Des O'Connor's singing came because I used to watch Des O'Connor, and I thought: God, you get on my bloody nerves, you. You're so handsome, you've got beautiful teeth, you wear lovely clothes, you're a good singer, all the women love you. I'm going to have a go at you. I stuck one line in one week, and the place erupted. And they're still doing them, now. We met when Eric's daughter was getting married. He said to me: 'I could never have bought that publicity.'

One of the first guests was Dame Flora Robson. I remember thinking to myself: I used to watch her in films with Errol Flynn when I was a kid! And I'm writing for her! I can't do this line here, can I? Well, I'll chance it, and if she objects we'll take it out. It was a front-of-tabs thing, and she came through wearing the actual Elizabeth I outfit she wore in the film with Errol Flynn. She looked breathtaking in this dress. She was carrying a football. Eric looked at his watch. She said: 'I'm sorry I'm late, but a young man kept asking me if I'd be fit for Saturday.' Eric said: 'And will you?' The audience loved it, because we'd pricked the bubble, when she did that line they fell in love with her: 'Ah, she's human, she's like us.' So I thought: this insulting people works.

Like André Preview – Mr Preview and Mr Privet. And then a bit later in the script Eric said: 'Mr Previn,' and André said: 'Preview' . . . In there is one of my treasured possessions: I had an LP *André Previn Plays My Fair Lady*. I knocked on his dressing-room door, and I went in and said: 'Mr Previn.' He said: 'No, it's André.' I said: 'Would you sign this?' He said: 'My God, you've got one of these? It's an awful long time ago.' He wrote on it, and I didn't even look at what he wrote: we just stayed and talked. I went home and looked: 'With great admiration.' I thought: This man is a musical genius, he is a man who at the age of twenty-six was the head of music at MGM music, and he's written to me 'With great admiration!' I never got over writing for big star names. I used to say: 'Bloody hell! Laurence Olivier! Yehudi Mehu . . . Mehudi Yu . . . Max Jaffa! Wow!'

And some of the lines! Peter Cushing, when he was King Arthur, and Eric came into the castle, and Peter Cushing said: 'What news of Carlisle?' And Eric said: 'When I left they were winning 2–1!'

DB: What aspect of the job did you find that you had consistent difficulties with?

EDDIE BRABEN: It's probably a cliché, but I think: the first line. The first line. I have actually gone into that room for a whole day, and not put one word on paper. I've come out at night and I've had to go and shower, because I've been saturated, and change my clothing. That's, say, on the Monday. On the Tuesday, the same. This is where you're chipping granite, now. I even remember three days, not a word. Maybe halfway through the third day, you can't get the words on paper quick enough, but only because you've sweated for two and a half days. How many times have you gone into that room, or in Southfield Park in Liverpool, and found me asleep over the typewriter?

DEIRDRE BRABEN: When we moved here I used to work in a hotel, just part-time, and my daughter and I sometimes used to come home at the same time, about midnight or after, and he'd be fast asleep over his typewriter.

EDDIE BRABEN: There were occasions when I've worked, as I say, I've worked all through this day, all through the night, all through the next day, and just fallen over, literally. That was the deadlines – the *Morecambe and Wise Shows* were quick turnarounds. It's put me in hospital a couple of times, hasn't it? Well, once, anyway.

DEIRDRE BRABEN: One night when he'd been working he had a shower, about nine o'clock, and we couldn't find him. He was on the bed and then he disappeared. My daughter was going away, and she was putting stuff in and out of her car, so I didn't take much notice that the front door was banging. We found him fast asleep on the bench outside.

EDDIE BRABEN: I had my dressing gown and pyjamas on . . .

DEIRDRE BRABEN: Fast asleep. Like a tramp.

EDDIE BRABEN: That was mental exhaustion, which sounds easy, but it's not – it's a terrible thing. I've had it two or three times; it wasn't very nice.

DEIRDRE BRABEN: Or sometimes he's been asleep and he just gets up, he doesn't know, and he just walks straight into the office and sits at the typewriter.

JMCG: For Morecambe and Wise you were writing situation comedy as well as gags.
EDDIE BRABEN: Nobody realised, and I didn't realise myself at first, that I was doing what we call a spot show – the opening, lots of little bits – and the sketch at the end was twenty minutes. So I was doing situation comedy within the framework of a Light Entertainment programme. I used to think to myself: I could have padded that sketch for a half-hour sitcom. The other night I timed *Coronation Street*. Do you know how long we actually got? Twenty minutes. Dialogue was twenty minutes.

DB: Did you find if you got stuck on the cross-talk you could move to the flat sketch and do a bit of that, or did you work straight through?
EDDIE BRABEN: I had to go from the top, and go through it right the way as you would see it, in sequence. I may have had the idea for the final sketch, but that was all.

DB: Within each show, is there a shape: is one item meant to balance something else?
EDDIE BRABEN: Not knowingly. Maybe I was just fortunate. I suppose the first show was right: it looked good; the shape was good. I stayed with it. I didn't want to change it.

JMCG: The dance routines, were they yours, too?
EDDIE BRABEN: That's the director, Ernest Maxim – because he's a song-and-dance man, and he was the best man in the world for musical numbers. Whenever it was dialogue, yes, I always did that, but the actual dance things I left alone. Ernest Maxim knew what he was doing – that *Stripper* routine was a classic, wasn't it? In the kitchen . . . I saw *The Stripper* again, and Shirley MacLaine was doing it, at the Montreux Festival.
   John Ammonds was the director originally. He had a great track

record: he was the sound-effects man in *ITMA*. It was done down
the road from here, did you know that? All the big BBC comedy
shows – *ITMA, Old Mother Riley* – they were all done in Bangor,
which is just down the road here: they took them out of London
during the war. I remember as a kid standing outside the stage door,
getting their autographs. Jack Train gave me his autograph; drew a
little train underneath with smoke coming out. I was evacuated; I
was only eight or nine. I lived in Anglesey for a while. I suppose
that's when the love affair started. John Ammonds did *ITMA*, and
he went on to Dave Morris, Ken Platt, and he did Eric and Ernie on
radio. When they got to television that was a plus for them, a man
who really knew comedy, and John did.

JMCG: **And he went to Thames, if you remember: after they did
a couple of shows there they got John Ammonds over to Thames.**
EDDIE BRABEN: Yeah, but they didn't get me, though. Didn't get
me. They'd already signed. I said: 'Sorry, I'm not going.' I was so
happy at the BBC, and Bill Cotton was there. Mind you, Philip
Jones at Thames, he was a lovely man as well, I loved Philip. I
couldn't see the reason for moving to Thames – obviously it was
money. And I couldn't see there was anything in it for me, except
money. But I've never been money-orientated. I've never had an
agent. I've never really appreciated my own value: put it that way.
I used to look at the cheques from the BBC and I'd think, By
God, this is better than being redundant. It was two years before
I went to Thames, but I didn't like writing for commercial television after the BBC.

   In fairness to Eric, it was probably good for him, because his
health wasn't good then. There were fewer shows and half-hours
where we'd beeen doing forty-five minutes – and the big one at
Christmas. Oh God, that was a nightmare. I can remember Eric
reading a script in January for a show we were going to do in two
weeks' time: 'We'll save that for Christmas, that piece there, that'll
be right for the Christmas show.' It used to hang over me like a great
big, black bat, that Christmas show . . . All of a sudden it dawned on
me: twenty million people, week in, and then twenty-six and a half
million people watching it . . . As Eric said, 'It's a million more than
the Queen got.' He said: 'Well, she's not very funny, is she? And
have you heard her singing 'Bring me Sunshine'? She's got no idea:
she's tone deaf!'

   But I didn't like it at Thames because it was half an hour, it was
less than half an hour, it was twenty-five minutes. Everything was
pared down to the bone, everything was condensed, everything was

cut down. I couldn't spread, I couldn't expand on anything, I couldn't do the long pauses – I used to love the long pauses. I didn't like this break in the middle. Commercials. You didn't associate a break in the middle with Eric and Ernie. You'd accept it with Benny Hill because he'd been doing it for so long, but not with Eric and Ernie; it broke the thread.

I was doing a Morecambe and Wise series once, and I had a telephone call from an Alexander Cohen, American producer (I didn't know who Alexander Cohen was), and he said, would I be interested in doing some work for him? He wanted to bring back *Hellzapoppin'* on stage with Jerry Lewis. I said: 'I'm sorry, he's not my type of comic. He always reminds me of somebody who's got some terrible illness.' He said: 'Have you ever seen him on stage?' I said: 'No.' He said: 'Well, how about Friday night?' I said: 'OK.' In half an hour he called me back and said: 'OK, I've booked the seats, and the hotel and the plane. He's opening on Thursday at the Olympia in Paris.' I said: 'Bloody hell, I thought he was in Halifax!' I thought he was in one of the big working-men's clubs.

I went over, we saw the show at night, and Jerry Lewis is God in Paris. Next day I went to his hotel with Alexander Cohen, we had a talk, and I happened to say that my daughter had been watching him in a film on TV. He said: 'You've got to take this picture. I'll sign it for her.' It was a big picture, and he wrote all kinds to Jane, and he brought out this envelope and it had in the top left-hand corner 'Jerry Lewis Inc., Hollywood', and underneath a little cartoon of Jerry Lewis. I said: 'Jerry, I've been in this business a few years now, I've met a lot of big names, but this is probably the nicest thing that anyone's done for me,' and I threw it the length of the room. He was on his knees, tears were coming down: 'I've gotta have this guy, I've gotta have this guy!'

He never got this guy, though, because I found out I'd have to go to America. I've always detested going away from home. That was the second offer I refused. The other one was actually Hollywood. I said: 'No, thank you. I don't want any part of that.' I must have been pretty hot in those days. The overriding factor was that I would be away from my wife and children and home. I've never been able to write away from home. I've never been able to write in a television studio or in a hotel room.

JMcG: **Where *do* you write?**

EDDIE BRABEN: Well, when I'm here, that little room there. When I used to live in Liverpool, eventually we moved to a rather nice, large house with a private park. I took the smallest bedroom. I said:

'That'll do me.' Any room that'll hold a chair and a desk and a type-writer, that's all I need, with things surrounding me that I'm famil-iar with, that I like to have around me. In there's a pigsty, but my wife daren't go in there to clean, she just leaves me in there.

JMcG: **You must have made the decision to change from what you were doing to be a writer.**

EDDIE BRABEN: I left school when I was fourteen, in the south end of Liverpool – the Dingle, it was then. It's now known as Croxteth, I think. I can still hear the headmaster saying to me: 'I'll see you in a few years' time, Braben, when you come to empty the dustbins.' Because I was as thick as the leg of a snooker table, I really was, and I went to work at Ogden's tobacco factory, knocking nails in boxes, and I thought, There's got to be something better than this. But what it was, I didn't know. I did my National Service and I was washing all those greasy dishes, and I thought, There's got to be something better than this. I still didn't know what it was. Then my father invested a hundred pounds – it was a hell of a lot of money – in a fruit stall in the Victorian building known as Liverpool St John's Market: there were about eight other stalls in this great, big, massive building – it was like a great railway station. And, God, I hated working on that. I thought, There's got to be something better than this. I still didn't know what it was, and for some reason I started writing lines on the back of brown paper bags, and the fruit was going rotten. I used to write about five hundred a week. Anybody can write five hundred lousy jokes a week, but you've got to write a great many before you actually write one that makes sense. I eventually did. I sold it to Charlie Chester for two-and-six, and the work gradually built up.

DB: **That was the one about how Hopalong Cassidy's mum knew he'd be a cowboy because he had a ten-gallon nappy . . .**

EDDIE BRABEN: That was the very first. I couldn't remember the one I wrote yesterday but I remember the first one with great affec-tion. Charlie was just a lovely man. My idol when I was in my teens was Dave Morris. They talk about surreal humour, but he was well before his time. He used to have this programme on the radio called *Club Night*. It was a working-man's club in the North; it was a great setting. Dave Morris was appearing in pantomime at the Royal Court Theatre in Liverpool, just outside the market, and he came to my father's stall for some meat – my father worked in the market, too – and my father said how much we admired him, and he brought him down to me. He had a straw hat on and his first words to me were: 'All right, son? Don't take any wooden money.'

I used to love radio – I couldn't believe the voices came out of this box. I thought: I'd love to be on the wireless. That stayed with me, and I wasn't satisfied until I went on the wireless, and that was when I did *The Worst Show on the Wireless* in the Seventies. It was me, Alison Steadman – it was her first break, actually – Bill Pertwee, Eli Woods.

JMcG: **How did you feel about writing for yourself?**
EDDIE BRABEN: I enjoyed it. I didn't have any funny lines. I was the poor idiot in the middle surrounded by all these other idiots. In one of them Alison played Mrs Turpin; she brought her son Precious to audition for the BBC, because he could climb inside a milk bottle and sing. The BBC man said: 'You can't possibly get inside a milk bottle.' Precious said: 'I can get inside a milk bottle. Give me a hand to take me accordion off first.' To my astonishment, it won the Best Comedy thing for the year, and I was quite thrilled with that.

DB: **Do you think there's a Liverpool flavour to your comedy?**
EDDIE BRABEN: There's a bit of disrespect in Liverpool, disrespect for authority. For pompous people. I've never really analysed it. People say: 'How do you do it?' Well, you don't know. How do you tell Beethoven how to play in goal? How do you tell Pavarotti how to do the splits? You don't, do you? It is a gift, and I don't wish to make this sound egotistical or big-headed, but when I lived in this private park in Liverpool, Southfield Park, it was a beautiful place to live. Of course, I didn't always live in beautiful places – two up and two down, outside lav. Anyway, in the winter, all the leaves – we were surrounded by trees, of course – they'd fall off and I could see right through, two hundred yards, to the main ring road. I used to start work very early in the morning, say half seven, and I could see buses going past packed tight with people looking miserable. I used to think, Well, maybe they're thinking: Oh, good, Morecambe and Wise are on tonight. I used to think, Well, that's why I've been given this gift, for those people. I honestly believe that. I'm not an overly religious person, but I could relate to those people going to work on the bus. I felt I owed it to them to do it. And that did help.

I used to have this feeling that one day the telephone would ring, and this very distant voice would say: 'Eddie Braben? It's all been a mistake.' 'Pardon?' 'It's all been a mistake. We're going to take it all back.' 'You're not, are you?' ''Fraid so. Bye!'

What are we doing being bloody old? We've no right to be old: we should be young again. I look in the mirror, and I say: 'Look at that!

Looks about thirty, that fella. Why are they all saying "Happy birthday to you, happy sixty-fifth birthday"? Bloody hell, I'm not sixty-five! Look at him: he's only a lad.' And the wife says: 'You're not sixty-five, are you?' Bloody am . . .

There have been two golden moments. One was Laurel and Hardy at the Liverpool Empire: it was an enormous theatre, and I'd never seen it so packed – every seat had gone; standing at the sides, standing at the back, on all floors. The interval had finished, and a total blackout, just one spot at the side, and then the piccolo started playing their tune. That's all it did, and the place erupted. They hadn't even walked on the stage, and when they walked on, it was unbelievable. So much so, Ollie just stood there and cried: the tears flowed down his face. I thought I'd never see that ever again.

So many years later, in Liverpool again, at the Royal Court Theatre, first half, interval, then complete darkness, then the band played 'Bring Me Sunshine' – and the same thing happened again. When they walked on, and crossed, I'd never heard applause like it: they were standing, and they hadn't said two words.

There's a golden thread between people like Eric and Ernie and Laurel and Hardy, between them and the audience. There's love. It goes beyond liking an act; there is a love between the two. It is a love relationship: they love those people. Why they love them, I don't really know. I don't think the audience would look at Eric and Ernie, or look at Laurel and Hardy and say: 'They are two stars.' They are two very warm human beings. Maybe if it was Sinatra or Judy Garland, you'd say: 'Wow!' But you wouldn't say 'Wow!' to Eric and Ernie, you'd say: 'Ah . . .' That's the difference: wow and ah; that's all I can say.

Michael Palin

Fish are funny, for some reason

Since *Monty Python's Flying Circus* burst on to the screen in 1969 and created an international cult, Michael Palin has extended his range to encompass film for television (*East of Ipswich*) and the cinema, as well as becoming television's long-distance traveller in series such as *Pole to Pole* and a novelist with *Hemingway's Chair*. A product of Brasenose College, Oxford, Michael is one part of the wave of graduates that swept into comedy writing in the Sixties. Work on *The Frost Report* brought him and his writing partner Terry Jones in touch with a group from Cambridge – John Cleese, Graham Chapman and Eric Idle.

Michael wrote for *The Marty Feldman Comedy Machine*, *Do Not Adjust Your Set*, *The Complete and Utter History of Britain*, *The Rutles* and *Ripping Yarns.* He led us through a maze of staircases at his north London home into a well-lit study at the top of the house, with working surfaces built over filing cabinets, from one of which he took some red spiral-bound A4 notebooks with the 'Silvine' brand name – part of the *Python* archive.

MICHAEL PALIN: There's a huge difference between writing on your own and writing with a partner or in a team. In comedy writing I nearly always worked with a partner. Didn't mean in any way that we wrote each alternate line – we very rarely did that – but it always meant that there was somebody else there that you trusted to test the material on, and it seemed very important with comedy. Whereas with my novel, for instance, I became quite protective of it, and didn't read much of it out to anybody else because it was a different sort of reaction I was looking for. Comedy needs ... the noise of the laugh, you need to know that it's made that electrical connection that causes someone to laugh, and for that I needed a partner. So I've always felt that was the difference between my comedy writing and, say, writing the travel books, which I've been able to write on my own.

When Terry Jones and I wrote together before *Python* we were quite disciplined because it was such a joy to be a scriptwriter. One of my childhood ambitions was to be a scriptwriter because I'd seen all the comic performers – the Norman Wisdoms, the Hancocks – and I was really interested in the writing behind it, and always looked at the name of the scriptwriter. Galton and Simpson were my heroes of comedy, possibly even more than the performers. So Terry and I were really just so pleased to be able to do this rather than banking, or insurance, or bus driving, so we worked very hard and took on as much work as we possibly could.

The first thing we did of any substance was *The Frost Report* in 1966, maybe '65. Then we worked for Marty Feldman, the Two Ronnies, all sorts: *Broaden Your Mind,* which was a thing that the team that became *The Goodies* did in 1967–68. We'd write for absolutely anybody. And Terry was employed at the BBC – he was on contract in the script department; I wasn't – so he had to do a certain amount of work each week: links for *The Billy Cotton Band Show*, things like that.

We wrote in quite a structured way and we used to work usually in the same room all day. As the work-load got slightly heavier and we had to write longer sketches, we'd work half a day separately or sometimes a day separately, and then meet up after that. To start with we had to get x quota of jokes out, so we'd work either down at Terry's (he lives conveniently nine miles away, right through the centre of London, in Camberwell), or he'd come up here. It went on like that with the early *Python*, and then gradually we began to write more separately. Sometimes quite long chunks of material would get written separately, but it was equally important to meet together and try the material out before it was then presented to the rest of the *Python* team.

JMCG: **And they had been writing on their own, too?**
MICHAEL PALIN: Yes, *Python* was a series of little sort of villages which combined into a city. There was Jones-Palin village, and Chapman-Cleese village, and there was Idle village which had only Eric in it! And there was Gilliam, who had a suburb of his own, a crazed ghetto for which he would produce material which no one else could do. We would get together for a session every three or four days, or sometimes after a week. There was much more collab-

oration in the early days of *Python*, in the sense of the group being together more often, than there was later on.

DB: **Were you and Terry Jones writing for you and Terry Jones, or were you working for a sketch without any particular casting?**
MICHAEL PALIN: The idea was that you would write for the group. Sometimes one would have a very clear idea that one wanted John or Graham or Eric to be one of the characters in a sketch, and you might write it specifically for somebody. We would perform the sketch as we were writing it, and in the actual sessions, the *Python* writing sessions, one member of the group would be appointed to read the material. So John read what Graham and he wrote, and I used to read what Terry Jones and I wrote – which very often gave you a good chance of getting that part. If you read it and it worked, everybody laughed; they'd say: 'Well, that's fine!' Because Eric was on his own and we all felt a bit guilty because he hadn't got a writing partner, he was indulged a lot.

John and Terry used to argue over material. They seemed to be the two separate poles of *Monty Python*. There was a base of material which went in straight away because it was very funny. Then there would be other pieces that you would argue over and it is very hard, as you know, to argue about comedy. It's so subjective, it's impossible: 'This is funny!' 'No, it isn't!' It's a silly argument to have, but then it gets on to: 'But it could be funny, if . . .' 'Maybe it wasn't read right, or something. And you were in the kitchen making coffee when I was reading that end bit of it.' 'But it still isn't funny!'

So there'd be these fights and Terry might tend to theorise a little bit about the feeling of *Python* and what it should represent. John wasn't very good on that sort of thing. Terry would be quite emotional, and John would become very, very cool and detached, and bait Terry for being Welsh, so Terry would get more and more Welsh and passionate and bang the table . . . It was all necessary stuff, and there was quite a lot of teasing and chiding going on amongst the group.

DB: **With you and Jones having been at Oxford, and Cleese, Chapman and Idle at Cambridge, was there an Oxford versus Cambridge contest?**
MICHAEL PALIN: Oh, very definitely, yes. That was the area where we could insult each other. Personal insults were not traded that much, but the Oxford–Cambridge thing was a very good substitute for the personal insult. John thought everybody who came from Oxford was hopelessly woolly, and we all thought people from

Cambridge were frightfully neurotic and over-competitive and generally rather cold and bitter, persecuted. It was all to do with climate,
I worked it out: because in Cambridge this cold wind is blowing
across the Fens all the time, whereas Oxford is rather pleasant and
balmy and has nice pubs around, nice places to go to. So the Oxford
people were often diverted by pleasure, which they quite enjoy;
whereas Cambridge people were taught that pleasure is a bad thing,
which only rots the brain and decays your moral values. So we used
to have a few laughs like that, and actually you can see there is a difference in *Python*. There's an edge of cruelty to the Cambridge
material, and there's an edge of whimsy in the Oxford stuff. At best,
both are extremely good ingredients. At worst, the cruelty is just
cruelty and whimsy is just rather silly and candyfloss-like.

**JMcG: Who had overall control of 'This is what we'll do'? Was it
Ian McNaughton, the producer?**
MICHAEL PALIN: No – in fact, we presented Ian with the material
that we put into each show. The actual judging of the material was
done by us. Obviously if Ian didn't think something was going to
work or wouldn't be funny, it would affect our final decision. But,
generally speaking, we took the decision as to what would go into a
show and scribbled it all down, in these strange notebooks. I suppose the final say was genuinely with the group. We were demo-
cratic in that way. We were quite acrimonious sometimes – there
would be very difficult sessions – but in the end, I think we all
respected each other's judgement more than we did any outsider's.

**DB: Was each series planned as a whole? Did you have six
episodes all worked out, or was some of it left to the editing?**
MICHAEL PALIN: I don't think, as far as I can remember, that
things were filmed and then put into shows in a different order from
what we had decided. Because we'd all started as writers we thought
the writer's prerogative of choosing material was very important,
and the writer's list was all-important. So it wasn't really a question
of director or producer or anyone else saying: 'I think we need this
weight in this show, or this weight in that show.' We would block
out six shows in advance, because that's all we had material for, and
we had to do that because the filming had to be done first for all six
shows. Very often some of the links would come a bit later on, but
basically we stuck to the order that we worked out.
    I remember *Pythons* being planned in a fairly casual way. That's
not really fair to the people who actually worked on them, because
they had to work very hard, but decisions were taken sometimes

very casually, and in an enormous rush – right from the day when the series began and we hadn't decided on a title. One department was calling it one thing, another department was calling it another, and it was really complicated because people were making costumes and labelling them for a programme called *Bumwackit, Buzzard, Stubble and Boot* and the make-up department would be putting things together for something called *It's*, which it was for a while.

DB: **Who hit the title in the end?**

MICHAEL PALIN: My memory is that it was Eric and John, actually, who got the two names together, but we were all tossing names around to go with *Flying Circus*. The BBC had run out of patience with our pathetic attempts to get comic names, and said it had to be something with *Flying Circus*. They said: 'Why don't you call it *John Cleese's Flying Circus*, or something like that?' But John, quite rightly, didn't want to be stuck with responsibility for a show that might be the biggest disaster of all time.

One attempt was after I'd gone to my mother-in-law's for the weekend and she had a Women's Institute magazine, and in it was a little round-up of all the various entertainments in the Bedfordshire area. At Little Snetterton parish church there was a talk on, sort of, rush mats from Brunei, and it was accompanied by so-and-so on the piano. One of them was a talk accompanied by somebody called Gwen Dibley on the piano, and I thought Gwen Dibley sounded a really nice name, and I came back and said: 'Why don't we call the series *Gwen Dibley's Flying Circus*?' It was just so nice to give someone their own series without them knowing, so that the *Radio Times* would come through and land on the doormat, and they'd say: 'Mum! Mum, you've got your own series! Saturday nights, 12.15!'

Well, John was very astute, and said: 'Hang on, hang on! She could sue us for all we've got.' So Gwen Dibley never got her show, sadly. It's funny now that in the sitcom *The Vicar of Dibley* the Dibley name comes up. So that was that.

I think it was at a session at John's flat in Basil Street in Knightsbridge when we finally got together *Python*. Someone suggested 'Python' and then someone said, 'What's a good name to go with Python?' 'Monty.' It just seemed to go very well, and the BBC were very stony-faced and said: 'Well, that's ridiculous. You can call it *Monty Python's Flying Circus* if you want, but it'll be known as *Flying Circus*.' Of course, quite the opposite actually happened. Wrong! Wrong! Still, it's not so bad. The problem is not working with people who are wrong: as long as they consistently think they're right, you have someone to play against.

DB: How did the break-up of *Python* come about?

MICHAEL PALIN: It was a group of six people, each coming into it from a different direction. That was the great thing: well, two writers never think exactly the same anyway, but everyone had a slightly different approach, played comedy a slightly different way. What held us together was an appreciation of each other's comedy and the way it all moulded together. You needed an Eric in the group, you needed a John, you needed a Terry. We felt we all complemented each other, but it was like a – what's the word? – a centrifugal force, all the time, that was just being held together. It was like an explosion that had happened, and it couldn't be held together for long, and this was what happened in the end. Even by the middle of the second series there was a feeling: I think John found writing slightly more difficult by that time. Maybe he thought about wanting to write something else, possibly there was a bit of stress between him and Graham because Graham was leading this wild life and would tend to arrive rather late. There was a period during the early third series of *Python* where Graham was in quite bad shape, and difficult for someone who's as disciplined and thorough as John to write with.

So all this began to change the balance, and I think by the time we did the third series John was really thinking of his next move and doing something else. I've never really discussed it thoroughly with John, what was in his mind, but he just wanted to get out. I think he felt oppressed by being part of a group. Once that started, it all began to fall apart, people whizzed off in all directions. Eric went off to do *Rutland Weekend Television*, and Terry and I began to do other stuff. In a way, Terry was the most conscientious of all the Pythons, the most concerned in keeping the group together. I think that Terry could see that there was a potential to do movies, and probably Gilliam could as well, and of course this is what happened. We wound down the television series and then, just by Terry harrying all the rest into the idea of doing a film, we began to get together and say: 'Well, what would we write and how would it be?' and we came up with *Monty Python and the Holy Grail*. And that gave us a second life, the films we made after that.

I think that came about largely because the two Terries wanted to direct, and felt there was something that we could do better than we'd done on television. We could not only create better pictures and better images but in the end we would have much more control, because with the BBC we had to abide by certain rules, like on the Thursday night or Wednesday night, when we did our recording, we had only an hour and a half to do the whole thing, and if we didn't do it in that time, that was that. It meant everything was a bit of a rush, and we used to look at some of those shows and say: 'These are appalling, a mess – wigs on the wrong way round . . . and someone got the line wrong there . . . we didn't have time for a retake . . .'

By an extraordinary turn-around of taste, those aspects of *Python* now seem to be what people really like! I thought 'Spanish Inquisition', for instance, was a disaster, because I had this hat put on me just before I went on. It kept coming right down, and my mind wasn't in the sketch at all. I kept thinking: I've got a fucking hat on, I can't see a bloody thing, and no one's going to be able to see me, and here I am doing this stuff . . . If you actually look, I keep trying to push back the hat. And everyone says: 'Oh, Spanish Inquisition: legendary.'

We did the Knights of Ni in *The Holy Grail*, and I was on top of a ladder and that wasn't right, and then there was something else and then it started to rain, and this helmet came right over, you couldn't see anybody in there, and the rule with comedy is you've got to see the eyes: the more you can see of the face, the better it will be . . . It was like putting a bag over your head, playing the Knights Who Say 'Ni' . . . I can remember feeling afterwards, at the end of that day's filming: God, if only we had the money to do this again the next day, it would be funny. And yet now people love that. So you can't really tell; sometimes things that look rough have that spontaneity to them which people really like.

DB: **Do your plans for a *Python* reunion include a TV series?**
MICHAEL PALIN: There are certainly no plans for a series. What there would be is possibly a stage show, which would be a revamped version of what we did twenty years ago, using that material rather than new material, but sometimes material that hasn't been seen on stage – so we might do 'Cheese Shop' rather than 'Dead Parrot'.

I think it's a dangerous thing to do. Not because as you get older you lose your sense of humour at all, but there's a danger that people identify you with performing at a certain age, and comedy is so precise and every single millisecond of performance or every single word-order matters so much. You just go slightly wrong and people think, Their timing's gone off. That would be dreadful.

I'd like to think we'd still be able to time it. John and I did the 'Dead Parrot' sketch on American television in January last year as part of the promotion for *Fierce Creatures* and it was OK. But there is a certain rawness you need when you're doing material for the first time. When you're doing it for the five-hundredth time it loses a bit of an edge. But you can only try it and see, really.

JMcG: **Who wrote the 'Dead Parrot' sketch?**
MICHAEL PALIN: John and Graham.

JMcG: **Things must be going through your mind as the lines are coming up?**
MICHAEL PALIN: Yes, like: 'Who's going to interrupt from the audience?' That tended to happen on stage, because we played to very large audiences – seven thousand at the Hollywood Bowl, three thousand sometimes – and it's quite a gentle sketch, actually, 'Dead Parrot'. But you'd have to belt it out, and of course people knew the lines so well. John would do his consummate comedy timing – i.e., a pause of about eight seconds before saying the line, like he does – and he's brilliant, John, brilliant pauser. But people would come in, and get him so ratty: 'I was going to say that!'

It's not an easy way to play comedy. We've tried to make a stipulation that if we do the tour we should play, maximum, two-thousand-seater houses, and of course no one's interested, because there's no money for anybody. They all want you to play Wembley Stadium, at the very least, nowadays.

DB: **Do you think there is a touchstone for what's funny? Is there a rule, a set of rules?**
MICHAEL PALIN: I really don't know how you make the rule. It's all in the eye of the beholder. It just depends what's going on in the mind of the person who's listening or watching, and you just honestly don't know. I think there are certain sure things: timing, of course, is vitally important. If you're trying to create a laugh, the pause and that moment of saying the line, choosing your moment, getting it clearly out – that's one of those things that's obviously very much part of comedy . . .

JMcG: **And would you do that in the read-through?**
MICHAEL PALIN: Sometimes the things I read worst were the things I really wanted to impress the others with. I'd suddenly get slightly aware that reading this was very important, whereas the best things were when you just had a pile of material and you just ran through them and you felt completely relaxed and you just knew how to play them. It's like when you're telling a joke – not that I'm good at telling jokes – but you know when you've got your moment, when it's flowing, and it just comes out. If you think all the moves ahead – How am I going to tell this? – you're lost. So if you start being self-conscious when you're reading material out, or even when you're writing it, it's not going to work so well. That's what I

love about comedy: it taps that completely imprecise area of inspiration; you don't know why you've written that, where it's come from, but you just happen to know that *that is funny*! Take one word out or do a slightly different voice, it isn't funny.

DB: On the page, how many times might you rewrite a line to get that precision?

MICHAEL PALIN: Again, I would say the best work that we did came out as it eventually was written and performed. I suppose there were certain areas where, yes, you'd play around with a phrase, or add another phrase. But the best sketches in *Python* came out fully fledged. Something like 'Dead Parrot', there was never a word rewritten in that. They just read it out and it worked. No one added anything, because John and Graham were really consummate, brilliant writers together, in a very odd way. As John would say, he'd write ninety-five per cent and Graham would write five per cent some days, but Graham's five per cent was absolutely essential because it was truly surreal. It may well have been Graham who suggested its being a Norwegian Blue, which changed it from being an ordinary parrot. An Amazonian Green or macaw is just not funny, but a Norwegian Blue, being extremely unlikely, is. And then, Norway is funnier than a lot of other countries, which one has to remember . . .

Like fish are funny, for some reason: haddock, halibut. We used fish a lot in *Python*, I don't know why they're funny but they are extremely funny, whereas many of God's creatures aren't so much. Birds weren't particularly funny – we used them every now and then – but fish were funny.

I think the best sketches just happen. 'Lumberjack Song', for instance, which I remember very well writing, because we'd struggled all day with this sketch about the barber. We thought the funniest thing was the sketch about the barber who had a terrible urge to wound his clients and a terrible fear of haircutting. 'Cutting, cutting, cutting,' he used to say, he just couldn't bear the idea of cutting. He became pathetic as a barber, and would put on a tape recording of snipping, and the guy in the chair would be talking, 'Oh, good match last night,' and all that, and would look round and there was no one cutting his hair, there's a guy cracking up!

We thought that was a good, funny idea, and then: how to end it? Which was never a great problem with *Python*, because you could go somewhere else. But we felt we had to do something, and I remember purely ad-libbing: 'I don't want to be a barber, anyway, I want to be a lumberjack!' Then that just wrote itself. I can remember we were writing here and it was about quarter to seven at night. That's not a good time to be writing comedy, really – the pubs are open, you've worked all day – but finally we just got on to this riff about being a lumberjack instead, and it just came out, and the whole song was written by quarter past seven. The next day we rang up Fred Tomlinson, who did the music – and said: 'We've got this song: it's got to be jolly!' Fred somehow managed to put it together with music, and that's how it happened.

We got to a stage where we knew each other's material so well that we would write things in John and Graham's style, hoping we could get it through, and we wrote a horoscope sketch. They loved using the thesaurus (like for 'Cheese Shop', they had a book on cheese), for things like 'Dead Parrot' – all the thesaurus words on death – they loved doing that. So we wrote a sketch about astrology, and we got about forty different words for horoscope. It was really just a joke, but at the end of it John and Graham said: 'We like that one; that's really good!'

You see, in this notebook, that's one that didn't go anywhere: 'The Party: A field. On a table, drinks are set out with glasses. Host and wife stand waiting. Speeded-up, a guest appears, then another, then another, until a party is formed. They all talk at the same time, then they move in different groups, to a bus stop. Then they get on, and we see them having a party at various places. A train goes past them at a level crossing; perhaps they go into someone's house. The people call the police to arrest them, a chase.' There, that never got anywhere.

'Filming in London: building site, misty, Shepherd's Bush street, brackets wife-swapping, doctor with stethoscope . . .' And we'd have the Thames symbol – we wanted to do the Thames logo: 'And now, a rotten old BBC programme!' We used to do all those things. All rather naughty things. Things in the news, or things people had just been to see: I remember when we'd been to see *The Wild Bunch* – every time someone got shot, blood just spurted out. Quite ridiculous stylisation, so someone would write that up. That was as near as we got to being topical. A lot of it, of course, was done from existing TV programmes. TV was showing new stuff all the time, so we could play around with that. I was hoping some American university would come and buy all this lot of notebooks. I don't want it here, if it's going to burn . . .

DB: **The other work that you do – screenplays, fiction – is there a thread running through it?**

MICHAEL PALIN: It tends to be the usual fertile comedy area of man against the system, the free spirit or the awkward character who always runs up against what I suppose we all see as a very conventional, respectable, responsible way of life. That's probably in all the work that I've done. That mischief-making character.

JMCG: **Who's your favourite film comedian?**

MICHAEL PALIN: When I was growing up in Sheffield, my favourite would be Norman Wisdom. Norman Wisdom was doing all that stuff . . . I loved the fact that there'd be all these people discussing D-Day and pushing things on maps around, and he'd be bringing them a cup of tea and putting it there, right in the middle of the map, and they'd be moving it: 'No, there!' When they were talking about moving troops, he was wondering where they wanted the cup of tea put. It was in *Man of the Moment.* And of course Jerry Lewis, too, I quite liked, because he did some very funny sight gags. Odd, gawky, strange, out-of-place characters who didn't fit in. Those are the people I've always been interested in. People who somehow stand at the back and screw up the photograph, or make the annoying remark when everything's going very smoothly. It's like in *Monty Python's Life of Brian,* when Graham appears at the window stark naked and addresses them all, and says: 'Don't be like this. Make up your own minds, you're all individuals!' And the bloke at the back says: 'I'm not!' Just things like that, I love that.

JMCG: **Did you contribute much to *A Fish Called Wanda*, to the character you played?**

MICHAEL PALIN: I had quite a bit of discussion with John exactly about that character. He just said: 'I'm going to write a character in a heist movie who can't get the words out because he's got a stammer.' He knew my father had a stammer and he said: 'How would you play this character?' So we talked about it and, yeah, I did add a lot. I said that normally people have got an awful lot to say: all the time, they're trying to say it, but they can't get it out. It's not that they're taciturn people; sometimes, quite the opposite. We worked out the idea for Ken that he loves animals because humans have let him down completely: so all his love is transferred to animals, which he started killing by accident. This is the frustration and this helps to build up the stammer. So the supreme moment at the end when he's the only person who knows where the loot is, he just can't deal with the tension of it. Except that Jamie, of course, gets through to him. There's that scene where she gives him a kiss, and he immediately and smoothly comes out with the entire information. So yes, we did work out all that stuff.

The good thing about *Wanda*, apart from the writing, was that it was kept to a small group and there was the feeling that they were trapped in this world, this inner group of people. Whereas *Fierce Creatures* could have gone anywhere; there were far more characters. Once people aren't trapped in a situation, the tension slackens, and comedy depends on tension, doesn't it, really? It depends very much on the fact that you can't go anywhere else.

I was watching a television comedy – I can't really say it by name – and there was some very funny material but the crucial moments were fabricated, they weren't realistic. They engaged in some action which was just not real, and then expected the consequences of that action to provoke comedy for the next ten or fifteen minutes. But it doesn't, if it's not real in the first place. In really good comedy, *Fawlty Towers* or something like that, there are no two ways about it. Cause and effect are so tight that you can't have any other way of doing it. That person cannot *possibly* have been in another room. This person *has* to say this remark at that time. He *has* to have burnt the . . . the kebabs at *exactly* that moment, and the smoke *has* to come through the door just then. John understands that, and that's why *Fawlty Towers* is so good, because there's no way out and you cringe, you think: 'Oh, God!'

It's also why one of the best new comic creations is Alan Partridge, because Steve Coogan creates this terrible strait-jacket for himself and his character. There has to be that tightness, you have to feel that only he has to be there. That's why comedy works.

And I really don't enjoy playing comedy unless I feel there's some sort of character there, even if it's just a quick moment . . . like the fish-slapping dance, which is something that John and I do, and which is one of the silliest things, funniest things, we've done in *Python*. It's a very modest thing, but there is a relationship between the two of them. It isn't just a tall man hitting another man with a fish. I like to think the character I played is slightly prissy; he's done a lot of folk-dancing in the evenings, so he's absolutely enjoying it, which is really irritating John. So in the end when he's hit with the fish it isn't just a piece of ritual, it's John working out exactly what he feels about this prat of a character. Which gives an edge to it all, really. So even for things as short as that you have to try and write a character in there. Otherwise, it's bland.

DB:　Do you feel happier writing those characters for performers that you're familiar with or can they just be put on the page and an actor can pick them up?

MICHAEL PALIN:　Certain people I just know are funny and know how to deal with comic lines. With other people, you hope that they will act their character so well that the line will come out. Something will be made funny by the conviction of the person playing the character.

JMCG: **What's the difference, when it comes to writing a film script, from the way *Python* used to work?**
MICHAEL PALIN: Well, the great difference is just in the kind of comedy. *East of Ipswich* was comedy of observation which depended on a reality. I wanted a perfect representation of an English seaside village in the 1950s, and in *Python* we would have kept that up for a short while and then one of the beach huts would have blown up, or a man with a cucumber would have appeared in the frame. You had to be much more disciplined with something like *East of Ipswich*.

JMCG: **And are you writing comedy at the moment?**
MICHAEL PALIN: I'm not really writing comedy at the moment, no. I'm doing something on Hemingway; it's his hundredth anniversary next year.

DB: **Does that mean you're a Hemingway obsessive like the character in your novel *Hemingway's Chair*?**
MICHAEL PALIN: No, I had to write the book rather quickly and chose a story that had been in my head about a mild-mannered man being obsessed by a legendary bombastic character. Hemingway was the right man. When I wrote the novel I had to do a lot of research into him. We're doing three or four programmes on him, we're going to Cuba to film.

Going back to comedy, I always think it works best when there is uncertainty and complication, and that's why *Python* is a paean to the hopelessness of the British, trying to get themselves together, or run a television company or an army or a church. Comedy is a way of coping with situations that aren't right. As soon as people have perfect situations, it doesn't work. That's why the Internet is uncomical. We should be making jokes about the fact that you have 'dot com slash'! – it's a silly way of communicating when you've got this wonderful language you've developed over hundreds of years – but people don't because the Internet is seen as a great benefit to mankind.

John Sullivan

Always trying to be different

The son of a south London plumber, John Sullivan joined the BBC as a props man to meet the stars, and was immediately ordered to keep away from them. He managed to get a script to Ronnie Barker, who passed it on to Dennis Main Wilson. A pilot in the *Comedy Playhouse* format which had been pioneered by Galton and Simpson led in 1977 to John's first sitcom, *Citizen Smith,* starring Robert Lindsey as Wolfie Smith, the Che Guevara of south-east London. It was the first in a string of successes that included *Only Fools and Horses*, which was immediately recognised as a triumph of characterisation and just as quickly taken to the heart of the public. *Just Good Friends, Dear John* and *Sitting Pretty* were followed by the innovative *Roger Roger*. John now has his office in his home, a substantial house at the end of a gravel drive in the stockbroker region of Surrey.

JMcG: **Does it help you to know who your cast is, who you're writing for?**

JOHN SULLIVAN: Oh, yeah. I did the first series of *Only Fools and Horses* without a pilot, so I wrote six episodes blind, not knowing who they were. Then we got David Jason and Nick Lyndhurst and made a few adjustments. Once I'd seen that first series, I was writing for them. You aim towards the strengths of the actor. You can hear the voice, see the face, see David's eyes, his looks, and Nick's open mouth. So a lot of the time Del would say something, and I'd just write: 'Cut to Rod', knowing full well Nick would give you the most wonderful expression and you'd get a great big laugh on it.

JMcG: **You put reaction shots into the script?**

JOHN SULLIVAN: For those two, yeah. Lots of them. And doing *Roger Roger* I put in 'Cut for a reaction' to someone. There's a couple of times in *Roger Roger* where I didn't put it in, and then afterwards thought, God, why didn't we have it? There's a natural reaction there and we didn't get it, and it's because it wasn't there in the script, so it's my fault.

JMcG: **Directors trained in television wouldn't cover the reaction. A director who's trained in film would.**

JOHN SULLIVAN: When I joined the BBC, I never knew how to lay a script out; I didn't know what was expected. So the first thing I wanted was a script, but what I realised years later was that I had a director's script, a shooting script, which had all the reaction, so that was the habit I got into: 'Cut to reaction, cut to reaction'. When I saw other writers' work I realised they didn't do it. But that's how I write.

DB: **Do directors sometimes feel that you're over-instructing them?**

JOHN SULLIVAN: Dennis Main Wilson was all for it. He was all for me coming to editing and everything, being heavily involved, and being on filming, and he talked to me an awful lot. Ray Butt was less so. He was protecting his area more. I've never had anyone complain, but of course after that I worked with Tony Dow, who then was an assistant floor manager. He came through slowly and we'd been mates – I was his best man and all that – so that at the time he took over directing we knew each other very well personally. Once Tony took over I became even more involved.

JMcG: **And you write music, don't you?**

JOHN SULLIVAN: I do the music for a lot of them and if I'm not doing it I'm there in the studio hearing what they're doing. Music used well is tremendously emotive. We've done some stuff where, by picking the right song, we brought so much out of the character. The scene when Rodney got married and Del was left alone, I chose that Simply Red one, 'Holding Back the Years', or 'Holding Back the Tears', whatever it's called, and people were actually crying in the audience. We use that in the studio, which is a bit dangerous for editing afterwards, but we got away with it.

DB: **And the songs that you yourself wrote and performed, when did they start?**

JOHN SULLIVAN: As a kid, I was always writing songs, but then you didn't have tape recorders, so by tomorrow they'd gone. Then for *Citizen Smith* Peter Whitmore actually chose 'The Red Flag' as the opening, and as the end thing as well on the pilot. I said to Dennis Main Wilson: 'It seems a bit boring, having the same thing. Can't we get another song?' He said: 'What are you after?' I said: 'Well, can anyone have a go?' So I wrote this thing called 'The Glorious Day', which Bob Lindsay recorded, and that was the first thing I'd written and had recorded. After that, for *Only Fools and Horses*, the music was in fact the original music that I'd written, but Ray Butt didn't particularly like it, so he got Ronnie Hazelhurst to do a number. Then David and Nick didn't like *that*, so Ray in the end sent my tape to Chas and Dave, who were then doing the beer commercials. The way I understand the story – although it may not be true, because people used to keep me very much in the dark – they were coming to the studio on a certain date and about three weeks prior to that they had this massive hit record, called *Ain't No Pleasing You*, which went to No. 1, and suddenly they were off touring. This is how Ray was – he was a clever sod – he said: 'Don't worry. Come down to the studio we've got someone.' So I've gone to Lime Grove, we'd had a couple of drinks, and I said: 'Who is he?' He said: 'It's you, mate.' I said: 'I can't do that!' Anyway, nine lagers later, I'm in there, and I did it. And I told my wife: 'Oh, Ray got some pub singer in.'

When we went to the studio for the show she was in the audience and she said to me she just froze when she heard my voice and she couldn't enjoy the show. Actually, she didn't realise there was an end number as well coming . . . So that was a bad night for her.

I got into doing it then. *Just Good Friends*, because we had Paul Nicholas, I thought: This would be great; we've got a singer. *Dear John*, I wanted Lynsey de Paul to do that. I don't know what went wrong, but we didn't get her. I won an award, best TV theme music, for the American version.

JMcG: **What did you think of the difference between the American version and the British version?**
JOHN SULLIVAN: When I first went over, my agent warned me that when you go in the studio you think you're seeing a different show, they change it so much. But a week or so before I arrived, there was a writers' strike in America. The Writers' Guild let me cross the picket line outside the studio and it was like *déjà vu*, because they were just doing my script – just place names changed, and I couldn't believe it.

Judd Hirsch played the lead. It worked ever so well. The audience

stood up and applauded and the head of NBC came up to me afterwards and said: 'You've got a series.' It was the kind of Hollywood
thing you see in films, where you arrive at the airport and there's a
limousine. Everyone assumes you're going to move and sends
brochures for the kids' schools. They just assume we come from a
backwater. I said: 'I don't want to go to America, I'm happy here.'
But because that script had worked they decided to stick with the
British scripts basically for the first twelve of them, and then the
American writers took over completely. It was fine for a while, but
one day I was over there at rehearsals and the characters were all
standing round, and one came out with the line: 'OK, group hug.' I
thought, That's me out, I've gone. That line finished my career in
America, really. 'Group hug'! But I had a lot of good times and they
were very courteous and nice.

DB: **Presumably the show would have continued in Britain if
you hadn't lost your lead, Ralph Bates?**
JOHN SULLIVAN: We suddenly realised this wasn't indigestion or
anything silly, and he was going into hospital. I was up in our bedroom here when we got the call from his wife on Saturday morning.
He'd had the biopsy and she was phoning to say it was cancer. He
was wonderful, and such a nice man as well.

DB: **It's got a quite different atmosphere from *Only Fools and
Horses*.**
JOHN SULLIVAN: I'm always trying to be different. I don't want to
get stuck.

JMcG: **Now in *Roger Roger* you've really got highs and lows of
comedy and drama.**
JOHN SULLIVAN: Before I'd even written it everyone was saying
that it must have an audience, and I was saying I didn't want one.
There was nothing on paper, and no one knew what I wanted to do.
I just dug in and said: 'It will not work any other way. I can't get
stuck with one set, an office set. I've got to show people with their
own problems, their own lives and their dreams, and the only way I
can do it is all film, and because of some of the areas I want to touch
I don't want an audience there.' When I'd written about three or
four scripts, Geoffrey Perkins said: 'I see what you mean. I understand.'
   I hope when we do the next series we're really into swift camera
movement. Rather than using the hard cut, using one camera to do
an awful lot. It gives life, movement . . . I've always argued that

where you're in a small set and you want movement, but it's difficult to choreograph that with all the actors and cables in the way – I've always said, well, whenever we can't actually use real movement, let the camera give us life. Even though actors are basically sitting down or standing, you get a feel of action.

I want to introduce a bit more music into the new series. The company who did the opening titles – young company called Red Pepper, young directors and cameramen – I want them to go out and film London bits – anything, down-and-outs, beautiful things, whatever, just film, film, film – and between certain scenes I'd like to put in a little ten-second bit with a little music across it . . .

JMCG: **Use it as punctuation . . .**
JOHN SULLIVAN: It gives that life. I've been told that at times it's too slow, but life dictates the speed of a scene. So if the actors have got to pause a bit, let them pause. You can speed it all up by those little breaks. They do it in *NYPD Blue*. Now, *they* do it because they're coming back from a commercial. We cut the commercials out, so suddenly you've got a new style. I like that: let's do it. You've got to keep your eyes out and see what's happening all around, if you're not actually inventing something new yourself, and don't be frightened to borrow something, change it slightly, but use it and move on, rather than just stay still for thirty years.

Roger Roger got criticised. One guy said: 'I can't really take this going from high farce to tragedy so quickly.' My argument always has been that my wife and I can be sitting in here celebrating something wonderful . . . the champagne's going . . . and over there, there could be a death in the family. That's why I want to use these other shots, to say whatever's happening: that poor sod's still starving and these people are still going past in their Rolls-Royce. I'm trying to capture as much of it as possible to give different flavours of what's going on in our life, to balance it against what I'm actually writing. It'll give it a quite bizarre feel . . .

Generally what I do is, I write characters. I used a minicab firm because a lot of characters come and go, and I can just take all these people from my head and hang them on the clothes-line for a while. That's all I do: character comedy, character drama, very interesting people.

DB: **Is that your usual method of working? Did you have the characters for *Only Fools and Horses* and then discover the black market as the milieu for it?**
JOHN SULLIVAN: They almost came together. Ray Butt, who pro-

duced the last lot of *Citizen Smith*, we knew that was coming to an end. I did a pilot show, a thing about a football team, which the BBC said they wanted; I got to episode 3 and they killed it. I didn't know what else to write, and I was desperate. We'd just got our first house and a young baby, and we'd got to pay that mortgage and put the groceries on the table. I was in the BBC Club bar with Ray, and in the past he and I had discovered that we had both worked in markets. His parents owned a stall in Roman Road and I used to work in Hilda Street Market, Balham. We discovered that our favourite character was the fly-pitcher. He's always funny, always a lad, and he was only there for half an hour, because he had to get away quickly before the market inspector came. You can have a good laugh with them, then they're gone. You barely knew their names but they seemed like friends. You never seemed to see them anywhere: where do they come from, where do they go? Ray said: 'Why don't you have a crack at that?' So I took this imaginary guy from the market where I'd been, and I followed him on an imaginary journey. In those days I had a lot of mates who lived in tower blocks. The lifts never worked and you always had to walk up to the seventeenth floor to get them to go to football. One of the things I wanted to say in it was: The lifts don't work in council blocks. Will somebody do something?

What's his life like? I knew a couple of guys. One is a fellow who works for me now, a mate of mine from my old street; he's got a brother who's about twelve years older than he is, and the brother has naturally guided him and led him and looked after him. And I knew another set of brothers, the same situation. And my sister is fourteen years older than I am, so as a kid she was never like a normal sister, she was kind of an auntie. It took me until I was twenty to really take her as a sister. I thought, I can do it in a way that he's got this kid brother: the mother died, and he brought him up. People will look on him as a hero because he didn't let the kid go into care or an orphanage, he brought him up. Even though he's a bit of a toerag, Del, and he'll sell you an iffy thing, he brought that kid up, so that's a great sound basis for a sympathetic man.

DB: For the settings of other shows, do you have a routine of research? Do you go and hang around in a minicab office?
JOHN SULLIVAN: No, I didn't do that, because I know so many minicab drivers. Virtually it's only myself and the guy who works for me, out of all that group of friends, that haven't been a minicab driver at some point. I'm writing this new comedy, and I'm writing it with a guy called Steve Glover. I've known him for twenty-some-

thing years, and even he was a minicab driver. I've known so many so the information and the background to that was pretty easy.

The new thing I'm writing is called *Heartburn Hotel*. The basic idea is this guy came out of the army after the Falklands War, with his army pay-out, and read that Birmingham would be the host for the 1992 Olympic Games. So he invested all his money in this hotel, and of course, for reasons best known to the Olympic Committee, it went to Barcelona, which took him totally by surprise, and his hotel failed, and now it's a DSS place, almost. He's got bed-and-breakfast and he's got illegal immigrants; they're putting everyone with him. He's a working-class snob. He should have been a general in the army, but no one recognises his ability – he's one of that sort. So he almost blames these poor people for the state of his life. He hasn't been as successful as he thought he would be, and he's a rather angry man, the last man in the world you'd ever have running a DSS place. I haven't been up to Birmingham, but Steve has done various bits of work in some of these hotels, so he's seen a bit of it.

JMcG: How will you work with him as a double act?
JOHN SULLIVAN: We started off trying to literally sit in the room and work together. But we've got very different styles. I take a long time thinking about where I'm going to go, I can't work to a set construction. I have to think for ages. He's a much faster type – he's younger than me – he's much faster. In the end I had to tell him to fuck off, I couldn't stand it any more, because he'd be getting in my ear-hole all the time. So we get together for a week or so and we crash out six possible good ideas. He'll take his three favourites, he'll go away and write them, I'll do mine and then when we're ready he'll send his to me, and I'll have a go at his. And we're there: I'm just finishing off the last one at the moment, and then we're just going to spend a week tidying up, and we start filming in early April.

Steve is some kind of second cousin fourteen times removed from my wife. That's how I met him, at various family weddings over the years, and then one wedding he said: 'I did this thing in a pub. I wrote some stuff for it.' Then three or four years after that [there] suddenly came through the post: 'Would you have a read of this, my first TV thing?' What he had was three good characters, crying out for a place to live. There was no reason for them being there, there was no background, and after a while I said: 'I've got this idea about a hotel, and I haven't got anyone living in it. Why don't your people move into my hotel, and we'll see . . . ?' I'm not sure yet if the producer realises it's different, he seems to be trying to think of it along the lines of an ordinary, straight sitcom. We describe it once as

Menopausal Mansions on Schizophrenia Street! You've got so many people trapped together with all these problems, it's going to be slightly crazy . . .

Of course I've had something like eighteen years writing all on my own, and suddenly to have somebody else in the room was at times like an invasion of my privacy. To get used to the idea of another writer being there was very difficult, and in the end we had to come to this other arrangement. Once I've done all the thinking I can write fast. Sometimes it's like you've got a hole in the head and these ideas are pouring out and you can't get them down quick enough. When I reach the stage where I'm perfectly happy and I know that the logic is there, that everything actually fits and makes sense, then I can go. But in that guessing period, I've got to do it on my own.

DB: Do you always work in the same room, with the same equipment?

JOHN SULLIVAN: Because I'm not very good with computers, I don't know where else I could ever go. So I always work here, on a word processor. Years ago, I'd go into rehearsals and do rewrites on an old typewriter. But I can't take my computer with me and I don't know how to do these laptops. But I haven't got any particular routine. Most days I go into the office round about seven, and kind of hope for the best, and if nothing's happening . . . I can't be one of those writers who will sit there all day looking at a blank screen, just waiting for inspiration. I'd rather just take the dog for a walk or go to the pictures or something. I give the day up after an hour. But then, if something happens, if I'm watching something or talking to someone in the house and it's eight o'clock in the evening and something hits me, I'll go and work from eight until two. Or sometimes I've woken up in the middle of the night, two in the morning, and something's happening. I'll get up and I'll work round until nine, ten, the following day. So I have no set pattern whatsoever, just how it comes. And I always find, something I hate about myself, I tend to do my best work when I'm under tremendous pressure. Because I'm like most writers, quite lazy. You don't work until you have to. So I generally find towards the end of a series that I'm working God knows how many hours – eighteen, nineteen a day, and I wish it wasn't that way, but the best stuff comes out then. I'd much prefer the best stuff to come out in a very controlled and civilised manner, but it doesn't, and people almost wait for me to be pressured so they can get the best, which is sad.

DB: Is there any aspect of writing that you dread having to do?

JOHN SULLIVAN: I don't look forward to that first day when you sit down: We're off! That's the worst day of the lot.

JMcG: **You've made notes before that?**
JOHN SULLIVAN: I always mean to. I've got so many of these tiny machines, they're everywhere, notebooks. And I'll be in a restaurant and hear something and go: 'Oh, yeah that's great.' So, backs of fag packets . . . I don't actually take too many notes, but I know where I want to get to. I very rarely sit down and go: 'Page 1.' I'll start somewhere – wherever, in the middle, anywhere, I don't really care. I'll go back to the beginning. I'll go to wherever I feel I'm strongest just to get going, to get moving, to get those words down, get into it. That idea of just 'Page 1' is a killer, and I advise everyone I ever talk to who wants to write, if you start on Page 1 and it's not working, well, go to Page 30. Start anywhere. Just start, start getting a flavour, start getting a taste of the thing for yourself.

DB: **What are you getting the flavour of, the characters?**
JOHN SULLIVAN: Yeah, because they start to change, as you move along. You start off with an outline, rough idea of a character, and as you go along you suddenly think: That would be nice, he loves Abba! Right, great, because there's a nice gag coming along about Abba! But if you'd decided he was a Beatles fan you say: 'I can't write that Abba gag, because he's a Beatles fan. No, sod that, I haven't written the Beatles fan bit yet, so I'll change it!' That's what I like: whatever his feelings are, his politics, you can change them as you go along, until now you've got the person, and then you can go back and say, 'Right, I'll go to Page 1, now I know who he is. We'll have him walking out of this club, that's how I'll introduce him. And the car, I know what car he drives now, that says something.'
    I'm never really happy with a character until I can actually go back to where he or she sat at school; it's a weird thing, his desk. What did he carve on his desk? I feel I really know them then.

DB: **Do you keep notes of these characteristics?**
JOHN SULLIVAN: No, they're in my head. Somebody's asking me about *Fools and Horses* (they're doing a book on it), and they said: 'Can we read your bibliography?' I said: 'Sorry? You want to say that again?' So they have to keep phoning me up: 'When did this happen? How old was Del?' I've got it in my head. It causes problems at times, with a lot of European countries wanting to do their versions of *Fools and Horses*. We've done one in Holland, and now there's a Scandinavian version apparently going to happen, and

German. Of course I send them copies of the scripts, but they phone my agent: 'Can you send the rest of it?' and I say: 'There is no rest of it. Get me a first-class seat and a nice hotel, and I'll come over and talk to you. It's all up here.'

I used to read other writers' stuff, would-be writers' stuff – I don't do it now – and they would actually write down what the character's all about. Then you start reading the dialogue and the actual story and there's no indication of the character. They think: I've done that.

DB: How did Del get his characteristic phrases?
JOHN SULLIVAN: What, the French phrases? When I started the first series we were slowly gravitating towards Europe, and I noticed every packet of food, although it's all in English, when you turn over there's French. And I thought: This guy, he likes to impress, he likes to think he impresses people with his rings; he doesn't realise that he's making the worst possible statement about himself. And I thought it would be quite nice, because he's selling stuff that's coming from Europe, that he would pick up on a few little things, and suddenly realise he's impressing Trigger. Anyone can! So we just introduced these little phrases, such as 'Fabrique Belgique', and they're all thinking: What a prat!

I'm always wary of actually trying to introduce catch-phrases. I think the only one I've deliberately introduced was in *Sitting Pretty*, where Annie kept saying 'phenomenal'. That kind of worked. But you can make a cross for yourself, because halfway through the second series that catch-phrase becomes quite boring. So you've now got to invent something else, or drop that character. Well, in reality, if that character said these things, they wouldn't suddenly drop them from their life. So if you do get a catch-phrase you should be careful how many times you use it. Becomes kind of lazy writing in the end: if you can't think of anything funny, 'Oh, I'll chuck that in.' That's the temptation, and if it ever crosses your mind you should take a long walk.

JMcG: Now you've reached the stage where you go in to the BBC and say, 'I want to do this,' but you know how it used to be, you remember what the BBC used to be like . . .
JOHN SULLIVAN: I took a pilot of *Just Good Friends* in to John Howard Davies and put it on his desk (he wasn't there). An hour later I went into the bar to have a drink, and John came in. He'd read the pilot and liked it, and asked: 'Well, how does it develop?' I told him and he just said, 'We'll have it.' And it was like that. In the bar, over a pint. Now you give it to the head, the head gives it to his

reader to read and the reader gives it to a committee, and then another committee, and you have to write a treatment to go before an accountants' committee . . . I don't know how anything gets made. It really is a long drawn-out process now.

When I did *Citizen Smith*, they put me on a contract and they wanted seven *Citizen Smiths* plus a pilot. You really wanted to write the pilots to get that cheque, and nothing ever happened to pilots. I wrote one pilot called *Dear John*, to which, again, nothing happened. Then *Fools* suddenly took off, and about eight months later *Just Good Friends* started. All of a sudden these old pilots were coming off the shelf, weren't they? Suddenly you were gold dust: you could do it, you had the touch. So I went away and did *Dear John*. That was madness anyway: three series a year, eighteen or twenty scripts a year, was impossible. That's how it used to be: seven and one pilot, all the time, for Jimmy Gilbert when he was head of Light Entertainment. Jimmy's favourite saying, I don't know if you remember, was: 'Will they understand it in Wick?' His family lived in Wick. He didn't like the title *Only Fools and Horses* and he said to me: 'Will they understand it in Wick? Can you think of something else?' So I retitled it *Dip Your Wick* and, being a Baptist, he didn't find it at all amusing. I almost got the sack on that one.

DB: **Is there a minimum amount of time between gags, or a maximum?**
JOHN SULLIVAN: It's an intuition, a feel you have. Particularly with something like *Fools and Horses*, where you can drop into drama quite easily, because you know them so well, I can go seven or eight pages without a real belly-laugh, just little character things between them. But when I've done that I like to come back with a big laugh if I possibly can, and it's quite easy because you get that big relief laugh: the audience want to laugh.

DB: **Is the structure important?**
JOHN SULLIVAN: Structure? That's an odd one, because I always fight and argue like hell about the structure when people want to make changes, and I go: 'No, it upsets the structure; the balance is gone.' Then we finish the show and they say: 'God, we're ten minutes too long,' and immediately I go: 'Oh, we can cut that bit, cut that out – fuck the structure.' And, sitting talking to you, I realise what I do. So the structure's important until you're ten minutes too long.

DB: **How do you know that something's funny?**

JOHN SULLIVAN: I tend to pace up and down and almost act it; I talk to myself an awful lot. I actually got out of going shopping with my wife through talking to myself in Marks & Spencer's. We've got a lot of mental homes around here and she started getting worried. When you go into the read-through you hear it and you know then. I make marks. If it's not going to work I put a circle round it and apologise. I don't know, you just know.

JMcG: Are you working to get a reaction from the audience?
JOHN SULLIVAN: If you've got a studio audience, you write for the audience. I'd written one *Fools and Horses* special, called 'To Hull and Back', and I knew it was all film, so I didn't write it with the idea 'I've got to put a gag in here to get that noise'. I didn't need the noise in the background. Then I did another one, that was supposed to be on film, but shown to a studio audience, so I was writing it with that in mind: 'I've got to get that noise around here, get that laughter in. And I'd better leave some kind of gap to get another laugh in.' Because you can't crowd laugh on laugh.
    Then there were various problems. I'm not sure if it was illness or what, but they suddenly said: 'We haven't got time now to show it to an audience,' so it was done cold. It lacked that noise where you needed the laugh. David and Nick had been told to act it in the way you would with an audience. So – this is not meant to sound insulting – David would come up kind of bigger-faced, if you know what I mean. He'd give it a bigger reaction, because it's going to an audience soon. Whereas on the one with no audience he gave it a much more subtle approach. We actually ended up in such desperate straits, the last scene was filmed in a studio by a camera crew who'd only ever done horse-racing. We whipped them straight back from Haydock Park.
    If you've got no audience, you can crowd two or three laughs. If they come naturally, you can bang them in because the people at home are going to get them, but obviously they're going to go right over a studio audience. Even if it's being done live, and the actors can pause for it, the audience get fed up with repetitious laughter.
    The thing I'm doing at the moment, I'd been saying to Steve: 'Take some laughs out! You've got one, two, three, four, five ... The audience are going to be fed up: save them!'

JMcG: What do you think are the most satisfying aspects of your own work? What are you best at?
JOHN SULLIVAN: Character writing. I'm OK at plots, but what satisfies me most is getting a good character. Of course, the only test

of that is when the audience have watched it. A lot of people say it doesn't matter if the audience don't particularly like the piece, you've still got a good character. But I look at it like the old days: you take a play and you put it on the stage. If they don't like it, they chuck tomatoes at it and you're off; if they like it, it'll run. I think that's fair. You're creating a product, you're putting it to the public, they pays their money.

Roger, Roger has never set the ratings alight – 9.30 Tuesday night against *Taggart*, it's not going to – but the reaction from both the press and the public has been so good that you feel satisfied. You think, OK, we're doing six million, which compared with *Fools* is no big shakes, but it's warm and nice and people are enjoying it. The letters are coming in . . .

At the end of the day it's those people who go into the post office and buy a TV licence – they pay my wages, they pay the heating in this place. And if I'm not keeping them happy, I'm not doing a good job, I feel I'm cheating. It's nice to get that response from them. So I think, OK, I'm doing a decent job. That's the most satisfying thing.

Richard Curtis

A slow-motion career

Richard Curtis is a beaming presence with a halo of curly blond hair in a bright, airy workroom with a polished wood floor, part of the shared office space he has set up for other writers and media people near the West London house where he lives with the writer-presenter Emma Freud and their two children. His writing career began at Oxford in partnership with Rowan Atkinson and he went on to write for *Not the Nine O'Clock News* and four series of *Blackadder*, collaborating at first with Atkinson and then with Ben Elton. *Blackadder*'s wild anachronisms culminate in a darkly affecting moment as the buffoons who have been amusing us launch themselves out of their First World War trench to certain death under inescapable German fire and the frame freezes in an echo of *Butch Cassidy and the Sundance Kid*. Richard himself turned to movies and has become Britain's most successful screenwriter after the phenomenal international box-office results from not only *Four Weddings and a Funeral* but also the *Mr Bean* film. When we visited him he was busy with a new film, this time starring Julia Roberts opposite Hugh Grant.

DB: **Do you work to a set pattern – always start early in the day, write on the back of envelopes, or whatever?**
RICHARD CURTIS: Things have changed a bit since I had a child – two children, in fact. I had years and years that were spectacularly ill-disciplined as far as time was concerned. I lived in a little cottage in the country all the time we were doing *Blackadder* and when I was writing *The Tall Guy*. I used to be as chaotic and self-indulgent as writers are allowed to be: watching eight or nine hours' television a day, watching *Neighbours* twice, and often not starting work until

three in the afternoon. But I'm not allowed to do that now, because I have to leave the house at ten and return in time to give the babies their bath and stuff like that at six-thirty. It may also be a sign of age that I used to have tremendous second wind – I could work until eight, have an hour's food and then work from nine in the evening until three in the morning without batting an eyelid, but I don't know that I can do that any more. My schedule is much more like someone in an office now. Indeed, I work in an office: I actually come in here and there are other people and we tend to have a sand-wich together.

I've been working on a computer for about a decade now, and I quite like the process, because there's a certain amount of fooling around you can do in terms of opening files, closing files, moving things, renaming things and stuff like that which allows you distrac-tion from doing the actual work. This new computer has a big TV screen in front of me, which perhaps is why I find it so comforting, because I like nothing more than watching television, so it's as though I'm watching television all day. It's just rather dull, poorly-produced television.

I try never to have the famous blank page. I've always left myself notes at the end of one day for the next so that I've got a help; the conversation, as it were, has started by the time I start the next day. So I'll always say: 'These are the ten things you should deal with tomorrow; this is what you should concentrate on.' I just have one go at throwing some joke into the ether at the end of one day so that when I start the next day it's easier to go on. Actually starting, I'm nice to myself. I don't torture myself by thinking: Today is the day that you've got to get that beginning done, or the end done. Very rarely do I do that.

When I'm advising people about writing, I say that the biggest hurdle you have to get over is how bad your own writing is. What horrifies people who start it new is that they think, Oh, I've got to do wonderful stuff. Or they read back what they've done and it's rubbish. After you've been writing for a while you know that when you get a finished film, that'll be one-thirtieth of what you wrote on the subject. Therefore you mustn't torture yourself with the fact that most of every day is spent writing stuff that's not great. It's basically all rewriting. Most of the process is to do with rewriting rather than writing.

JMcG: Do you find that you've got some sort of pattern inside you – the point at which you've got the elements of a piece dis-posed properly?

RICHARD CURTIS: You can have that and it turns out not to have been a true moment; it can turn out to have been infatuation, not true love. One can be convinced that one's got a rhythm, that one's got an answer to a problem, that everything has gone completely right. That's all part of the learning to rewrite, of learning to be fussy enough, not just saying, 'That's a funny scene,' or 'That's an interesting scene,' but saying, 'That's the start of a funny scene. How can I make that better?' By going on and on and on working at it and being willing to sacrifice it later on, when you realise that another scene that you've written has replaced the need for it. The main thing you find out at read-throughs is that you have covered the same ground more than once, and therefore stuff can go. But there are definitely good moments when you think it's right. When I was much younger and lived in a sort of communal house, I used to judge things by whether or not I wanted to read them to my friends when they got home. I never *did* read them to the friends, but you knew whether or not you'd done it right by whether you wanted to tell the tale, whether you wanted to tell the joke to someone else.

I've been very lucky in that in a way I strong-arm my girlfriends into this. I'm very lucky now to be with a girl who basically is my script editor and with whom I work really closely and show the stuff during the day. The real editing process goes into just deciding: 'Well, will I show her?' I absolutely trust her, and there was another girlfriend before her who transpired to be a very fine writer herself, so perhaps I got lucky there. Emma is a very good critic because she has no second agenda, and indeed very few personal prejudices. She's heard me talk about it, she knows what I'm aiming for, she knows where I'm letting myself down, where I've changed it from the time before, so it's really like a second, slightly less excitable me who comes in and quietens it down, and criticises. It's an unbelievably important part of the working process. She's now not scared of my enthusiasm. So if I charge downstairs and say, 'Funniest thing in the history of writing,' she's not scared to go, 'Oh, oh, oh, not really.' It's a fantastic pleasure.

JMcG: **You said you had something to say about repetition ...**
RICHARD CURTIS: It will be spotted, if anyone ever read all my stuff together, that they're about the same thing happening again, but bigger: man gets hit by a smallish piece of wood, followed by a bigger piece of wood, followed by a huge piece of wood. It's something which I started to do when we were working on *Not the Nine O'Clock News* and it has gone on being the first process, or one of the first processes, that I do on the seed of any comic idea. So if I

want a chap to have a difficult date with a girl in a film, then I know that I'll try and make him have *four* difficult dates with girls: have the first one and then build it up, have the second one, and then the third one, and then the fourth one. So with *Four Weddings and a Funeral* it's one wedding, and then it's: 'Let's see what I can do with the next one,' and 'Let's see what I can do with the next one after that.' I actually have quite a simple technique: having thought of one thing, I just exaggerate and expand and move it around and look at it – a very simple straight line of expansion and repetition.

DB: **Curious that you've hit on four, because many writers think of a rule of three.**
RICHARD CURTIS: Ben and I used to talk about this a lot at *Blackadder*, because in that slightly rococo stuff there were a lot of threes. It would be the Duke of Westminster, the Duke of Glastonbury, and the Duchess of Nibblepop. Then we said: 'That's too many. Why do we have the boring second one?' We went from the rule of three to what we call the rule of two, where you just have one straight one and then a silly one. Ben finally got fed up with that, he said: 'This is a waste of time. Why do we have the Duke of Westminster?' So we eventually developed the theory of the rule of one, where you simply say your funny line and get on with it. Like, eventually, Ben decided that what he was writing were no longer *double entendres* at all, they were just single *entendres*: there was no possible way of misinterpreting what he'd written.

JMcG: **Do you find it difficult to look back on past work?**
RICHARD CURTIS: I've got different feelings about different things. We can't look back on the stage work – that's just memories of, like, standing behind stage with Rowan, changing tights. *Not the Nine O'Clock News* we never saw for a decade, because it was a topical programme and it was never re-edited, and it's quite interesting to watch that now, because I can see things I find quite funny in that still. The major interest in watching *Not the Nine O'Clock News* is just seeing how young everybody is. And then the *Blackadders*: the first series was a bizarre thing, and I like it whenever I see glimpses of what we were trying to do and it was so extreme. I haven't for years watched the other *Blackadders* – I have your traditional double reaction: you can't believe how bad some of it is. There are a lot of sitcoms where the first eighteen minutes are good, and then the last twelve you were trying to get yourself out of the plot, and you just can't believe how far you stretched it.
   My theory is basically that no matter how hard you try on sit-

coms, out of six episodes two are good, two are all right and two are weak. The charms about *Blackadder* are, one, it's quite lovely to look at because it was so lusciously designed and dressed, and, secondly, it's very dense, there are more words in it than one would expect and sometimes those give me pleasure. And I like *Four Weddings and a Funeral* a lot because I think it's aesthetically a pleasing film. It's lit beautifully.

I'm very involved in the film production process; that's perhaps the oddest thing about me. I think I saw *Four Weddings* about sixty times, and the last twenty I obviously didn't laugh once. In fact on the first night someone sitting next to me complained: 'You must have found *one* thing in that film funny.' But I still thought it was quite lovely to look at. I don't mind looking back on old things.

JMcG: **What about the discipline of writing a film, and working with that sort of people, in comparison with the sort you work with in television?**

RICHARD CURTIS: I've had a very protected career. I've worked with people I know very well, except, I suppose, on one occasion. So I've been lucky in both formats in that I tend to have been involved in a very consultative process, and sometimes it's extremely painful being consultative to such a degree, because you have to sacrifice your independence and you can't be tyrannical. As we got further into the *Blackadders* the number of people who were good at comedy and in the same room and very strong-willed became hard to bear, but I've never looked at an episode of *Blackadder* and thought: It would have been better if I'd been in charge. For all the agony of it, the torture of that poor body of the original script that went on, the plastic surgery made it better. I hope I never cross the line into thinking that other people's contributions will not make a lot of difference. But it's a funny old line, because you've absolutely got to hang on to your own theory of why something's funny and what was the purpose and never let it go. So what you've got to hope is that you meet people who are close enough in opinion to you that you can have all those arguments and let them have as much input as possible without having to sacrifice what you think is funny.

Film is where that system is meant to break down, but the first film I did was *The Tall Guy*. I was working with Mel Smith and Rowan, both of whom I knew extremely well, and Emma Thompson and Jeff Goldblum. And Jeff should have been the fly in the ointment but wasn't. He's really sweet. Maybe he's not when you get him on a sound stage with dinosaurs, but over here he was just heaven: he couldn't have been more interested in the process, wanting to try things lots of different ways. Whenever I see Jeff the thing he's keenest on is teaching acting, and he was a bit like that when you were working with him. We were terribly consultative on that and always insisted on a read-through ages beforehand. I sit through all auditions for movies, because that's the way of finding out whether or not your script's any good, and you can listen and make all the changes while the auditions are going on, and by going through the auditioning process you and the director realise you both understand what the character's meant to be – so there's not that awful moment when you suddenly find out that you meant something different and no one's realised it.

The film which should have been difficult was *Four Weddings*, where I was working with Duncan Kenworthy, whom I knew socially but I'd not worked with before, and who is not a comedy producer, and Mike Newell, who's not a comedy director. We had to go right back in Mike's work to 1968 – when he'd done this wonderful Jack Rosenthal script called *Ready When You Are, Mr McGill*, which was a great masterpiece – to be sure how funny he was. But, again, the way we worked was by being endlessly in each other's company. We were quite lucky because it was delayed twice; we lost the finance, so we auditioned the whole film twice and Mike believed in interviewing very thoroughly for every part in auditioning, so by the time we got on to the set there wasn't that much room for misunderstanding. I'm there every single minute of every single day of the shooting and Mike did get cross with me a few times because I'm so keen to be heard. But that, I think, is all right until I start telling directors how to direct, which I've never done because I don't have any opinion on where the camera should go, or how it should be shot or lit or anything like that. I've sometimes got opinions on how the lines should be said.

I don't know how writers let their work go in the way that they do, and I've never met a person who was glad they had. I suppose the reason must be sometimes time, nay money. It takes me for ever to do a film. This new film, when it's finished, will have been four years. I know that I'll be working on this film for the next fourteen months – and I've completely finished it: I could just hand it over to someone now, and turn up at the première. So I'm making the choice, instead of writing two new films, to just stick with this one. But I think it's worth it. It means you're a producer of sorts, for much more time than you're a writer. That partly comes from trying to work *in situ*: I don't know what it's like working within an American system; I've made the choice of staying here and working with Working Title and Polygram, and working with people who trust me and know me. This new film of mine, ironically, because I've got less energy now that I've turned the corner and I'm forty, I decided to set the film within a hundred yards of where I live, so that I could get up every morning and walk to work. But they've got in this fantastic designer, who instantly looked at Notting Hill and thought it wasn't up to scratch as Notting Hill, and is rebuilding it in Shepperton. So I'm now going to have to drive an hour every morning to get to my own front door.

DB: **Do you face any particular problems with translating your work into performance?**

RICHARD CURTIS: There's one thing that is emerging about the more naturalistic stuff that I do, which is not *The Vicar of Dibley* or *Blackadder* but is more *Four Weddings* and this new film. I haven't got to the bottom of this at all, and it could easily be that I'm a bad writer, but I think there are very, very few people who make what I write interesting. I think there's a slightness of characterisation in what I do. Now I'm sure when I'm writing these lines that I absolutely know the voice that it's going to have. I know when I'm writing a line for one character, when I'm writing a line for another character, I'm not just trying to be funny generally and putting the name of the character in front of it, I'm really very sure and I understand the subtleties and I feel as though I know the character. I feel I'm doing proper writing. But when we audition people, ninety-nine per cent of the time nothing comes across. People do the lines quite well, they don't seem to be making any mistakes at all, but it's not either funny or interesting. And it seems to be that there's just a particular type of performance, or character or accuracy which sings with the way that I write. It's not something a lot of people can do, and it doesn't mean that the people that can do it are necessarily the best actors in the world. With *Four Weddings*, we interviewed sixty people to do the part that Hugh Grant did, and initially I had a lot of reservations about him, because I was hoping that the film wouldn't come across as being too upper-class, and he'd certainly portrayed a lot of upper-class people before. But he was the one person who suddenly came in three-dimensional when he read the lines, and with everyone else there were two dimensions. That is the strange thing about the way the lines that I write come out. It requires a particular kind of . . . I think I would call it exuberant naturalism, someone who by being completely natural still manages to have a kind of extraordinary extra sparkle about them which moves them back in the direction of where I started, which is the heightened performance of people like Rowan. So that's turned out to be a peculiar thing: I think that my work needs a lot of very careful casting, otherwise it would just come over as being plain.

JMcG: You were saying there's a difference between your television work and your movie work . . .

RICHARD CURTIS: I'm very happy with a kind of heightened reality in TV. Obviously that was the case with *Blackadder* because that was historical. But what we've done in *The Vicar of Dibley* is what we do in the films in reverse, in that we start with big characterisations, people we can't forget, people who say the same word all the time, people who are completely stupid, and then we try to add heart to that. So little Emma Chambers, she's playing somebody completely thick, but she's such a heartfelt and sweet and affectionate performance, and I would entrust any member of my family to those sweet little arms. I start with the big jokes and the big idea, whereas what I've tried to do with films is the other way round: to start with natural characters and then try to make them say lines which are funnier and closer to the comedy lines that I used to write for TV sketches and stuff. I seem, either through cowardice or taste, to try to write films as a naturalistic medium.

It started because I wanted to write about some things where I absolutely knew what I was writing about. *The Tall Guy* was not autobiographical, but pretty close to it. I wanted it to be not misinterpretable, not something that could be taken out of my hands and turned into something else. I wanted it to be just a small, acute observation of things I absolutely knew, and I think I've stayed in that mode. The other day I did the first draft of a treatment of a movie of *Bewitched*, the American sitcom, and I rather enjoyed that, so I think it's just by chance that I've ended up writing these rather intimate, personal movies.

This third film, which is also about a guy finding true love, may be the last of those that I do. Partly because I think I've found it – I've been completely happy with the same person for years now, and therefore the next thing that I'm going to write is I'm sure going to be autobiographical, but a cheat . . . is, in fact, going to be about a couple right at the end of their lives, and it will to some extent be about my parents, but also I suspect, secretly, it'll be about what it's like to live with someone you love, which is a famously dull subject. I read somewhere that 87 per cent of sex in the movies is for the first time; they don't like to show people who've had sex before. If I tried to write a comedy about a happily married couple *per se*, that would be hard. But you can write about a happily married couple, one of whom is going to die soon, and I think that's going to be the next thing I write.

Nowadays, because I'm involved in production and I do Comic Relief as well, which takes up about a third of my time, I've got a slow-motion career. I think of quite a lot of ideas, and because it's four years until I eventually get writing them, only the ones that are somehow true to me and the things in life that I find interesting survive the waiting process. Just as if some people you knew were waiting outside your front door, but only the one who really loved you would still be there if you made them wait four years. This idea about an older couple: I did the first draft of the first act – because I think it might be a play – five years ago, and I'm still interested in the subject. If I'm going to spend four years on something, there's got to be something at the bottom of it which is of interest.

JMcG: **Quite a lot of your work is done with a collaborator – how does that fit into your working pattern?**
RICHARD CURTIS: Ben Elton and I collaborated on *Blackadder*. We were both single men then, we had a deadline and Ben would write a draft and then send me the disk; I would write a draft, I would rewrite his draft and send the disk back. We never sat in the same room, ever . . . because we were far too interested in pop music. Put me and Ben in a room, and we were only interested in Madonna and Madness and talking about pop and the Beatles. We didn't care about comedy enough to waste our time talking about it. *Mr Bean* was written with Robin Driscoll and *The Vicar of Dibley* with Paul Mayhew-Archer, and we did the same sort of process, but I think people who work with me now know that it's going to be slow.

DB: **What do you find most difficult in writing comedy?**
RICHARD CURTIS: When writing *Blackadder* the most difficult thing was definitely thinking of the similes. Ben and I used to put that off for ever, so Ben would send it to me and the line would say: 'You are as stupid – as my knob.' That's what it would always say. We can't use 'my knob', so I'd have a go at it, and then he'd have another go at it, and when we got into the rehearsal room everybody would have a go at it. So that moment when you realise you're nearly there but you've got to make it funnier, that is really tricky. Very difficult thinking of titles if they don't come straight at you. My new film's called *The Notting Hill Film* because I've never thought of the perfect title, whereas *Four Weddings and a Funeral* was called that the day I started writing it. The Americans tried to get us to change the title, but it was always that as far as we were concerned.

But the hardest bit of writing, the very hardest bit, is when you suddenly realise that all the lovely little things that you've written, and all the jokes, and all the characters just don't add up. It isn't exciting enough, it isn't interesting enough, it doesn't quite make sense. And that's when writing is really hard, when you've got to use all your logic and all your intelligence to try and wrench it into a position where it'll work. It happens both in films and sitcoms, and in sitcoms you tend to in the end just fail, you cobble it together. You know you've got twenty minutes of quite funny stuff and you hope the audience don't notice there's a glitch. In films it's much harder and much more worrying, because I believe that audiences, even if they don't realise it on the top level, at the bottom level, in their hearts, they know that something has gone awry.

Beginnings and endings, those are hard. I've been quite lucky with endings, but sometimes you just have to establish so much at the beginning. *Four Weddings* was the classic example of a really lucky break, in that we actually thought of a beginning and it was very simple and worked. Whereas in *The Tall Guy* I wanted to lay down so much information – I wanted to lay down that the guy worked in a theatre show, that he didn't like his boss, that he lived in Camden Town, that he lived with a girl who'd slept with lots of people, that he had lots of old girlfriends – and the first fifteen minutes of the movie really is a muddle. Sometimes it's very hard furnishing all your information before you can get on with the story, and sometimes it's unnecessary.

Mr Bean is a kind of glitch in my film-writing career – thank God, because it's done fine. The joy of *Mr Bean* is all to do with the rehearsal process. With *Mr Bean* Rowan and I and all the people involved get in a room with a tiny little idea which was worked out at home. I would be in a strait-jacket if anyone ever saw me working on the *Mr Bean* stuff, because you have to *do* it. I thought of him meeting the Queen Mum, waiting in a line, so what it involved was me standing in my room for two and a half hours just looking at my body, trying to work out 'What can I do with just this body?' We used to roar with laughter as we worked out the *Bean* stuff. The film therefore was a different kind of writing: we thought of the basic jokes, but we would work them out in a rehearsal room, so half of the movie was in a way written in a rehearsal room, the rest was written in the usual way.

DB: **But there are very few sight gags in, say, *The Vicar of Dibley* ...**

RICHARD CURTIS: I should apply the *Mr Bean* experience more to my work than I do, and there's a scene in *Four Weddings* when Hugh gets stuck behind a curtain in a room with two people who are having sex on their wedding day, and that was an idea I wrote for *Mr Bean* and never used there. It has a different texture in *Four Weddings* from the other jokes.

When I'm writing I sit down and I do a whole day on each character. I spend a whole day pretending I'm one of them and checking that I've got a beginning, middle and end to my story, and that I've got something to say in every scene, which is a way of just making sure that the characters are thorough. What I never do, which perhaps I should, is spend a whole day saying: 'Are there any visual possibilities in this scene?' So those tend just to be thought of at the very last moment when you're rehearsing. It's words for me and that's both a plus and a minus. It's a minus because I don't therefore think through the economy of film as well as I should.

At the moment I'm watching a lot of films and I notice the scenes are too damned short. People aren't saying enough. It's not idiosyncratic enough, it's all sign language. It's eight clichés one after another, and they're clichés because they're too rich: the lines are too well worked out to make it short, so everybody's expressing exactly what they mean, there's no drift in it. You see people giving wonderful performances off the lines, but their performances are all there is, and therefore they tend to be generic sad, generic happy, generic discontented, and not as specific to that film as they should be. So when I argue with people about leaving lines as they are, it is partly because you want to go on defining why it's a different kind of misunderstanding, or a different kind of sorrow or a different kind of joy. The editing process, which is so easy on film, means that you often cut the lines then. One of the most interesting edits that was made on *Four Weddings* was at the second wedding: Hugh meets Andie again, takes her back to her house, and they sleep with each other one more time, and there's no dialogue at all: there was reams of it, but we cut it, because in the end the richness of the situation was entirely achievable through their looks and through silence, whereas I'd written lots of real clunky dialogue which said all those things. Definitely pictures are more elegant and subtle and truthful if they can give you enough detail.

DB: **So in that case you're quite trustful of the audience ...**

RICHARD CURTIS: I assume that the audience are in key with what I think. The most important thing about comedy writing is that you don't think about whether the audience will laugh. You have to laugh yourself; you have to have perfected a joke you've thought of.

When I first started in 1978, you know, on *Week Ending* or something, you went in and you were told what was funny that week. You were told, it's funny that the Chancellor has done this, it's funny that British Rail have done that. That was a disastrous way of writing, because I didn't find any of the things they mentioned funny. I only write stuff because I like it, I think it's funny and I assume people will share that. If I think that I can see something going on in the scene, then I'm sure the audience can see it as well. That said, of course, I am trying to manipulate the audience all the time, emotionally.

JMcG: **I'm taking it you set out to write comedy, that was your intention . . .**

RICHARD CURTIS: Well, no, I set out to be one of the Beatles! I fell into comedy writing at university. I thought I was going to be an actor and I turned out to be an atrocious actor, a very bland actor; I was always cast as Fabian. So in order to get on stage and perform I had to start writing comedy and then I teamed up with Rowan. It turned out to be the thing I most instinctively did. I didn't start writing poetry; I didn't start writing short stories; I started writing jokes.

It turned out to be an extremely lucky profession for making a living in. I do feel bad about comedy writers from twenty and thirty years ago, when you think about how little Galton and Simpson were allowed to exploit their work. They were just paid like normal writers, and they are very great writers, and someone like me . . . we did *Not the Nine O'Clock News* and the first album sold 500,000 copies and then suddenly video tape came in; *Blackadder* video tapes have sold 10 million. It's turned out to be a fantastically profitable and lucky area.

I set out by chance and it's been a logical route from sketches to sitcom, from sitcom to film. I don't know how many more sitcoms I will write now. There is a specific rhythm about that half-hour which you can learn. There's a lovely thing about planting the information and then letting one plot go, and the second, then taking time off in the middle to be as stupid as you like and then winding it up and reminding people of something that happened. There seems to be a rhythm which is a joy.

Victoria Wood

You have to write from the heart

The phenomenal Victoria Wood is able to sell out the Albert Hall as many nights as she likes to perform there, and still get full houses wherever she goes on tour with her stand-up comedy and infectious songs – which her fans recognise from the first bars of the introduction, as if she were Ella Fitzgerald beginning 'Manhattan'. She has also made an unforgettable impact on television with series such as *Victoria Wood – As Seen on TV* making use of a brilliant stock company of comic actors led by Julie Walters, who was her co-star in *Pat and Margaret,* the TV film based on Victoria's script. She has established herself firmly in the affection of the public because her comedy encourages women to laugh at themselves without feeling humiliated, and men to join in without feeling threatened. Our conversation with her began just after noon one day at the house in north London where she lives with her husband, the magician Geoffrey Durham, and their two children. On one side of her workroom stood an upright piano with a Mozart sonata open on the music stand; on the opposite wall hung a photograph of Dizzy Gillespie leaning on a lamp-post at the corner of 52nd Street and Sixth Avenue.

DB: You've written for the stage, and *Pat and Margaret* for television. Are plays in a different compartment from sketches and stand-up?
VICTORIA WOOD: I think they're shades of the same thing. At the moment I'm writing a comedy series, but there are echoes of what I've done in my drama, and also echoes of what I've done in my sketches. I think you can meet in the middle where you've got some reality and naturalism and you've also got the dialogue heightened

enough to get big laughs. To me it's all on the same spectrum. But there's always got to be some link with comedy: I couldn't get out of bed if I wasn't going to write something funny. I wouldn't have any interest in it. But I want it to have some reality as well.

JMCG: **You've regular interpreters, chiefly Julie Walters. Are you writing for her specifically?**

VICTORIA WOOD: Yeah. She does things that nobody else can do. I find that I can write things for her when I would have difficulty explaining to anybody else how I wanted it done. I find that with a lot of the people that I write for. The thing that I'm writing now, Julie's in it, Celia Imrie, Duncan Preston, Anne Reid, Thelma Barlow – I'm working towards what I know they can do, because then you can take it up on to a higher level. You just know they can interpret it. They're tuned up to do it. We've just auditioned and we've got a couple of girls, and I think they're going to be good, but they're not that experienced. So I've crossed out all their big speeches and given them to me, and given them a bit less!

DB: **Do you like to write for yourself? Or would you rather somebody else performed your words?**

VICTORIA WOOD: I've been writing this series since January, and when I wrote the first two episodes my husband said: 'You're not in it!' And I said: 'Well, I am, I'm standing there with the kettle,' and he said: 'You're not saying anything.' So I had to go back and insert myself all the way through and I did find it hard to alight on a character for myself. It's a temptation when you're writing to give yourself all the qualities that you'd like to have in real life. Well, that's nothing to do with writing comedy, that's really another issue altogether, so I had to block that out, I had to write myself a funny part and a part that only I could do. It was really quite difficult. I've hit on it now, I think, because I'm on episode number five. I want to be in it because I want to get out of the bloody house!

DB: **What's the most difficult task you face in translating thought on to the page? Is there something you dread?**

VICTORIA WOOD: I think it's having the bottle to start it at all, because when it's in your head it's perfect. And when I write first drafts they're really, really bad. They're really bad, but they're better than nothing. There are no jokes in it, there are a lot of people plodding about. But at least it's starting to take a shape. Then I do another draft, then another draft, and I think: Now I know who everybody is, I can really get going. I haven't written a series for a long time, and the last series I wrote were all sketch shows, which are easy: you just write as many sketches as you can and put them on the carpet and divide them into six piles. This is an ongoing story, episode to episode. It's only one set. It's the same people. But I've got to get them in and out – why *do* people walk about? Where can they go? What can they do? I found it all quite unmanageable. I was scared of starting it because I thought: It can't be as good as it was when it was just an idea two years ago. So I'm always scared of just . . . bringing it to life.

JMcG: **As an idea, was it a story or was it a set of characters?**
VICTORIA WOOD: It was a situation. It's just a group of women in a factory canteen. I was interested in how people are when they come into work. You gather from what they're saying what their real lives are about – especially with people who do quite a dull job. The focus is not the job but what is actually going on the rest of the time. Characters are what appeal to me, I suppose. You have to be interested in them, you have to have a bond with them on some level. I can never really cotton on to a comedy that is so bizarre I can't recognise anything realistic in it at all, because then it becomes farce to me and I've never liked farce. I find it very cold: it's so mechanical.

I put words in people's mouths that they would never say. And yet when you overhear people talk they say bizarre things, because they know what they're talking about. It's because we *don't* know what they're talking about that it sounds odd.

In fact, people do talk in brand names, they talk in half-sentences, they refer to things from their past or from just now, and it's that slightly odd effect that I'm trying to capture. It is also very naturalistic. If you take a transcript of something that somebody's actually said and type it out, you can't read it yourself, you can't act it out, because it's so particular, the way people speak. They 'um' and 'er' and tail off and repeat themselves. I'm putting in a lot of that, and cross-conversations, and people saying: 'Oh, did you see so-and-so?' and then five minutes later somebody saying: 'What did you say?' I'm trying to weave everything together. I'm trying to make it real, and I'm trying to develop characters that audiences will care about . . . I'm just trying to push it in a direction I haven't pushed it before.

I plot out each episode, and I don't think one episode's yet finished the way I meant it to finish. I just finished one at ten to twelve – I was in a bit of a rush! Just before you came I was desperately trying to get it done and it went off on another tangent, happily, and I had a good finish to it, which I hadn't had before. I'm trying to surprise myself, really. I don't want to just write something I know where it's going to go. I want it to go off in another direction.

JMcG: And are there men in it, too?
VICTORIA WOOD: Two men. Which is enough. Five women and two men. I'm pleased with my men, actually: they're not just token men, they're two really good characters. I'm more interested in men now than I was a few years ago. My knowledge is about women, obviously. I think male writers' main characters tend to be men. Women could never have written *The Goon Show* – that comes from a masculine environment, from the army. Obviously my main characters will always be women, I think that's perfectly appropriate, but that's not to say I can't write a decent man's part once in a while.

DB: What's the women's equivalent of the army? What shared experience do women have?
VICTORIA WOOD: I suppose it's work – that's what I'm doing. I've got a bunch of women opening tins of beans and frying eggs all day every day. The equivalent of the army is any situation where you're in a bunch and you have somebody in authority over you.

DB: I'm wondering where women learn the common language of women.
VICTORIA WOOD: Well, you see, women talk; men don't. Women communicate when they talk. Men talk to take up space and make a noise, a lot of the time. Women talk in whatever situation they find themselves and they link together very easily. Men tend to use talk more as a sort of territorial thing, to say: 'This is where I come in the pecking order.' 'I'll tell you this joke and then you'll understand who I am.' Women don't do that so much; we're not so hierarchical.

I wouldn't presume really to know how men are when they're on their own, because, obviously, that's not a side I ever see. I know what it's like to be in a mixed group and it's different from what it's like to be in a group of women. But all I care about, really, is getting laughs, number one, and people, I care about people, and writing about people and writing about people's experiences and relationships, that's what I'm interested in. Getting laughs, that's the most important thing.

JMcG: Do you find that difficult, constructing the laugh?
VICTORIA WOOD: Not hugely difficult, no. I've worked on it, I think I've refined it over the years, but I clicked into it the day when I wrote my first sketch, when I found that something had been

eluding me before, of how you construct a joke and what's funny and what's not funny. I just fell into it right then, like learning to ride a bike, really, and so, what's hard, I think, is finding a really huge laugh. You can write medium funny and you can see it often in feeble sitcoms – that they've got an idea of what makes a joke and how a sentence would proceed towards a punch line, but it doesn't really get you. What you have to do is to push and push and keep on and on and on until you get that really funny line. That's what I'm interested in . . . and the bizarre word or the odd thing that nobody could ever have expected.

DB: **Do you assess your own work or do you try it out on anyone?**

VICTORIA WOOD: Try it out on the audience! You can't test it out. With this series we had some auditions, so I got a good listen of it, but it only confirmed what I already thought about some of it and I was going to change that anyway.

DB: **Does the show have a title yet?**

VICTORIA WOOD: It's called *Dinnerladies* at the moment. They're very keen to put it on BBC 1. I was wanting to slide it on through the back door of BBC 2. But there's going to be a bit of press attention, whatever I do. I can't sneak it in completely unnoticed. I might just as well go for broke and have it on BBC 1. At about half past nine, I think.

JMcG: **When can you, in television for instance, step back and allow a director to do something?**

VICTORIA WOOD: That is a problem; I don't know how we're going to be on the series. The feel that I want to get is like *E.R.* and those things, where people are moving about. The camera's very skilfully placed: you always hear what you're meant to hear, yet there are always about seventeen people talking at the same time; it's very smooth.

   The good thing we're doing, which has not been done before, is that we're recording it twice, like the Americans record their dress rehearsal. We're actually going to do it in front of an audience on a Friday night and do it again on a Saturday night. So we'll get a good look at it on a Saturday morning and see what's worked and what hasn't worked. Also, if the timing's a bit off we can cut down the dialogue, rather than editing it by actually snipping out bits of video tape: we can actually chop the dialogue down. So I'm quite hopeful about that.

DB: **You come from Bury, north of Manchester ... Do you think there's a Northern quality in comedy?**

VICTORIA WOOD: You can't deny that most of our best comics have come from the North or Scotland, really. There's something about the way people construct language and people's attitude. It's a laconic quality that Lancashire people have – they never get excited about anything – and it's a very useful way of getting laughs. And the word order, everything going back to front, saying: 'Did they not?' In fact, when I wrote my first sketch, I had a whole thing where somebody says: 'You can't do that!' 'Can I not?' – 'Did I not?' I'd never been aware of it until I found myself writing it.

Lancashire people will never be impressed by anything; they just take it all on the chin. I was in a chip shop near Morecambe, and somebody came in and said: 'The pier's burned down!' and this woman just said: 'About time!' That summed it up.

DB: **How did you absorb the dialect?**

VICTORIA WOOD: I had such a strange upbringing living in this house that used to be an anti-aircraft place up on the hill. We never had any visitors at all, because I had such strange parents, and all I did was watch the television – and yet something was going in ... some language was going in. I was the youngest of four but they'd left home; they were quite a lot older than I was. So I did spend a lot of time on my own just eating and watching television, but somehow I absorbed that way of talking. My family were middle-class, lower-middle-class. My father was an insurance underwriter; my mother was a teacher. But I tend to write better for working-class characters and I don't know why that should be, because it's not my own background. I went to a grammar school. But I have a much stronger accent than my sisters, so it's sunk into me somehow. I used to get told off: somebody would phone me up and my mother would say: 'It's one of her "gorra gerrit" friends.'

DB: **We noticed that you admired someone we both knew in Manchester, Peter Eckersley...**

VICTORIA WOOD: Yeah. His picture's on the wall, there. My first play, *Talent,* was on at the Crucible in Sheffield. He went to see it and bought it for Granada, where he was head of drama, and that's when I met him. I started working with him and he commissioned two more plays after that and then I got my own series and we did a pilot, and the year that we were going to shoot a series, Peter died. We did the series but I think it suffered from the lack of Peter, and I didn't work at Granada after that. I didn't want to – it was working with him I was interested in. I didn't feel I would be in such good hands as at the BBC, so I moved over. I found Peter so clever and so helpful and an inspiration, really encouraging, because I'd not done a lot until then. My big break was having this play on at Sheffield, and then Peter buying it – those were the two things that kicked everything on. I never stopped working.

JMcG: **Did he help you with editing as well?**

VICTORIA WOOD: Yes, he did – he had a very good sense of what you didn't need in the script, which was very useful to me. I would slash, and he'd go: 'No, hang on – don't take all that out!' and I'd say: 'I will, I will. It needs to be about three pages long!' He never tried to alter what I'd done, but he had a really good editor's eye, and an overall sense of what we were working on, and the length of something and the pace, and he was very tasteful. Really good sense of humour. Good laugh. Now I work a lot with his wife, Anne Reid, so it's a good link with Peter.

JMcG: **So you started basically as a writer?**

VICTORIA WOOD: Well, I started off as a singer-songwriter. I started off in television when I was twenty and I was at university. I was a barmaid at a pub in Birmingham, where a lot of the BBC producers drank. I was at a party . . . I must have been drunk myself to play the piano in front of all those blokes. One of them said: 'That's absolutely marvellous. You must come to Pebble Mill and audition.' The next morning the phone rang and they said: 'Where are you? We're all here!' I never thought people were serious. I went down and played all the songs I'd written, and one of the guys who did the opt-out programme at 10.30 on a Friday night said: 'I use songs, topical stuff,' so I started working. They'd say: 'Write a song about money or about food.' And I would write one to order: two minutes ten seconds. I sang at the piano, so that got me an Equity card. Then I used to do *Start the Week* on the radio, deadly programme, with Richard Baker, and *That's Life* on television, another deadly programme, with Esther Rantzen.

I had a lot of exposure as a singer-songwriter but I didn't have any idea how to make that into a career. I just hoped that somebody would give me a job and then I'd write a song and go on telly and do it and get sixty quid. But it was very stop-and-start. Eventually I'd been on every programme that ever wanted a topical song – there weren't that many in the first place – and it all seemed to grind to a halt. At the same time as I was doing these programmes at Pebble Mill, I went on *New Faces*, which was a high-rated talent show at the time. I won the first heat but I didn't win any more. ATV did a comedy series using winners from *New Faces* - it was probably the worst show that's ever been on British television. I've never met anyone who saw it – and it had Marti Caine, Lenny Henry and me and three other people who never made anything of themselves.

I did these odd shows, but I didn't do live work at all . . . I wasn't writing; I didn't know what to do with myself, really. I was twenty-one. I was living in a bed-sit on my own in Birmingham. I'd been at university there, but now all my friends had left: everybody with any bottle had gone to London. So I was sat in this very large room in what is now a private hospital, eating mince out of tins. My plan was to be famous. I thought, I can't be in rep or anything like that: I don't look right, I don't sound right, I've not been properly trained. I didn't know what to do. I suppose I was hoping something would happen and somebody would say: 'We'll make you a star,' because that's what I wanted to be, a star. This went on for a few years and the people at the dole office were getting really fed up with me. They were saying: 'We don't understand: one week you earn a hundred pounds and then you're on the dole for twenty-two weeks. We don't understand what sort of career this is.' I didn't really have much to say in reply.

Then I met my husband, who's a magician but was then an actor, and we went to live in a flat in Morecambe because we'd seen an Alan Bennett play about Morecambe and we thought that would be funny. Actually, it wasn't, but we were a bit mad.

I'd met a BBC radio producer, and I wrote a radio comedy and sent it to him. He wrote back and said it had too many jokes in it, too many one-liners! God, he should be so lucky! And then he died. I was getting very, very depressed, now. I felt I'd had so many good chances and I'd blown them somehow. I'd done a few businessmen's cabarets, where they thought I would be blue and glamorous, and I wasn't blue and I wore jeans, and I had to get my dad to come and take me home. Geoff decided to stop being an actor and be a magician, so he was out of work. So that was two of us eating mince out of tins and being miserable . . .

Then I met this comedian called John Dowie, who I would say was the first alternative comic. This was the late Seventies. He didn't tell jokes, and he was a bit aggressive; he looked a bit punky and a bit strange, and he was a lovely bloke. He's never really got on in television, because he doesn't want to change his material and it's not suitable for television. He was doing a little tour of arts centres and things like that, and he asked me to play the piano and do bits of my own, so we did a few sketches together, and we took it to Battersea

Arts Centre in '78. Dusty Hughes, who was running the Bush Theatre, was in the audience and he asked me to contribute to a revue they were writing, called *In at the Death,* with Snoo Wilson, writers like that.

I said I would write something but I didn't want to be in it. I didn't want to be in Shepherd's Bush for three weeks, because I thought it was so horrible, and three weeks in my career was a long time because I'd only ever worked anywhere for one night a year, so I thought: It's a bit of a commitment, three weeks! We went to a meeting, I think at Snoo Wilson's house, and they said: 'You've got to write four things all to do with the week's news. And it's all got to be about death!'

Well, Guy the gorilla had died, so I wrote a song about Guy the gorilla, and there'd been a thing in the paper about somebody being killed joyriding, so I wrote a thing about that. And another piece about an assisted suicide, so that was three songs. Julie Walters was at the meeting and I really liked her and I thought, Well, if she's going to be in it, maybe it would be quite a good laugh to be in it, so I said, 'I've changed my mind, I *will* be in it.' For the fourth piece, I said to Dusty: 'I can't think of any more songs to do. Can I write a sketch?' And he said: 'You can if you want to.' He didn't care really: he was always mending his car. None of the other sketches were funny – they weren't meant to be funny: it was a very serious revue, very hard-hitting, and a bit dreary. I wrote a sketch called 'Sex' and it was the first thing that I'd ever written that really resounded with me. I thought: Nobody else could have written this. I felt I'd found my voice in it. It used to go a bomb every night because it had jokes in it and nothing else had. David Leland, a theatre director who was doing a season of new plays at the Crucible, said: 'Why don't you write a play?' So, suddenly, from doing absolutely nothing, I'd written a sketch and I sat down and wrote *Talent* in three weeks. I didn't even think about it, it all came pouring out, and we did that at the Crucible. Peter saw the play, and that's how I got going. So 1978 was my good year, but I'd had four years of pissing about until then.

JMcG: **And you'd done a drama degree?**

VICTORIA WOOD: I'd just scraped through. I hadn't coped at all well with being at university and my way of not coping was to ignore the whole thing. I'd go off and write songs and play the piano. I couldn't get involved with what anyone else was doing at all. They were very discouraging. You were expected to be able to be a Shakespearean actress or a very good stage manager; there was no room to be a bit barmy, and be a . . . struggling writer: that really

didn't come into it. Fair enough, it was an academic institution. I
didn't deal with it very well. But I got on the telly and I got my
Equity card, so that didn't really matter. Now you know the
history: it was writing that propelled my career.

DB: **But you hoped to become a comedian: how old were you
when you got the ambition?**
VICTORIA WOOD: About eleven, I suppose, twelve. I was writing
things at the piano, just for my own amusement. I spent a lot of time
on my own, because I didn't have any friends near where I lived, as
there weren't any other houses. I was in a youth theatre from when
I was fifteen, so I was always aiming in that direction.

JMcG: **Did you do the songs at home for the family? To enter-
tain your relatives?**
VICTORIA WOOD: No, I didn't have any relatives. I lived in this
weird house where we each had a room of our own. I had a room
with a piano in it, and a television, and I sat in there, and my dad was
in his own office writing radio plays. My mother was in another
room, sorting wool into cardboard cups, and my other sisters were
out having a good time. We didn't eat together, and we didn't do
anything together after I was a certain age, so I was on my own. We
were totally dysfunctional. We didn't work as a family at all. We
were all busy, all in our different rooms.

My dad was great, but he was a very odd person. He was very solitary. He was alone in his office, tapping away. He wanted to be a big
playwright, and he had one play done in the theatre and a few radio
plays on. I suppose he didn't quite manage to do what he wanted to
do.

Sometimes my dad would come in the room and I'd be watching
television, and he wouldn't sit down. He'd stand there, as if about to
leave; he could stand there for an hour. My mother never watched
the television at all: she didn't approve of the television. It had to go
back every summer: we only had it in the winter, then it went back
to the shop. I was devoted to television. I watched it every hour that
I could – there wasn't that much then, but I must have seen every sitcom there ever was. Once when I was doing exams, my father
decided I shouldn't watch television because I was supposed to be
revising, and he wrapped it up in a raincoat. I came in one day and it
was all wrapped up in this bloody mac! He didn't say anything!
Nobody in my family ever said anything. I just came in and it's all
done. 'What's happening? Why didn't you say?'

DB: **Can we discuss your music, because that's where you're unique among the writers we're talking to ...**

VICTORIA WOOD: I know, I can get off with a song, I'm lucky. I don't have to say: 'My name's ... thank you very much,' I can bugger off with a bit of music. It doesn't loom very large in my life, music, really. But I find it incredibly useful for the show. My dad played: he was a semi-pro, and wrote shows when he was in the navy. My dad was a very nice pianist. He used to take popular songs and change the words – put in jokes about insurance companies and sing them at the works do. I can't remember what I write first, words or music. If it's going to be a good song, I've usually written the tune first, because they're few and far between, good tunes; they don't come to me easily. So with the best songs I get the tune and an inkling of the idea, and one of the key words, and then I'm well away. The last few songs I wrote for my last show I really enjoyed writing – I love writing lyrics. Once I've got the idea and the tune, I love just fitting it all together and getting that exact word that's going to get a 'whoof!' – I adore that. There's nothing worse to me when people put the stress on the wrong line, just to fit in with the tune.

When I first started as a stand-up comic I was too nervous to stand up, so I sat at the piano because I had a piece of furniture there. And when I first stood up I would only stand in the crook of the piano, so I had something to hold on to, and it was ages before I could actually step away from it, and then I would hold on to the microphone. Now I have a mike in my hair, so I don't have to touch anything or hold anything, which is brilliant. But the piano is real security.

DB: **You've got a mike in your hair?**

VICTORIA WOOD: Not *now!*

JMcG: **Do you have a regular working day when you're writing?**

VICTORIA WOOD: I work from nine until about half three and then I get my children from school, or they get got, I give them a snack and then I go back and do a bit more. So nine to five, basically. But that includes doing the laundry and things, I don't work continuously. Or if I go to the gym it's, like, eleven until five. But I do it five days a week. I'm getting really tight for time so I'm going to Yorkshire tonight, and I get a day and a half without the children. I reckon I might be able to do an episode in that day and a half, which would be brilliant. Because I wrote six and then I put two in the bin, so that put me back.

JMcG: **Do you take a laptop, or something?**

VICTORIA WOOD: I write longhand. I can type, but I don't. I've tried writing straight on to the computer and it doesn't seem to work as well. So I just take a pad of paper. I'm used to the size of the paper, so I know how many pages is half an hour.

DB: **And you can write dialogue directly and it'll stand?**

VICTORIA WOOD: Yeah, a lot of the time it will stand. Most often I'll do three drafts, but a couple of these episodes are just one draft – that's when I'm well up and running: I've worked all the characters out, I've had a really good idea, and I don't write it too quickly. But because I'm a bit pushed for time, I'm going to try to do, like, eighteen hours in a day and a half, and I might get it done. I worked through the night just recently, which caught me up a bit, and I did three hours this morning before you came. And that finished that episode, so I've only got one to do. If you hadn't been coming, I would have taken all day to do it.

JMcG: **Do you write the stand-up act in the same way?**

VICTORIA WOOD: I don't write in such good handwriting, because nobody has to read it except me. Then I work it on stage and it gets changed, so the handwritten copy bears not much resemblance in the end to what's being done on stage. The process is less literary and more to do with performance. I often find if I'm working on stage that I've left out a whole chunk of something and that's because on some level I've known it wouldn't work: I've instinctively cut it as I've gone along. On the page it looked all right, but as a stand-up comic I can judge it better.

DB: **And does that differ from one night to another?**

VICTORIA WOOD: No. Once it's all fixed, I keep it the same. Obviously if something happens in the theatre then I'll improvise a bit, but basically I have the routine and I stick to it. That's my way of working, to refine the performance every night until it reaches a certain standard. Then it starts to fall off and you have to pack it in. Hopefully not until you've finished the tour!

DB: **Have you ever worked with anybody else, as a writing partner?**

VICTORIA WOOD: I haven't ever collaborated with anybody really. I think with John Dowie we maybe struggled to write a couple of things together, but I don't remember that it worked. I had an editor on *Pat and Margaret*, which I found incredibly useful and

very helpful: like with Peter, just an outside eye on the overall shape
of something. If you're writing a screenplay it's handy if somebody
else says: 'Suppose they don't go there, suppose they go to the petrol
station, suppose they go to the hospital.' You think: Oh, yeah! If I
did a screenplay with a great big story I might work with somebody
else in that regard. I can't imagine writing dialogue with anybody
else; I just can't picture it. I'm quite a solitary person, I suppose. I
just come in here and do it and I don't show it to anybody. My assistant, Cathy, types one while I'm on the next one and then I amend
what she's typed. So I've had to let her see rough drafts and things
like that, which I've never done before. I was a bit dubious about it,
but she's very tactful. I used to have a typist who was about
seventeen years old and I used to give her a piece and she'd say: 'I
suppose it means something to you.'

JMcG: Everybody – Denis Norden for one – admires your skill
with bringing in references to brand names. How did you hit on
that?
VICTORIA WOOD: I don't think about it; it's just part of what I do,
I suppose. When I wrote that very first sketch, there was a reference
to Mothercare. I suppose it's part of my ordinary life. I don't do it
deliberately: I don't think, Well, I'll mention a brand name and that
will strike a chord. In my last show on stage there was more about
people, I think. Because when I went to Australia with it, I had to
go around all the supermarkets changing all the bloody names. I
couldn't just say Vegemite, I had to find something that is in
Britain as well as Australia, and they're buggers, they don't have
Jammy Dodgers and I adore them. One of the punch lines was
Jammy Dodgers and there's really no substitute for that. 'Jammy
Dodgers' is such a funny name, and they don't bloody have them!
In the end I said: 'Stop the car. I've got to go in this supermarket to
find something that looks like a Jammy Dodger.' Well, they have
things called Lamington Fingers! That was all right. I coped, but it
was a bit of a strain. I thought: Why do I do this? It's so particular.
Why can't I just write about bollocks, like everybody else does,
or sperm? Easier.

DB: Apart from the actual brand names, do you have a struggle
to find the *mot juste* or does it drop out of thin air?
VICTORIA WOOD: It's like most things: sometimes it's, like, a gift
from God and sometimes you're having to chew at it to get the right
thing. It's nice when it lands in your head: 'Where the hell did that
come from?'

DB: Are there any elements that comedy has to have?

VICTORIA WOOD: A rhythm; it tends to have a rhythm. There's a right rhythm and a wrong rhythm, and if you haven't got it you just haven't got it.

DB: And is there something that you really would like to write about but the opportunity hasn't arisen?

VICTORIA WOOD: No. I've been thinking about this series for a long time and I loved my last tour, but I can't tour all the time, because of the children, and also I'm too knackered. I think once this is over I'll just take a bit of a breather and see what comes into my mind. I've got a couple of ideas for stage plays. I like to keep free a little bit, so if an idea comes in I can follow it through and see, well, is it a sketch? Is it a play? What is it?

DB: Is there a subject that ought to be tackled in comedy?

VICTORIA WOOD: I think comedy can take anything on board if it's dealt with intelligently. What you can't do is just tack an issue on to a bunch of crappy dialogue to make it hard-hitting. You have to write from the heart. If you're not writing from the heart, you have to give up.

What I see a lot at the moment is very sloppy writing: nobody's cut it down, nobody's refined it, nobody's worked on it. Not that I'm harking back to the past as being better, but, say, on *Morecambe and Wise*, you knew they had so much rehearsal, and they worked on all their routines, so they could lift off. There was room to bring in Peter Cushing or somebody like that and it actually went in a different direction, just because they had been doing it all that time. There was that rock-solid thing of working on stage all the time. That's the only place you learn: on stage, doing it with a live audience. You don't learn much from being on television, except how to be on television.

Paul Merton

As serious as any art form

In private Paul Merton is a less intimidating figure than he appears on television – bespectacled, smiling, and apparently slimmer – and his truculence and terseness are replaced by a free-wheeling conversational style and a ready laugh. It is as if he put on a matador's suit to go on television, and the *machismo* to go with it. The public Paul is a character he has created for himself, but one that fits him so well that it appears quite natural. There is similar careful preparation for his part in *Have I Got News for You* on television and *Just a Minute* on radio, the kind of preparation that is largely invisible to the public but nevertheless allows him to communicate directly. His rapport with an audience is very clearly seen in his appearances with the Comedy Store Players in London on Sunday evenings, when improvisational games give him an opportunity for a sort of instant writing which can be turned immediately into performance. He takes an enthusiast's interest in the comedy of previous generations: as an example, he introduced himself to Joe because of his admiration for the Peter Sellers movie *The Magic Christian*, which Joe directed and co-wrote with Terry Southern. Our talk with Paul began in the early afternoon at the Savile Club, and ended after dark, ranging over more subjects than comedy.

JMcG: **As a writer, what is your relationship with yourself as a performer? Do you find yourself saying: 'No, he wouldn't like that'?**

PAUL MERTON: I often write with an old school friend of mine, John Irwin: we wrote the Channel 4 series together and a radio series together and there is a restriction on writing for me because we can only write stuff that I can do. It doesn't test our range as writers: we now write very well for my style, but that means we can't write a scene with two old women sitting in a room talking about something that happened before the war, or something like that. There's no point in putting me in a wig, because I'm not that kind of performer who would, you know, disappear into a part that someone like Peter Sellers or Steve Coogan would. Equally, I can do other stuff that they can't do. My personality comes out of the person I am anyway, but it's a rather amplified version of me, a more confident version. If you're going to have me as a Cavalier you can put me in the clothes, but you're still going to get me.

JMCG: **How about writing for characters other than your own?**
PAUL MERTON: I've written with Julian Clary, for a show called *Sticky Moments* which he and I put together years ago. That's a completely different style of writing. Julian's stuff is basically double meanings and within ten minutes of talking to him everybody in the room is doing them – you can't help it. The stuff I write with Julian is not something I'm ever going to go: 'I wish I had that joke!' You can have it: it's yours, Julian. In general we just write something that I'm not in. As soon as you take me out of it, you can write about anything.

DB: **In your experience as a stand-up comic do you suddenly in front of a audience discover things that you wouldn't have thought of on your own?**
PAUL MERTON: Writing a new idea, it never worked the first time I did it. Second or third time, I knew whether it was worth sticking with or whether to abandon it, because the audience inform you what's funny in the end. You've got the funny idea in your head and you've got your set-up over here and your punch line over there and it's very funny to you, but the audience don't know the bit in the middle. So sometimes you have to break it down a bit and add a bit of information for them to make the leap that you've made. You don't want to spell it out word for word, but they need just enough of a carrot to lead them down the line where they'll get there at the same time as you do. That is a great feeling.

   The only way to shape a stand-up act is to do it in front of an audience. You have no idea how it will go otherwise, unless, of course, you stick to some formulaic way of writing where you say, 'Well, I'm known for making jokes about fat bus conductors, that's my routine,' so you just do loads of jokes about fat bus conductors.

DB: **In your improvisation work with the Comedy Store Players you have a very intimate relationship with the audience – which**

is actually providing the material, for one thing. In other work, do you miss that instant access to audience reaction?

PAUL MERTON: At the Store you've got this huge interaction with the audience and their reactions to what you're doing can lift you to higher levels of inspiration. But if they're not laughing it's like walking through thick concrete. They sometimes shout out during a scene, shout out a line that's occurred to them, and it kills what we're doing stone dead. If you're doing a stand-up gig and somebody shouts out, you can come away from what you're doing, put them down, then come back to the next joke. With the improv thing, you're concentrating so much on what the other people on stage are saying that, if suddenly somebody shouts out, your attention is no longer on the stage. The audience never sees this but the whole thing just falls to the floor and you have to gather it up and get it going again.

I did one of Galton and Simpson's TV shows with Josie Lawrence and there was one line in the script that I was worried about because people kept saying: 'It's very gentle, isn't it?' I thought: Gentle? No laughs, then. But of course we started doing it and the audience were great. They made it a better show than it might have been. Ray and Alan's stuff is so good anyway, and the audience is telling you it's funny. Even in a TV studio they can lift your work up, as well as in a live environment.

Film is entirely another thing. In the days of Laurel and Hardy or Keaton they would have the sneak previews; Harold Lloyd would have people sitting in the audience with stop-watches timing laughs and if a laugh was the wrong kind they went back and reshot it. You can't do that with film now, so you just have to be very certain what you're saying, storyboard it and look at it through the lens. But it's got to be you in the end who says, 'I think that's going to be funny' – and nobody can ever know for sure.

JMCG: You're talking about some very visual comics. Do you think the lack of sight gags in TV comes from the fact that a lot of writers started in radio?

PAUL MERTON: You could audiotape some shows and listen to them back and you wouldn't really miss anything. Funnily enough, even the people who haven't done radio still write like that. One sight gag we did on the Channel 4 thing is my favourite. Very short, very simple, it was a shot of two people in a roof garden, and there are two chairs and a table. And the dialogue goes something like: 'You've done a very nice job of this, Alan.' And I say: 'Yes, I'm very pleased with it – would you like some tea?' And as I pour you see instead of the tea falling straight down from the spout it's going at 45 degrees, and the camera comes round and you realise you're actually on a pitched roof. In the final shot there's a woman lawn-mowing; you see her pushing the lawn-mower up this bit of grass and then disappearing over the top. Now, it was one simple little joke: you've got a roof garden but it's not a flat roof. It's 10–15 seconds long and there's no other point to it. We disguise what's happened and then we reveal what's happened. But, you know, you quite often look at this sort of thing on the page and it probably doesn't mean anything to anybody who can't read a script.

You occasionally write things you think nobody's ever going to laugh at: one we shot anyway because John was very keen on it – I put the blame on him. It was a shot of somebody by a safe, just turning the little dial on the safe with a stethoscope, listening and turning. Then the bloke stands up and says: 'Well, it seems fine to me,' and the safe gets up and walks out and says: 'Thanks, Doc,' and it's got legs and arms. It was worth doing, but the audience didn't react at all, and we thought: It's too much for your general public – it's just an idea.

You get interviewed by journalists, and they have no idea of the process. When we did the first Channel 4 series some guy from *Esquire* magazine came along for two days in the rehearsal room to watch us rehearsing and putting it all together. The tone of his article was that he was amazed how seriously we took it. There was some argument about what was a funnier prop – I can't remember what the props were now – was an ostrich with a frying-pan funnier than a bear with a Coca-Cola bottle? He thought there's no difference. In fact, the difficult thing is trying to concentrate on what that difference is.

He imagined you sit around laughing; of course there's a bit of that, which is what makes it such a great job. But generally speaking you're talking about a particularly thorny problem and it's as serious as any art form. Groucho Marx had the line on it really: he said that people have no respect for comedy because they think that it's easy. If it works and you see something like *The Producers* it just seems to be like water flowing. But it's also the best film that Mel Brooks has made by a mile and he's not been able to reproduce the quality of that film, and not through lack of effort.

DB: **Do writers get stretched too thin by the British method that a show is written by one guy, or two at most?**
PAUL MERTON: Somebody told me about a British writer who sat in on a *Cheers* script meeting once, with ten guys round a table. The

reason why you get such a high burn-out rate among writers in the States is because it's very much a young man's game, young woman's game, and you have to just brainstorm your way through these sessions. Somebody says: Norm comes in through the door of the bar, he has a joke to get him to the bar. Sam comes out of the office. What's the gag between Sam coming out of the office and Sam getting to the bar? What's the joke for that, what's the joke for this? And the best of it when it works, like *Cheers,* is fantastic. But in my own heart I prefer the British way of doing it. You couldn't have had a series like *Fawlty Towers* unless it was written by two people. It has to be a personal view.

David Renwick, who writes *One Foot in the Grave,* which has been sold to the States, was telling me that Americans are very thrilled – you know, 'great, love your show, Bill Cosby's very up for it,' and all that sort of stuff. He goes over there, sits around the obligatory swimming pool for a few weeks and comes home and then he gets this message: 'We've been looking at the scripts, and it's a bit depressing that he's out of work, isn't it? I think we're going to lose that element: he's going to have a job!' And of course the whole premise of the show was that he's lost his job after so many years and he doesn't know what to do with himself any more.

I remember seeing an episode of the American equivalent of *Porridge* and, again, they liked the scripts a great deal but just two people were not enough, him and Richard Beckinsale in the cell, so they had six people in the cell. They each had a funny walk, they all had their own personal little quirks, and they'd got Ronnie Barker's lines split up between them. So you'd got five really funny people in this cell together, and it was nonsense.

JMCG: **Who are the successors to the great comics of the past?**
PAUL MERTON: There aren't people of that stature around any more. Spike Milligan, Peter Sellers, Tony Hancock, the Marx Brothers – people who were considered giants. Peter Cook was one of the last people really that you could say was like a sort of giant in the stature of his work. People are very popular and some people have good careers but nobody talks of Steve Coogan in the way that they talked of Peter Sellers.

I think TV actually reduces personalities of performers. If you were a Cary Grant fan in the Thirties, Forties and Fifties, the only place you could see Cary Grant was at the pictures. Cary Grant, under the old system, would have made two or three films a year, so you go and see Cary about every six months. You might hear Cary Grant in a radio interview if you were lucky, but other than that the only time you ever saw him was on that huge screen, so that gives him status, it gives him stature . . .

And everything looks fantastic and his face is 60 foot across and he's got a great profile. And also black-and-white has that other-world quality to it that colour doesn't have. *The Third Man* in colour? Well, you wouldn't have been able to do half of those shots, because they relied on shadow.

So you sat in a cinema laughing with a load of people and said that was fantastic, you came out, you knew you'd see Cary Grant or Peter Sellers in a film again in eight months' time, when he was, you know, when he was particularly productive in those late Fifties. There was a sense of occasion. You had to arrange your evening to go and see it; you didn't just sit at home. But now if you have a successful TV series then it will be out on video. So if you want me on *Have I Got News for You*, it's as easy as walking into Woolworths and spending £10 on a tape. I don't think that people are any less talented; there's a lot of talent, but because it's on that small screen it's more accessible and therefore it's more life-size. Whereas the old stuff was beyond life: it was . . . heroic, romantic.

It sounds pretentious, but the audience should be taken somewhere other than where they come in. If you go and see Bernard Manning – and nobody disputes he tells jokes very well . . . he's been doing it forty years, he should be able to time a gag – he'll do the Pakis and all that sort of stuff. He is reinforcing people's prejudices; he is saying why you live in a shit house and you've got a shit job is because the Pakistanis down the road are doing this, are doing that and whatever, so he's just reaffirming people's small-minded ignorance. If you go and see a show, you want to be taken to somewhere else in an imaginative way so you leave the venue in a slightly different state of mind from the one you went in with. This all sounds very crap – you wouldn't really verbalise this normally – but the audience should be moved in some way. You tell a story where you can manage to create a marvellous visual image in people's heads so they are seeing the same thing that you're seeing, and you've done it through the power of words and just a body movement – that's a life-affirming thing.

Ian Pattison

Better than a nine-to-five job

Ian Pattison, the creator of Rab C. Nesbitt, and Joe began by circling each other as two Govan-born lads were bound to do, establishing that they were on opposite sides of the Great Glaswegian Divide between Celtic and Rangers, but settling into a friendly truce when it was clear that they were both too wise to let such sectarian matters concern them. We had gone to see Ian Pattison on his own patch in Glasgow where he works in the Comedy Unit, a company spun off from the BBC and headed by his producer-director Colin Gilbert, the son of Jimmy Gilbert, the former head of BBC Light Entertainment. A character as closely attuned to the Thatcher era and its aftermath as Alf Garnett was to the Sixties, Rab C. Nesbitt, as played by Gregor Fisher with the support of a formidable ensemble of actors, transcends his roots in Govan as the thinking man's scum. He is an inspired creation based firmly on the material available in Glasgow's streets, and probably the first figure in comedy since Will Rogers to approach the public in philosophical mood. (Note: his audience throughout Britain have been quick to grasp his meaning, but some non-Scots might be helped by knowing that a *dookit* is a dovecote or pigeon-loft, and *the malky* is a term for extreme brutality derived from a notoriously violent individual whose first name was Malcolm.)

JMcG: **How did you discover Rab? You're political, obviously.**
IAN PATTISON: It's implicit, then – if I'm political, it's not explicit. It's based on what I saw around me. The only thing that annoys me really is when critics say, or the Glasgow culture police say: 'This is giving Glasgow a bad name. It shouldn't be on,' and I think, Well, you can't take that away from me, because that's my experience

you're talking about. You might not recognise it, but I come from a place where that kind of behaviour goes on. OK, it's sometimes exaggerated, and sometimes it's *underplayed*, funnily enough, but it's there, and it's a piece of fascism to try to take that away from me, because that's what I do, that's what I taught myself. Rab was based, the *spirit* of Rab was based, on an uncle of mine who died two years ago. But he was a good-looking fellow, he was very smart: he didn't look like Rab looked. The look was based on what you see around you – guys who in the Sixties and early Seventies would be walking around on a Saturday afternoon with their vest on, because they're keeping their one clean shirt for going out on Saturday night. That's where it comes from. And, of course, Gregor. I can't take credit for that. I just write the words; he breathes the life into them – so it is really a double-act.

We can't film in Govan any more, because Gregor gets too much hassle. People either want to ask for his autograph or beat his brains out. Occasionally both: that's the way it is. So now we've got a house up in Springburn. But we're getting hassle there too, because you've got real, live neighbours all around you, who are doing mental things like eating social workers. So we'll move out. We built flats inside a sound stage so we can do all the interiors.

Here in Glasgow they can say 'Hello' like it's a declaration of war. Once you get through that reserve, it's OK, people are nice. There is quite a lot of anti-English hostility from middle-class people. It is terribly boorish and I feel quite embarrassed when I take some friends into the pub or somewhere like The Ubiquitous Chip. Horrible. Working-class folk, salt of the fucking earth, I'll tell you, man, no problem.

DB: **Apart from the fact that you're writing about a Scottish subject, a Scottish place and a set of Scottish characters, do you think there's some special Scottishness about *Rab*?**
IAN PATTISON: I hope not. For me it's just almost incidental that it's set in Scotland. It's set in Govan because I'm from there, but I don't think it would make any difference if Rab was from Liverpool, or Manchester or the East End of London. The references would be slightly different. To me the social conditions create Rabs, and those social conditions prevail in cities up and down Britain. I've been through Hulme in Manchester, for example. A friend of mine, a journalist living down there, she took me through this place, and I thought: God, if we think Govan's bad, Govan's Las Vegas compared with this . . .

DB: **The immediate reaction to Rab in the South was: 'Can't understand what he's saying.' Have you relied on the audience learning to keep up with him?**

IAN PATTISON: Some people still say that, but why should we make concessions? If they see *Goodfellas* they don't expect Robert de Niro to speak in Received Pronunciation, so *they'll* make the concession there. If it's good, people will get into it the more they watch it. If we start diluting it, they will detect that, and we will lose that quasi-documentary, hand-held thing that runs through it. We're not trying to clean it up, we're trying to make ourselves comprehensible. Obviously there are colloquialisms that we will put in or not.

DB: **Have you invented any of the colloquialisms?**

IAN PATTISON: I don't know any more. Because I would think 'I invented that', and people would say: 'I remember we used to say that,' or: 'My granny used to say that.'

JMcG: **What about something like 'the malky'?**

IAN PATTISON: The malky is a real word, it's a real term. I was working in a day-release shipbuilding course when I was sixteen, with all these Greenock guys talking about getting malkied at the weekend. So: 'Excuse me, run that past me one more time?' The malky, yeah, it's just stuck, I've regurgitated it. But you place it in a context – that gives people a fighting chance of understanding it. We had a conversation about the word 'dookit'. You'll know what a 'dookit' is, Joe, but you, David, *won't* know what a 'dookit' is. We had this noun at the end of a sentence, and I remember saying: 'No, we can't have that there, because it doesn't give it a context.' So we will always think about where we're placing it. It enriches the colloquialism when you hear this kind of patois coming through, so we try and keep it.

DB: **When you're starting on a new series, do you see it as a whole?**

IAN PATTISON: I don't know what happens between finishing one series and starting another; it just seems as if instantly the moment's upon me when I have to start again. Usually I'll have six words, or three or four words – 'cancer' or 'sexual harassment' or something – and I'll try and write episodes about them. There are guys who have written successful series and they will give a producer eight outlines, and every scene will be outlined and there's a ten per cent imaginative bit built in just to see if it'll go somewhere else. These guys know exactly what they're doing, and they will say to him: 'Pick six out of these eight,' and go away and write them. I could never do that, because I don't know until I've written it. To me, it's like saying to a painter: 'Show us the painting, and then go away and paint it.'

JMcG: **Do you relate to anything like that, painting or music? Do you like music?**
IAN PATTISON: I like both. I know people say there's a sense of music in writing, and, a boy from Govan, I'm very wary about stepping down that path. Ballerina, I'm not. But, yes, I think there's a sense of rhythm; whether that's the same thing as a sense of music, I don't know. If a script comes out cleanly, it's as if you can't take any credit for it. You go: 'I was just there. The lightning hit me.' It's the ones you've got to struggle for that you think more of. It's a process of discovering the inevitable. That's the way it seems to me: it's there, and all you've got to do is push the shit away to get at that inevitability. It's as if the form already exists. I know that's probably a philosophical concept. I don't know which philosopher came up with it, but certainly it's there; it's just a matter of seeing it and dusting it like an archaeologist almost – although hopefully the jokes aren't that old. That's the rough parallel, *Rab* and music.

DB: **Do you have a method for clearing the shit out of the way so you can see the thing?**
IAN PATTISON: Basically, I let the characters give me the plot – plot's a bad word for me, I'm not good on plot – story. Characters can introduce story. You think: What could they do this series? Maybe A could have an affair with B – how would C feel about that?

JMcG: **Do you enjoy writing?**
IAN PATTISON: I find it a lonely game, and the older I get the deeper the shelf gets into the sea, and the further out you go, and that's the way it seems to me. I come back to what Flaubert said: 'A writer's life is a dog's life but it's the only life . . .' I'm addicted. I couldn't do anything else. Anything that isn't writing is relaxation to me – paying the gas bill or anything. Writing takes so much of my emotions that there's not much left for anything else. So I'm a very placid fellow. I remember Jilly Cooper, of all people, saying that the one common factor she'd found about all these guys who were savage on the page was that they were pussycats off it, because they got rid of all their aggressions on the page. I think I'm one of that category. Whether I'm a savage or not, I don't know.

JMCG: **At school did you reveal any talent?**

IAN PATTISON: Talent? Do you have a dictionary? If you were brought up in Govan, you'll know that there are no precedents for becoming a comedy writer, or any other kind of writer. I was at Fairfield Infants – that was Govan's school – and then there was one of the clearances that took people out of the slums. Some people went to Drumchapel, some to Easterhouse. I went to Johnstone, which was about thirteen miles outside Glasgow. They were building a new estate four miles outside Paisley. It was like going to the promised land: trees and grass and stuff. You don't realise that there are more colours in the world than just slate-grey and black. You don't feel deprived in any way, but it just seems remarkable when you see a field. The only thing I could do at school was what they call up here 'compositions'. I could write essays, fairly effortlessly, but everything else was just a daydream to me. Something happened after the age of twelve: a daydream set in and it never went away until I left school. The only thing I could do and that I was interested in was writing these essays, but where do you go with that? Your teachers live in the same grotty wee town as you do. The only difference then was that they were the other side of the desk and paid forty quid a week for living in the same shit-hole that I was. So, what could they offer me by way of a bigger horizon? They hadn't seen it themselves. Maybe everybody should be educated there, because it just makes you unhappy and you have to resolve these internal crises, which is good for writing.

So you have to find your own way, and that can take decades, and the turning point for me, I suppose, was going to London, having done dozens of jobs up here and been thoroughly bored and miserable. Went down to London and met some people who said that it's not such a reprehensible thing to want to be a writer. It was a bit like being gay: you didn't want to admit it. I might as well have said to my father, 'I want to be a ballerina,' or something.

I was living in bed-sits and working in restaurants. A friend and I went down at the age of fifteen. I'd seen this play on telly called *The Making of Jericho*, by Alan Owen, and that was a turning point for me. It was all about this shipping clerk who's thoroughly bored with his life, and happens to go to this pub where all these artists are hanging out, and by a strange quirk he becomes an artist too. And I really thought: Fuck, if I go to London, that'll happen to me! Sadly it didn't.

I went down, slept in gutters, did the stuff that Sixties kids did: homelessness isn't new, it's just more of an industry now than it was then. Then came back to Glasgow; parents had split up by this time

. . . I couldn't keep away, really. When I was in London I felt home-sick, and when I was in Glasgow I was sick of home: it was that kind of thing. All my friends were in Glasgow, but all the work was in London. This is all going back to when I was about sixteen. I can't even remember it myself very well. What happened then? What the fuck happened then? I went to work in a holiday camp at Ayr. I thought, I'm going to shag myself silly. I'm eighteen and I'm still a virgin. I thought, This is the life for me; and on the first night I met the girl who was to become my wife. So I had one shag, basically, the four months. I think I timed that one wrong. And then I went to Newcastle and I lived there for about fifteen years, because she was a Geordie girl.

In a five-year interim period the two of us, me and my wife-to-be, went to London and lived in Putney, I remember, and by sheer fluke there was a fellow downstairs who was living with his girlfriend, and he was keen to develop my interest in writing.

He was called George Kay. I hope George has done really, really well. I don't know what became of him but I remember the two girl-friends meeting, his and mine, and they were both from Newcastle it turned out, and they said: 'Both our boyfriends are closet writers. Let's get them together.' We each thought, Fuckin' hell, this guy'll be a boring bastard. And we met and we talked all night, we just got on so well.

George's name was George Kazinsky (he was of Polish extrac-tion), but he called himself Kay. I really wish I did know where he was. He was a labourer, and he was trying to write the great novel, of course, as all labourers do. You don't get a job as a labourer unless you're a novelist on the side. We all have a George in our life, I sup-pose. And he said: 'You should do this thing: you're talking about it, not doing it.' So I tried to write the great British novel, as we all do – well, I kicked off in poetry, because it's shorter, and you think: You can write ten lines, you've got a poem. Then I slid right down the greasy pole into this skid row of writing gags for telly, and here I remain.

I also had all kinds of shitty jobs: anything that didn't require me to think about it or invest anything in it, I would do. I wanted my head space free, and I would come home and work on scripts in the evenings. The theatre was the thing for me, but you can spend three months or six months writing a play: you send it out to the Bush Theatre, and you get a two-line rejection three months later. The only encouraging theatre was the Glasgow Citizens'. They were very encouraging about a play I sent. Didn't do it, but they were very encouraging. Anyway, I thought, Fuck it, I'll do a television play. I sent it to BBC Scotland. A woman called Maggie Allen, who was then script supervisor, says: 'Your play's shit, but you've obviously got some comic talent. Send something to Sean Hardie.'

Sean had just come up to take over as Head of Light Entertainment at BBC Scotland and he was working then with Colin Gilbert as his underling, and both of them had worked on *Not the Nine O'Clock News*. Sean took me on to his exclusive band of one million and one freelance writers. Then there was a big bust-up over a show called *Sin on Saturday*, which the incoming Director General, Alistair Milne, took off as a show of strength, and Sean resigned in protest. And out of the ashes of that explosion came the Comedy Unit with Colin Gilbert at its head. Colin realised something had to be, there had to be a platform for Scottish writers if he was going to encourage local talent, and so he came up with a radio show called *Naked Radio*, which was listened to by three men and a dog, and about three weeks in, I got a phone call just when I was about to give up writing. I'd thought, I'm going to be Mr Additional Material for the rest of my fucking life. If that's the case, I'd rather not do it.

Colin offered me a two-minute commission, so I thought: Well, that's all right, that's twenty quid. It was the commitment that he was prepared to offer me a commission, however meagre – you can imagine what radio budgets are like. So I thought, Well, I'll give it another go, and gradually got more and more stuff on. And then Colin had to put together a sketch show for television, and racked his brains to think of a cast that would be appealing to the Network. It was only at the last moment that it crossed his mind that: 'Wait a moment, I've got a sketch show on radio, why aren't I thinking about putting those guys on television?' Answer: because they're Scottish, and the Network won't accept those voices. So, it was with some trepidation that he took that step, and out of that came Gregor Fisher, Elaine Smith, Tony Roper, all the people who are in *Nesbitt* now. Elaine Smith, what a great soulful voice she's got. She's as good as Gregor is in that way. She has to be as strong as Gregor, otherwise it's an unequal contest.

DB: **When the *Naked Video* and *Naked Radio* shows were going, were you working in a team, or were you just firing your pieces in?**

IAN PATTISON: That was living in Newcastle, firing odd pieces in – firing *loads* of pieces in. Anybody outside would look at the credits on a sketch show, and see about ten names and think, That must be great: there are ten guys round a table, and they're all having a great time, knocking gags back and forth. But no, nine of these guys are all over, up and down the country, working in estate agents' offices and one thing and another, and there's one guy who's a script editor, working under an assumed name. There's no *bonhomie* about it.

DB: When it comes to actual production of *Rab C. Nesbitt*, are you there on the floor?
IAN PATTISON: Well, no. My rule of thumb is, if you trust a director you don't have to be on the set, and if you don't trust him, you don't *want* to be on the set. I think by now Colin can be left to get on with it. We've now got the luxury of the read-through, would you believe? On the sixth series, we've managed to establish that. Isn't that astonishing? The lowest, cheapest form of theatre has that above even the most big-budgeted television piece. They can hone it, hone it, hone it until they get it right in theatre. In television it's got to work first time. Nobody builds in a provision for dealing with the script element. They don't understand how it comes about, so therefore they can't legislate for it. We've now got a read-through for *Nesbitt*, and it's a tremendous luxury just to be able to cut and hone and stitch up and all of that. But after that, it just goes cold on me. By the time it's hit the screen, I'm just not interested any more. There are very few *Rabs* that I can enjoy watching. One or two, perhaps.

DB: What *can* you watch with pleasure?
IAN PATTISON: If I want pure comedy, if I want a laugh, there's very little I'll tune in for except Harry Enfield; he's brilliant. I like a lot of *The Fast Show*, but I don't like it all unreservedly.

JMcG: What about the American sitcoms?
IAN PATTISON: They're brilliant, they're wonderful, but it's like overdosing on soufflé: they're so well-honed and refined. I want something with a bit of roughage to it. The cartoons they're doing, like *The Simpsons* and *King of the Hill*, you can imagine the studio saying: 'How can we get rid of these highly-paid actors? By series three, they'll all be wanting triple money. So we'll use cartoons and if the guy who's doing the voice-over says, "Give me more money!" we'll just tell him to fuck off, and get another voice.'

JMcG: Where do you write?
IAN PATTISON: Because I was brought up in the real world and had to do real jobs, I've got a real work ethic, I've got to go out to work.

Sitting at home working – I live alone – is just to wither on the vine for me; I need the stimulus of other people. Even if I'm a surly bastard who doesn't talk to them, I like to know they're around. It's nice to hear office noise – fax machines and telephones and all that. It's not a distraction. I think it helps. So that's when I work, and do nine to five. Here's a joke that occurred to me: somebody said to me, 'Why did you become a writer?' 'It was better than a nine-to-five job.' 'What hours do you work?' 'Nine to five!'

I use a typewriter. I've got an Apple Mac that's been sitting in a box with a printer for two and half years now. I don't open it because I know that way madness lies. At the BBC we're all using typewriters until suddenly, we went home on Friday, I come back on Monday and word processors have taken over. The BBC got rid, overnight, of all the manual typewriters and they stored them all in a big Portakabin in BBC Scotland. So when Colin Gilbert and I left to set up the Comedy Unit I managed to persuade them to part with three or four typewriters, so I'm OK for the next three or four years.

DB: **And the Comedy Unit is your outfit, yours and Colin's?**
IAN PATTISON: Colin's the senior partner, I've got shares in it. We have 'creative meetings' every so often, stuff like new projects. But basically I just come in, go in a box in the corner, because it's a big open-plan office, go there, write, and go home, and sometimes don't speak to anybody all day, but I like to know they're around. I'm just an oddity in there. I just do it, go away, and let them talk business.

Graham Linehan and Arthur Mathews

You try and amuse each other

Like many writers who work closely together, Graham Linehan and Arthur Mathews have a habit of picking up each other's half-spoken thoughts and continuing them. We met them in their basement office at a TV production company off Tottenham Court Road the day their last series of *Father Ted* was being launched for the press and a fortnight before the sudden death of Dermot Morgan, the actor who played Ted himself, at a tragically early age. Later they added this: '*Father Ted* depended so much on Dermot that its success was largely due to him. He is irreplaceable and we owe him a huge debt.' Graham and Arthur contributed sketches to *Alas Smith and Jones* and *The Fast Show* before writing *Father Ted*. Their current projects when we spoke were both for the BBC: a sketch show called *Big Train* and a new sitcom set in the Sixties, *A Bunch of Hippies*. We asked them what they thought of the present state of the sitcom genre.

GRAHAM LINEHAN: There are certain types of sitcom, it's like someone suddenly thinks: Do you know what we really miss, do you know what's not on TV at the moment? A sitcom about a family! It's amazing that hundreds of people have this idea at the same time, and I just don't understand what motivates them. We did a sitcom called *Paris* with Alexei Sayle which seemed to us a fruitful ground. Every episode was based on a different aspect of the time: there was one about the rise of Fascism; another that was about jazz coming in. I think it didn't get a second series because the dynamics of the characters weren't worked out well enough and that to me, now, is the most important thing in the world.

ARTHUR MATHEWS: No one disagrees with that rule, do they? It all has to be character-based.

GRAHAM LINEHAN: But after writing *Ted* I wonder how much of that is luck, happening upon a bunch of characters who spark off each other.

ARTHUR MATHEWS: Plus cast as well: we're very lucky in *Ted* with the cast we have.

DB: Did you originally write for those actors?
GRAHAM LINEHAN: Arthur used to do Ted as a stand-up in Dublin years ago.

ARTHUR MATHEWS: Not in any big way. In a very small way, actually.

GRAHAM LINEHAN: So Ted was a voice that Arthur could call on and if I felt that Arthur could say a line in that voice, then you'd know the character was working. Dougal came from the name 'Dougal', because it was a funny name, we thought. He was originally a far more intelligent man. Arthur would describe him in the stand-up: he used to be chased from villages by angry villagers. Mrs Doyle – there's always a housekeeper: there has to be a housekeeper – probably came from the idea of not accepting 'No' for an answer when she offers a cup of tea. That was the first thing that led to everything else she's ever done. And Jack, Jack was interesting because Jack originally was dead.

ARTHUR MATHEWS: We had written a spoof documentary about a priest who goes back to his old seminary and one of the people he visits is a priest who is actually dead, but he doesn't know: he thinks he's just asleep.

GRAHAM LINEHAN: He's based on a certain type of priest that you would hear about occasionally – just the old nasty side of the Catholic Church. So it's our one concession to satire I suppose.
    People are constantly asking us if this is going to be the last series. People don't actually realise that they're getting sick of a show. You'll meet someone out and they'll go: 'Oh, I hope you do another series of *Ted*.' 'Well, it's on tonight.' 'Oh, I forgot to tape it.' That's

what we want to avoid.

It's also possible that you can go to other areas in comedy. People will be disappointed if our next sitcom doesn't have a surreal edge to it, but if we eventually found ourselves getting bored of that, or losing it, we might move into comedy dramas, or films. One of the reasons why we do want to give up *Ted* is because the surrealism, funnily enough, gives you fewer options rather than more. A realistic sitcom you can write for ever, but a sitcom that's surreal . . .

ARTHUR MATHEWS: Especially for Mrs Doyle and Father Jack and Dougal, you run out of things. You could write for Ted for ever, really . . .

GRAHAM LINEHAN: Ted is in the real world . . .

ARTHUR MATHEWS: The other three are kind of caricatures, and that's their appeal, their limit.

DB: Do you find any difficulty in translating your words from page to screen?
GRAHAM LINEHAN: I would say no . . . Arthur and I seem to have a very visual imagination. There are certain jokes we write and you can trust the actors to know where they should be standing, whether they should be standing or sitting or whatever. But other jokes are very specific, someone has to be in a certain position, and we always write them as clearly as we can into the script. I think it comes from reading a lot of scripts myself. Before we started writing, I bought lots of film scripts and books of sketches.

ARTHUR MATHEWS: You nearly always want to shorten things, rather than lengthen things, when you see them performed. When we were writing for *Alas Smith and Jones* we used to write sketches that'd be five pages long, six pages long. But we learned that about a page and a half long is nearly always long enough.

GRAHAM LINEHAN: We spent about a year writing very closely with Griff Rhys-Jones and Mel Smith and I think that was where we really learnt how to do it. The worst thing in a lot of comedy are jokes that don't have anything to do with the plot or character, they're just gags. And we started kind of losing them and it was painful at first, but now I think we both feel it's actually quite liberating and enjoyable to throw away stuff.

ARTHUR MATHEWS: Yeah, once you get over the pain it's a good thing to do.

GRAHAM LINEHAN: In the first episode in the second series of *Ted*, we didn't want to lose one thing from the first scene. And we saw it back and the first scene seemed to go on and on, and it just drives us up the walls now when we watch it. So we've gone the other way. Now our scenes are really short. I think this comes from watching *Seinfeld*. And we've become far more plot-driven.

ARTHUR MATHEWS: More things happen.

GRAHAM LINEHAN: We've tried to be fair on the actors because Frank and Pauline in previous series didn't have as much as they should have done, and they're both very funny comic actors, so it's great discipline to write a scene and say: 'Oh, Mrs Doyle isn't in this scene. How do we get her in without it getting flabby?'

ARTHUR MATHEWS: They're so sharp: Channel 4 sitcoms are, like, twenty-three or twenty-four minutes by the time you've had the break and title music and credits at the end. We had a read-through of one, and because there's a lot of stuff on location as well, literally it's eleven minutes in the studio, that's all they have to do.

GRAHAM LINEHAN: But an interesting thing happened when we did the Christmas special. At the read-through we were something like eight minutes over, and we asked for an extension from Channel 4 and got it. And I wish we hadn't. I'd love to cut eight minutes out! I think twenty-four minutes, I think the time we have on *Ted*, is enough to do what we're after.

DB: **Do you have a source of material or ideas that you're conscious of?**
ARTHUR MATHEWS: Not really . . . Just recently a friend of mine had these old films from the Sixties made by this Irish language organisation called Gael Linn, and one of the things was the annual blessing of the aeroplanes at Dublin airport, with the priest blessing these big jumbo jets. But better than that was the annual blessing of the scooters – two hundred mods passing by a priest who was blessing all the scooters . . . And there's a great book, *Beyond Belief,* mostly about Catholicism in Ireland, but other religions and all; it's just full of these types of things.

GRAHAM LINEHAN: It's really useful that they're all priests, because all the exposition is taken care of by their uniforms. We don't have to explain anything about them when they walk through the door. When we start writing we think of 'The Detective Priest', 'The Heavy Metal Priest' or whatever, and all they express is their character. You don't have to say where they work, or what they do. They're celibate, or at least they should be celibate, they believe in God or they should believe in God, and there's all this baggage that comes with them. That means that we have to do less writing. It's so easy: you just put anything in front of the word 'priest.'

The other useful thing about them all belonging to the priesthood is that, like any organisation when you're not a part of it, it is vaguely mysterious. You can make up, you can apply your own interpretations as to what it is exactly they do. So because the FBI are mysterious, in *Twin Peaks* David Lynch was able to claim that they actually studied the paranormal, and who can disagree with him, except the FBI? With *Ted* we can have parties in the Vatican and priests who do nothing except play Ludo all day because no one really knows exactly what their days consist of.

DB: **And Ireland is exotic to the Brits, because they don't understand half of what goes on there . . .**
GRAHAM LINEHAN: One of the things which works to our advantage is the one-way traffic of information from England to Ireland. We've grown up with English TV, English comedy shows and American films and all these influences, but English people know very little about Ireland. So we can make up stuff about Ireland that's nonsense. Like, we were going to do a documentary about Dublin, with not one fact true: Arthur used to have a thing called 'Disappearing Dublin' which is all about landmarks that are gone, and we were going to get photographs and change them so that we could have the thatched skyscraper, which blew away, and Hitler's cottage – because Ireland was neutral during the war, so Hitler used to visit, take two weeks off the war. It's death to comedy writers, once you know *why* something is: it ceases to be funny. But when people have little information, you can tell them any nonsense . . .

ARTHUR MATHEWS: But we're just not conscious that the priests are Irish or that it's set in Ireland. We don't hear Irish accents. We just forget about that whole area.

GRAHAM LINEHAN: We did have to stop people from putting on more Irish accents.

ARTHUR MATHEWS: Generally our actors are great. A lot of them are not used to TV – they're in the Abbey Theatre, they're used to doing *The Playboy of the Western World*, and they presume with *Ted* . . .

GRAHAM LINEHAN: We occasionally have to stop someone from going: 'Hello, there!' It's kind of a defence mechanism: it's easier to act if you're not yourself, if you're putting on a mask. We want a show where Irish people can be themselves, on an English-produced show. We don't want anyone putting on a little green hat. Oh, God, it would be nice to put a stop to acting. It's the great scourge of the world today. It's strange, it's this mystery. In America they mystify it with Method and all that sort of stuff but over here they mystify it with this kind of RSC performance.

DB: Do you come to work in this room every day?
GRAHAM LINEHAN: Eleven is our starting time and we might not even start working then; we probably just talk and smoke for half an hour or an hour, depending on how busy we are, and then we usually write until about five, half five. I think when you relax a bit you actually write more than if you're worried about blank pages and so on. It's disrupted when we're filming *Father Ted.*

ARTHUR MATHEWS: Graham directed the location stuff on *Ted* this time, and we're associate producers on it as well, so we're a lot more involved than we used to be.

GRAHAM LINEHAN: But we don't direct the studio, because you have to be paying attention to so many things. When you get into the studio the audiences laugh so much more than when it's on the monitors. You can compose a joke beautifully but they'll still laugh because the actor's in front of them, just to be nice. They are occasionally useful, though. Sometimes you can have a niggling feeling about a joke, and the studio audience will confirm it. When you know a joke is great, and they haven't got it, it doesn't matter: they'll get it at home. Our biggest problem has been . . .

ARTHUR MATHEWS: Yeah, taking off laughs in the edit.

GRAHAM LINEHAN: We take off loads of laughs, because I think there's nothing worse than sitting at home and hearing a line get a laugh and going . . .

ARTHUR MATHEWS: 'That's not funny.'

GRAHAM LINEHAN: Because you start to feel cheated and you start to feel also it might be canned, so . . .

JMcG: **Do you use any canned?**
GRAHAM LINEHAN: No. If we do a scene twice and it doesn't get a laugh the second time but it got a huge laugh the first time, we'll get the laugh from the first time and put it on the second.

ARTHUR MATHEWS: You shouldn't notice laughter really on comedy shows. It should just be like music.

GRAHAM LINEHAN: But there are certain kinds of humour that do need it: I think *Ted* really needs a laughter track to work.

ARTHUR MATHEWS: It's a sitcom, it's a standard British studio audience.

GRAHAM LINEHAN: Because it's so conventional in certain ways, it needs that laughter track. I think it would be quite dead without it. Something like *The Larry Sanders Show* would be dead *with* a laughter track, because the jokes are so subtle and understated.

JMcG: **That has always been the big argument in Britain: with an audience or without an audience?**
ARTHUR MATHEWS: We've learned that they're completely different things. You have to write it differently, the gags are different.

GRAHAM LINEHAN: There's a certain kind of quiet gag that's great without an audience. It also requires a kind of confidence in your own writing, which I hope we have now, but in the early days we might not. But it might be interesting to try something now without laughter.
    In sitcoms the Americans have such an advantage over us: they get to rehearse all week on their set, which we don't. We have to go to a rehearsal room. They do it on a Friday night at seven o'clock, after doing a dress rehearsal which they film, then they film the one in front of the audience. Then they get the audience out, another audience in, and they do it again. As the Americans go, it's such a big country, and so much money behind it, I don't think the question is, 'Why do they make so many good comedies?' it's 'Why don't they have more?' There are a lot of bad comedies.

ARTHUR MATHEWS: And for such a big country as well, there is a lack of variety. Apart from, strangely enough, animation: that's where they differ, because *The Simpsons* is really good.

GRAHAM LINEHAN: Animation in the States is where you get the most satirical and savage comedy. In America the family is a political issue, and for *The Simpsons* to have a go in the way they do is extraordinary.

DB: You don't think animation is just a way of saving on actors?
GRAHAM LINEHAN: Possibly . . .

DB: Just going back to your routine: you've got one keyboard in this room, so one of you is typing, the other one's walking up and down?
GRAHAM LINEHAN: Yeah, except we've never been so . . .

ARTHUR MATHEWS: Rigid.

GRAHAM LINEHAN: Rigid, as one is the typist and the other is the pacer.

ARTHUR MATHEWS: I had very bad typing at first. I was very slow off the ground doing my stuff.

GRAHAM LINEHAN: Say, if I come up with an idea, I'll write two pages, and get to the point, get to the main joke point or get as far as I can with it, and then Arthur will come in and read it and edit it and suggest changes. Or we do it the other way round. But the thing that we're always doing is, we're sitting beside each other and I'll write something and I'll go: 'Don't look, don't look, don't look!'

ARTHUR MATHEWS: Because you try and amuse each other.

GRAHAM LINEHAN: You have to get these instant reactions. I can actually almost feel Arthur's eyes passing over the line I've written and if it doesn't get a laugh, it's: 'Oh, shit.' You see sitcoms on TV and I can't see a writer laughing as he writes some of the things. I've seen shows that are ambitious and fall down, like *Sunnyside Farm,* which two friends of ours wrote and they laugh their heads off while they're writing. It didn't quite work, for various reasons, but there are other shows you see where there's, say, a cheeky kid who comes in and says a few boring Americanised cute phrases, and I just can't picture a writer being amazed at what he's written and leaning back in his chair and roaring his head off. Me and Arthur, it's a very bad day if we haven't been laughing a lot.

JMCG: Do you feel that there are any subjects that are neglected, even if they're not things that you want to cover?

ARTHUR MATHEWS: We have these crazy flights of fancy about where to set a sitcom, and we had one set in the world of orchestra leaders, Formula One motor racing and the international tennis circuit.

GRAHAM LINEHAN: Chess champions . . .

ARTHUR MATHEWS: Chess masters, yeah . . .

GRAHAM LINEHAN: There's definitely something to be done about chess masters, because they're all so highly strung. But the thing is, if we came up with a really good idea, we'd do it. So, I don't feel that we're being ill-served by the amount of things out at the moment. I think the only thing that England is missing as a whole is a good TV animated comedy.

Charlie Higson

Just keep distilling it down

Appropriately for the author of a darkly humorous psychological thriller with a bleak urban background, Charlie Higson – as he prefers to be called – has a look reminiscent of the young Raymond Chandler, staring at life with the eye of a disappointed romantic, perhaps. Charlie was a presence mainly behind the camera in the first series of *The Fast Show,* concentrating on his work as producer but emerging to play Ralph the landowner and Coughing Bob. His novels – grim, often violent, but also often very funny – are set among people on the margins of society in Hackney, a few miles east of his present home in north London, where we talked in an upstairs sitting-room.

DB: **Can we talk about how you divide up your work between the two activities for performance and . . .**
CHARLIE HIGSON: Writing and performance? I started in television as a writer, although always in the back of my mind I thought it would be nice to do some performing as well. I've always written comedy for television with Paul Whitehouse, and the way we start writing anything is by performing it, and sort of mucking about and getting the voice and bouncing ideas back and forth. So, even in the writing in the early stages, there'd been a certain level of performance. But Harry Enfield wasn't particularly interested in me as a performer – he wasn't particularly interested in me as a *writer*, but I came as a package with Paul so he didn't have much say in it, because he wanted Paul. Paul and I had done a couple of series of Harry's show, and we'd done the *Saturday Live* and *Friday Live* stuff with him, but we'd never intended to be known just as Harry Enfield's writers. We wanted to do a thing of our own, which is how *The Fast*

Show came about, and from the start it was always understood that I would be performing little bits and pieces on that – although not that much on the first series, because it was testing the waters, and we ended up, almost by accident, producing it as well, which we hadn't intended to do. But comedy is a very small world, there are very few good producers and directors around, and all the producers we liked were busy on something else. The BBC said: 'Why don't you produce it?' because we had been involved in other projects in semi-producing roles, so we said: 'Yes.' So on the first series of *The Fast Show* I was concentrating more on writing and producing. Particularly when we came to the studio recordings I did very little performing, so that I could be up in the box keeping an eye on things.

The way the series tend to work is that Paul and I spend about five or six months writing it. We do, I suppose, about seventy per cent of the writing and the other performers write their own bits and pieces. We write some for them. Then we go through another six months of production and post-production, during which we're also acting. This is why we may be taking a break from *The Fast Show* for a while, because it's a year of your life: normally on a show like that, the writers would work for four or five months and then they wouldn't have anything more to do with the project, so they could be getting on with other stuff, or writing the next series. There is a certain level of frustration in not having the time to really spend writing, particularly writing other projects. Paul has been doing *Fast Show* and Harry Enfield back to back for nearly five years, with no break, so he's pretty fed up with sketch shows.

JMCG: **How do you get it down on paper?**
CHARLIE HIGSON: I've got an office here in the house and we work about four hours a day, I suppose, five days a week, for how-ever many months it takes, really. We are quite boring on that level. Paul's never got to grips with the technology of word processing so I sit at the machine and he wanders around throwing out ideas and we perform little bits and pieces. Then I tend to structure it and do the nuts and bolts stuff, and then once the ideas are written up, just keep rewriting it. We generate as much material as possible, and then keep going back to it and working over it – particularly when we get into pre-production, when you're then approaching it from the point of view of a producer, and you're having to say, obviously, what locations you've got, what things aren't going to be practical, so you just keep tightening it and focusing it and distilling it down.

The Fast Show is very much a team, and they're all fairly vociferous in what they like and don't like and what they think's going to work. So the creative process carries on: I suppose since the whole industry opened up, since Channel 4 and all the independents, writers have been allowed a lot more say. Which most of the time is a good thing, but there are some writers who shouldn't be allowed near the production process because they don't understand it and they can get very precious about what they're doing.

DB: **At what point do you integrate the other contributors?**
CHARLIE HIGSON: Theoretically, whilst we're working they're also writing scripts, but their scripts tend to come in at the last minute. We have a handful of other writers who are just writers who also write bits and pieces, and we inevitably get huge piles of unsolicited scripts in, which we try and wade through, but it's always a bit dispiriting, although probably in the series we would put in four or five sketches of unsolicited stuff.

It is nice when you get something completely out of nowhere. You always think, Wouldn't it be great to discover this great comedy talent that no one else has heard of. For the first series we got in two writers we liked who hadn't done anything at the time, Graham Linehan and Arthur Mathews; they came up with the characters of Ted and Ralph that we do, and of course since then they've gone on to do *Father Ted* and various other things, so they're now too busy to write for us.

DB: **Do you have some overall plan about how each strand of the show is going to fit?**
CHARLIE HIGSON: We try and write as much as possible for all the characters. For the main characters we try and get at least six major sketches, but that may mean that we write ten and only use six. We don't sit down with any huge masterplan other than to say: 'We'll start writing and we'll write what we think is funny.' At the end if there's one character we haven't written any sketches for, we'll say: 'We haven't got any ideas for that. We'll drop him.'

In the last series we had a major new character we thought was going to be massive. We filmed about ten sketches with him and it just didn't work, it didn't go in at all. It would have been fatal up front to plan the whole thing around that. There are certain characters, like Ted and Ralph, who have more of a storyline, where you say: 'This one has to go first and then that one and that one,' but that's as far as it's structured. You get to the edit and you've got God knows how many hundreds of bits and pieces to put together, and you start by organising them. You put them into group order and you start building up so each show then starts to come together. In the editing process it is like a movie, in that you want it to flow. You've got two countryside pieces in a row, so one of them will have to move. You have a fast one and then a slow one, and you might have one that's a bit more downbeat, and you need to put something a bit up. The editing process is quite fun, and new technology has really helped that, with digital editing. You've got to keep moving one thing from one show to another, which in turn changes everything in *that* show and what's on either side of it. With digital editing you can keep doing it to your heart's content.

JMcG: The Ted and Ralph characters, did they come out of a political attitude?
CHARLIE HIGSON: Well, we'd been down the pub with Graham and Arthur while we were still putting together the first series, and they sent in some fully formed ideas, and then just right at the end of the evening they said, 'We've got this idea. We're not really sure about it,' and they sort of acted it, this relationship, and there just seemed something very charming about it, and different, and it seemed very funny although you couldn't put your finger on why. It is sort of the love that crosses every boundary of race, age, sex, and class.

When we first played the characters to studio audiences, there was complete silence, they were totally mystified. It was almost touch and go whether they made it in, but we just felt there was something there, and people did appreciate them as they watched from week to week, and now I suppose they are among the most popular characters on the show. Because there's a bit of genuine drama and emotion there.

DB: How much are you dependent on the audience?
CHARLIE HIGSON: They're useful, but they're not the ultimate test. Ultimately Paul and I go on what we like, what we think is strong and what worked well, and what works with the studio audience is by no means always what works well with the home audience. Live audience, they quite like big stuff played out, and of course the more obvious stuff they go for as well, because it's hard for them to concentrate, there's a lot going on. When we make the show we do about three weeks' location shooting, and then about four days in a multi-camera studio without an audience, and four nights with. So compared with a lot of sketch shows we don't do that much with the audience, and the stuff we do with them tends to be the more obvious, old-fashioned sketches, like the Suit You

tailors and Chanel 9 Neus and any longer piece that is a more traditional sketch.

JMCG: Do you think you need an audience for television comedy?
CHARLIE HIGSON: We had big arguments about this on the first series. Most of the cast didn't want to do it with an audience. But people are used to seeing comedy on television with laughter, and it changes it quite drastically if you don't have that laughter. I also find that it really does help people's performances when they've got an audience. The ridiculous thing about TV is that when you get the audience in you've got one shot at it, one night when you've got to get through x amount of stuff and you haven't got time to keep going back over it. You may have spent months preparing, and 'Bash!' you're out there, it's all going 'Bish! bash! bosh!' and it's off and that's it! And you think: All this money put into it and we've got this one shot.

I like the American system where they record the same show twice in one night. You have got a second chance: if something really just didn't work, you can fix it; or you can play the same thing to two different audiences and get completely different reactions. But it is a very expensive thing to do. And *The Fast Show* is expensive. We've got a core cast of seven major performers; there's a lot of location work, a lot of filming, a huge number of costumes and wigs, and about thirty-five different sketches per show. That all adds up. Whereas if you've got a sitcom, you've got the same set every week, the same four actors. I've always fancied that as a challenge, to do a pure sitcom with no location stuff, three sets. They managed it on the *Blackadders* after the first series.

DB: Do you think there's a chance for a fresh spirit coming into sitcom?
CHARLIE HIGSON: I don't see why not. At the risk of sounding arrogant, before we did *The Fast Show* everyone was saying: 'Oh, the sketch show's dead. We don't want to do that any more,' and since we've done it, everyone's saying: 'Let's make some more sketch shows!' It only takes a couple of good writers to come along and write a good sitcom and suddenly everyone says: 'Oh, sitcom's a good thing.' At any given moment there are two or three good sitcoms on, like *One Foot in the Grave* and *Father Ted*.

I don't think any comedy form is inherently dead or unworkable, it just depends on where the good writers want to work. Recently, because of the bad feelings that people tend to have about sitcoms – God knows why – a lot of writers haven't been interested in trying to write them. You do get so viciously attacked if you do a sitcom that doesn't quite work or isn't as funny as people hoped. That's always mystified me: why comedy gets so much more scrutiny than any other TV form. You get a bad drama on and you're not saying: 'How dare these people do a crap drama? Don't they know that the drama's dead, and the Americans do it so much better?' But you put some little sitcom out, unpretentious little thing, and suddenly it's 'My God, what do you think you're doing?' If comedy doesn't make people laugh, it seems to make them angry.

It takes a couple of series to get things right, and the BBC, in the past, used to give people the benefit of the doubt, if they liked it, to make more. I don't know if that's happening less now – ITV never really have done that.

JMcG: What about the difference between the standard of BBC comedy and ITV comedy?
CHARLIE HIGSON: It's a much easier environment at the BBC. You're talking to the people who own the channel, basically, and they could decide. If you go to an ITV company they're fighting with all the other companies for the slots. Every couple of years somebody from ITV turns up and says: 'Will you come and do some comedy for the ITV? There's a potential slot in two years' time: eleven o'clock on a Sunday night. We're up against a few other people, but that's the slot,' and you think, I can't work like that.

In *The Fast Show*'s very early incarnation we were developing it with Hat Trick Productions, and they were very keen to break into ITV. They had very positive meetings at LWT, and a year later nothing had happened, so we took it away from Hat Trick and away from ITV and took it to the BBC, and they said: 'If you bring it in-house, not via an independent, we'll commission you now.' At LWT, we'd go in and say: 'We want to do this new sketch show, and we want to put together a team of new faces. Paul Whitehouse' – he was relatively known from working with Harry – 'he'd be about the biggest name, but everyone else, you won't have heard of them.' People would say: 'Great, something new!' A month later they come back: 'We really like it, but where are the stars?' You say: 'Don't you remember us saying it's not a star vehicle? You can't do a new show with a new team if it's all the same old tired faces.' 'Yeah, you're right, yeah.' And a month later: 'We really like it, but where are the stars?' That's what they need on ITV, and it's got to come out instantly with huge ratings. The BBC would nurture talent if they liked it: the first series of *The Fast Show* was not a resounding ratings success, but they stuck with it.

You would have to watch two or three to get the hang of it: we felt it would be nice not to insult the audience's intelligence and that through repeated watching they would develop a relationship with the programme. Enough people did stay with it, and with repeats and video it built up a good word of mouth. There's a lot of stuff you might miss the first time round and it's only when you've got to know a character, and you can go back and watch an earlier one, it would appear to be that much funnier. So we always had in our mind that a lot of TV in the future is going to be recycling stuff – video, all the new cable channels . . . things will be constantly on. So we thought it would be nice to have something that, rather than getting boring the more you watched it, would actually get funnier as you get to know it and you see all the running gags which you maybe didn't spot before.

DB: **And of course you've been able to take that out into Hammersmith on stage at the Apollo and . . .**
CHARLIE HIGSON: Yeah, we had no idea if that was going to work or not. It was interesting to see the amount of warmth that people had for the individual characters: they just loved seeing them and there were big cheers of recognition. It's three and a half thousand seats, and we sold out thirty-two nights. About a hundred and ten thousand people came in. It's a very difficult place to play. It's big and cold, but the audience were so up for it.

DB: **What do you find personally the most difficult part about writing comedy?**
CHARLIE HIGSON: I suppose it's trying not to get bored with what you've written. You have to keep reminding yourself that when you first wrote it, it made you laugh. There's a great danger in comedy that you keep changing it simply because you're bored with it – and you're not improving it: you're writing sideways.

JMCG: **What about working on your own?**
CHARLIE HIGSON: Well, I write my novels by myself, and I'm working on a couple of film scripts. It's a nice change, particularly writing the books. It's so different from doing TV comedy.
I never set out to be a comedy writer. I was writing stuff from an early age, but it was novels, that type of thing. And I ended up doing the TV comedy by accident, really. I knew Paul, I knew Harry, I knew Vic Reeves. Harry wanted Paul to start writing stuff for him. Paul didn't have a word processor and I did, and Paul wasn't comfortable with the whole idea of being a writer, so we worked

together and just found out that we worked very well together, and we could do it. I kept the novels going because I like it, and you can explore those areas which you can't really do in a TV sketch show. Maybe it makes you go a bit too far down that route, but I do find it a nice release to get rid of all the pent-up anger and poison that you develop living in London . . . that you can squeeze your pus on to the page or whatever . . . The discipline is the same, just making yourself go into the office and sit at the machine and do it. And that's the same whether it's a book or a comedy. The thing about the comedy is that we discipline each other. We make an arrangement. I think: Paul's coming round, we'll have to work; and he's thinking: I've got to go round. We'll have to work. So even if neither of us actually wants to do it, we always think the other one does.

I normally would start a book in those periods when Paul isn't around, so if he was going off to do Harry's show I might have a three-month gap when I could get the book started. Once that start is under the belt I find it much easier; I can work on it before Paul's there and after he's gone. I don't know if I could actually *start* a major other project whilst doing *The Fast Show* or working with Paul, but I could certainly finish one off. I used to just write at all hours of the day and night, but since getting married and having two children that can't be done any more so I do sort of try and keep office hours.

DB: Were you setting out in the novels to build a fictional Hackney in the same way as Raymond Chandler built a fictional Los Angeles?

CHARLIE HIGSON: Well, it was Hackney because I was living in Hackney when I was writing them and I don't like doing research, so it was easy to set it there. I write the type of books that I like to read – and I certainly used to read when I started writing the books – which were a lot of quite dark American psychological thrillers: Jim Thompson, Charles Willeford and people like that. So I just thought: I'll try and write the type of book I like to read, but I obviously can't set it in America, so I'll set it in Hackney. In fact in the last two books there's been much more comedy than there was in the earlier ones. I don't know if that's starting to spill over from the comedy writing, or if it's just I'm a bit more relaxed about things these days.

Arabella Weir

Standing in the corner

Arabella Weir kept one eye on us and the other on her new baby, Isabella Agnes, who spent most of the interview asleep in a high-tech cradle but eventually emerged for a feed. We were in the house in North London which Arabella shares with her partner, Jeremy. Arabella, a diplomat's daughter, was befriended as a child by the director Karel Reisz and his actress wife, Betsy Blair. Arabella herself trained as an actress but began to write as well after joining the cast of Alexei Sayle's television show. Her roles in *The Fast Show* include Insecure Woman, and she suddenly burst into the best-sellers with a novel using the character's catch-phrase as its title: *Does My Bum Look Big in This?*

JMCG: **Was the idea in *The Fast Show* to give every character a catch-phrase?**
ARABELLA WEIR: It's not how we invented it. But you know so much about the characters because of what they say every time. It's probably easier to write, to think of the catch-phrase that gives you so much information about that person – 'I'm afraid I was very, very drunk' – and then work backwards. But I didn't work that way with No Offence or the others. I'd just keep hacking away at it and end up with the catch-phrase that I think is best. That character I did in a couple of the last series, Girl Who Boys Can't Hear, there's no catch-phrase there. She just talks and the men don't pay any attention to her, and then they have the idea themselves. Somebody said: 'Where did you get that character?' And I said: 'Working in comedy.' First series of *The Fast Show* I could say anything and everyone would be, like: 'Right, Simon, what do you think?' And I'd be, like: 'Am I in the room?' I'd written an article in *The Guardian*

about that character, and several women wrote to me and said: 'Oh, you don't know, that's me.' A lot of women can identify with that. In fact most of the guys could too; most of the guys went: 'That's a good character.' Bizarre.

DB: **Are you writing for women?**

ARABELLA WEIR: I'm not consciously doing it. I hope everybody will find it funny. After the first series a couple of blokes, who in my view haven't got a very good sense of humour, said, either to friends or to me: 'I like that woman who says "Does my bum look big in this?" but it doesn't really work because you haven't got a big bum.' Or: 'It doesn't really work because you don't see her bum.' I said: 'Do you think that you need to see a shot of her big arse for the gag to work? Well, you don't get it.' That's an offensive Benny Hill type of thing: look at the big fat woman waddling down the road and we'll make comments about her arse. *This* is about every woman's generic paranoia; it's in her mind. It's to do with her thinking that she's outside some special club. Inside that club everyone's got the right ear-rings, small arses, fantastic sex-lives with their lovely husbands, and teach their children to read and play the violin! I hope that men find the characters funny. Lots of men like No Offence. So I'm not writing for women specifically, but I don't mind if guys don't get it.

DB: **Are there new opportunities for women in writing and performing comedy?**

ARABELLA WEIR: No, I don't think there's greater opportunity for women as long as the controllers, the commissioning editors, are men, and they still far and away are the majority in comedy. At the BBC, where we all live, they are mainly blokes and they still think Nick Hancock doing something based on football is hilarious. Women will watch something which is very bloke-ish, like *Men Behaving Badly*, and go: 'That's just like Johnny! That's just like Peter!' But men – I'm talking about men as a large group – if they saw how women really are together, would be not only intimidated by it but slightly repelled.

A group of women will be much more lairy and saucy than men expect – not only working-class women but middle-class women now have girls' nights out and stuff. It has seeped over into all different walks of life and I think men find that threatening. *Men Behaving Badly* is to me the quintessential example of a show that would not be accepted if it was the other way round, although it would be equally realistic. Men would feel sorry for the girl who liked the boy upstairs: they wouldn't be able to see her as a lairy kind of go-getting girl who just fancies this fit man who lives upstairs. They would think: Oh, God, she fancies him and he doesn't seem to be responding and that makes me feel awful and I feel sorry for her. Any woman who isn't fancied by the object of her desire is *ipso facto* pathetic. You don't see Neil Morrissey's character as pathetic. Men are uncomfortable with women's needs, and are so often protected from them: 'Don't worry about Mummy: she's fine.' They're brought up with that. If Caroline Quentin's character was like Martin Clunes's and she was behaving as badly as he does, she'd just be a bitch and a cow; she'd be seen as a ball-breaker.

It's difficult for a woman to play somebody who's badly behaved because once you're thirty-plus people expect you to behave properly. And if you don't, you've either got to be on telly, mad, a witch, a right old cow, a slag, a tart, or a man-eater. You can't just be a woman who's lots of things and doesn't behave particularly well, and lives in a flat with a bunch of other people because she feels like it.

To be palatable to the BBC, a piece still has to be about Northern working-class women – it can't be that they're women we know. God forbid that any of them are educated and middle-class or that it's a mixture of women. That thing *Playing the Field* about women footballers – lots of unwanted pregnancies and gritty stuff – the attitude is: 'Oh, they're more lairy because they're like that up North.' But if they're like that down here in the South, then they're slaggy types.

JMCG: **Is that attitude the reason why so few women do stand-up comedy?**

ARABELLA WEIR: It's back to that thing about what's acceptable from a man and what's acceptable from a woman. Stand-up is in itself quite aggressive. We know blokes shout at you from building sites and shout at you in bars, but people are uncomfortable with women talking in that out-front, lairy way, which is why women who do stand-up on their own, like Joan Rivers or Jo Brand, are taking the piss out of themselves. Regrettably, audiences are comfortable with that; they're going: 'Oh, good, she's being horrible about herself, but I don't want her pointing at us, because that's not ladylike. Then she'll confront me and I'll have to hit her. If a woman's rude to me, my machismo will be challenged.' It was interesting when I did No Offence to the audience at the Hammersmith Odeon – Labbatt's Apollo – in the live *Fast Show*. I'd go to a woman first, and the gag went: 'I'm promoting a new line of perfume for the

older lady. It might be of some interest to you, my dear.' The women
would laugh, but the woman in question would laugh as well. Then
I'd pick on another woman and say: 'Can I give you a few beauty
tips? Women who are desperate to get married, like yourself...' and
the last thing was: 'You've let yourself go in a shocking manner. No
offence.' Big laughs. From her, and all her mates poking her, right?
And then I'd get to a bloke, and I'd say: 'Can I interest you in a whiff
of Mel Gibson's crotch?' and there was a whole bunch of material
about Mel Gibson's 'line of perfume', and then I'd say: 'But you're
probably not interested, are you? Because you look quite tight,
you're dressed a bit miserly...' And, almost without exception, the
blokes would be really chippy, and one bloke I thought was actually
going to get up on stage and whack me.

Of course, I don't know him, or whether he's tight or not. But he
felt affronted. And I thought, That is such a stark difference, because
what I was saying to the women was much more offensive: about
repulsive lesbians and stuff. Women were howling, and men howling – everybody howling.

DB: **If there were better outlets for comedy by women, what
would it be like?**
ARABELLA WEIR: You could do comedy that was self-deprecating
à la Woody Allen – 'Look at me, I'm shit' – that didn't make people
uncomfortable. It's only men who are uncomfortable about it.
Loads of women have read my book – I would imagine principally
women – and they go: 'It's so funny. That's just like me. I thought I
was the only person who does that thing of changing her skirt three
times...' But all the men that have read it, bar one, have gone: 'Oh,
it's quite sad! Is she really like that?'

And I explain that that's like all women – I'll be saying to a girlfriend: 'I looked in the mirror and I thought, Jesus, I've turned into
a Kentish Town mother, I'm wearing slip-ons and a caftan,' and
she'll laugh, and then I'll be saying, 'But then I went out and had a
brilliant time.' I won't be going: 'I've turned into a Kentish Town
mother. Now I'll kill myself.' So I think there's a market out there:
women are self-deprecating and that's what they find funny. They
are generally more able to laugh at themselves because they've got
less investment in being the macho, Ferrari-driving bread-winner.

JMCG: **Do you know what's funny?**
ARABELLA WEIR: I know what *I* think is funny, and if they don't
think it's funny they're just wrong. But I wrote a double act for me
and Alexei Sayle, where Alexei was dressed as a woman, where we

were two lesbians running a bike shop called 'The Menstrual Cycle', and Alexei has a much more surreal sense of comedy than I do and so he would think gags that I thought were just OK were brilliant, and he'd throw out a lot of the stuff that I thought was great. I remember thinking, You're wrong. Of course he was right for him. But that's what I don't want to do any more.

With the success of *The Fast Show* I was asked to write for other people. Disaster. Cannot do that. I had no interest and no motivation sitting at my computer if I was writing for somebody else. I realised there's no point in me writing the material for someone else because, even if somebody else wants the material, I don't want them to do it differently from how I would do it. I want them to do it exactly how I would do it and that's always going to be on a hiding to nothing because I'm going to be thinking they're wrong no matter how good they are.

So that was the first thing that I discovered, that I couldn't write for anybody else, or that I *wouldn't* write for anybody else, and luckily so far I haven't needed to. When I write for myself, for a few weeks prior to writing the character I'll have been doing her in my head and looking round the house and thinking: What would she think about that? She'd have something unpleasant to say about that sofa. Then I'll sit at the computer and 'do' her; then I'll read it out and think: Oh, no, she's got to speak differently. I probably write as a performer and when I wrote the book I found the only way I could check if it was funny or not was if I read it aloud to myself, because I think if something reads aloud well, then it'll read well to a reader.

DB: **Obviously you've got at least one solidly established character in the Insecure Woman: do you look for material for her, or do you continue to develop other characters when material presents itself?**
ARABELLA WEIR: The latter. The good thing about Insecure Woman, and I think the reason she became so popular, is that she was specifically designed not to be a woman but to be *every* woman, which is why in one sketch she'll be a judge, in another a policewoman, in another a doctor. She's supposed to be everybody, and she's not supposed to be like the other character that had quite a lot of popularity, which was Different With Boys. She was supposed to be one specific woman who always behaved like that in front of men. She was one way with women, she was another way with men. I've never had to look for material for Insecure Woman, in that every day presented stuff that an insecure woman would be thinking.

When we were writing the third series, I wanted to do different

characters. The one called No Offence developed out of doing a
South African accent. Paul and Charlie said: 'You must do someone
who speaks like that.' I just happened to see a woman in a department store and I thought: That woman's values are very old-fashioned. I fantasised that marriage would be all, even if it was cheesy,
to that woman, and developed her out of that.

DB: **Is there stuff floating around which you haven't yet found
a character to express?**
ARABELLA WEIR: I will observe something and my worry will be:
'Is that universally recognisable enough to make it into a character?'
That happened with Charlie in the last series. He did a man which
ended up on the cutting-room floor, which has never happened in the
show before. It was something for which you needed a long-term
narrative, like a sitcom or a film. He was called Mid-Life Crisis Man,
and he was a bloke that you saw as a stiff lawyer, and then he was in
leather jeans and a pierced nose with a young girlfriend. We see it happen all the time, but it's not funny in an instantly recognisable way.
I've got a new character that I want to do, and I'm afraid she'd only
be recognisable in upper-class and media circles. She's the Matron
Wife: you see very public school, effete men who to all intents and
purposes are gay, but they're married to jolly-hockey-sticks, often
large, matron types. You think: You're a poof, and you've married
your mum. I've been thinking about her for ages now.

JMcG: **What's the thing you find most difficult?**
ARABELLA WEIR: Writing a book. Oh, writing, writing's so hard.
Writing on my own, writing a book, that is hard work. I know a lot
of writers and had a lot of writers in my upbringing, 'proper' writers
like John Lahr and Clancy Sigal, and my mother was an English
teacher and she's written a lot. People had said to me: 'If you can
write like you speak, you'll make your fortune.' But what I didn't
think was ever going to happen – well, how could I have anticipated
this? – was that the performing and the writing would happen at the
same time. I did that book and it was, it *is* being, very successful and
then I did a proposal for a second book, but in my fantasy I'd have
all the time in the world to do that. And that went to auction and I
got a fortune to write that and that's a comic novel, too, but much
more— in my fantasy, it's a kind of Roddy Doyle. I remember
thinking my first book was very, very hard work. But that just seems
like a day at the beach next to this next one. And so I haven't started
writing it yet and I have no idea how I'm going to be able to . . . I am
getting a nanny: the advance made it possible to hire someone, the

most expensive kind of child-care, which is someone coming to the house and only looking after your kid and I hope that I'll be able to write in the morning until Isabella needs a feed at lunchtime. So I'll write for three hours in the morning and carry on for three or four hours in the afternoon and at weekends as well. Don't know how I'm going to do anything else.

JMcG: **Would that be the same as a pre-baby working stint?**
ARABELLA WEIR: A pre-baby working stint was 9.30 to *The World at One* because I'd think: Great, I can go down and listen to other people. If I was really spoiling myself I'd listen to *The Archers*, but most of the time I'd wait until the Sunday. Then I'd come back up at twenty to two and work until about five, six, seven, but if I was on a roll I'd keep working later. With the first book I had this rule that whatever happened I had to write a thousand words a day, not including weekends, but if I missed a day because I had a meeting or whatever, then I'd have to write two thousand the next or make it up at the weekend.

A friend gave me a piece of advice: 'Write everything that's in your head, don't edit yourself. Worry about that later. Don't get halfway through a schtick and then go: "Why would anybody care what she's doing at Sainsbury's?" Just get everything out.' Which I can't do with the second book because it needs to be more structured – so now I'm just panicking about the second book.

DB: **So you went through the first book just in one draft and then you went back over it?**
ARABELLA WEIR: I'd write down everything I was going to write in the day, and then I'd go back over it the next morning, so I was editing as I went. When I presented it to the publishers they didn't ask for rewrites, they asked for more: they said they wanted to hear more about one bit and they wanted stuff fleshed out. Someone said: 'How does it feel to be successful now?' and I said: 'Listen, it doesn't feel like anything. I feel like I've been at the wretched party for years, standing in the corner, and everyone's going: "Oh, not her!" All of a sudden the boys are queuing up, going: "Can you dance with me?" And I'm going: "Why didn't you want to dance with me fifteen years ago? I've been here all the time." They're going: "Yeah, but that was then; now you're hot." I'm the same person that I've always been. Obviously I'm more experienced now, but I do feel like I've been standing in the corner for eighteen years going: "What about me?" and people going: "No, thanks." Then all of a sudden they're going: "You! You!" '

Caroline Aherne

People just saying funny things

Caroline Aherne is one of the young writers and performers who leaped suddenly out of Manchester in the Nineties and somehow hit on the chat show as both haven and target: Steve Coogan as Alan Partridge and Caroline as Mrs Merton. Her new show, *The Royle Family*, is about a Manchester family, but the name suggests that this will not be the glamorous, triumphalist Manchester strutting the world stage from a base at Old Trafford; instead we are likely to be relegated to the wry, often despondent view of the downtrodden supporters of United's poor relations, Manchester City – managed by Joe Royle. Caroline was rather flustered after climbing the four flights of stairs to David's central London flat carrying handfuls of bags from a morning's shopping for her mother's birthday.

CAROLINE AHERNE: I write with two boys, Henry Normal and Craig Cash; Henry Normal also writes for Steve Coogan, and some other people as well. We sit in an office, the three of us, and basically we think what makes us laugh, and then we see if all three of us think it's funny. Sometimes we vote on things and if two people think it's funny, then it's OK. Well, we're always voting on everything. The first time we've written dialogue is for the comedy dramas that we've just filmed for BBC 2, called *The Royle Family*. Ricky Tomlinson, Scouse actor, he played my dad, and it's about a working-class family. All the action takes place in their living-room . . . They get a phone bill in the first episode and that's as much action as is in it. We wanted to see if we could write something where the humour just comes from characters and not events happening. So nothing much happens; it's about a family watching telly, basically.

DB: **Is his name really Henry Normal?**

CAROLINE AHERNE: No, he changed it. He's called Peter Carroll really – he changed it when he was younger. I think he regrets it now. We get there about eleven o'clock and me and Craig would just mess about, but Henry says: 'Come on, we've got to work.' He's always the one who does that, and he also types everything, and then Craig sits there and doodles on a pad, and I pull this drawer thing out and prop my legs on the drawer, and we have to do that every morning, that's the way we do it. Then we sit there and think of what to say at the intro, and then think of sorts of questions to ask. And then I might want to make phone calls to people and Henry says no, and I say: 'Oh, please, Henry,' and he says, 'OK,' and then Craig's allowed to make a phone call, but Henry rules us.

Before we had Henry, me and Craig never used to do anything. We just used to sometimes have some pizza, because he used to say, 'I can't write without pizza,' and then he'd have to have some red wine – he'd say, 'I can't write without red wine' – and then it would be too late for him to write, he couldn't think any more. With Henry it's great because he's like a teacher: he makes us work. We actually go into an office every day and we work from eleven until half four or, if we're feeling particularly creative, until five.

I'm probably the best at, like, with *The Royle Family* I thought up the idea and what would happen, then Craig's very good on gags and dialogue, and Henry's very good at saying: 'You've used that word four times.' So the three of us together, it's the perfect team.

The Royle Family is set in Manchester and you just see a half-hour in this family's life – no other scenes, no time-lapsing. The first episode the dad gets a phone bill, and there's a number in it, somebody's rung Aberdeen, and he goes on and on about who's rung Aberdeen. And I look through the catalogue with my friend from next door, and – it's very childish – I say: 'Close your eyes,' and she gives me a finger, and then I put it on the men's dickies, and when she opens her eyes they're on the men's dickies in the catalogue. The telly's on the whole time in all six episodes and the dad comments on it all the time. Like, you can hear Chris Evans's voice and Dad goes: 'Look at him on again. He's all about like shit in a field, him.' I say: 'Oh, but he's a millionaire,' and he goes: 'Don't care if he's a millionaire, he's still got ginger bollocks.' And there's a pause and the mum goes: 'Oh, that reminds me: there's some tangerines in me fridge.' I love it when comedy comes out of people just saying funny things, rather than things happening. So that's what we've done, which is quite different, and there's no laughter track and we did it on film. It's sometimes like watching documentary – there's that sort of edge to it.

JMcG: How did the BBC stand up to you wanting to do it without an audience?
CAROLINE AHERNE: They rowed and rowed and rowed, then I cried. When I'd done two series of *Mrs Merton* they said: 'We'll tie you into a deal to do another two series and two Christmas specials and any other projects you want to do.' So I said: 'I want to do this thing about a family in Manchester.' So they said OK. But then they wanted it with audience laughter, and they wanted it to be filmed in front of a studio audience. In the end I was very childish, and I said, 'I'm not doing it, then,' like that, very childishly, and I *think* I cried. I'm so glad I stuck to my guns there, because it would completely ruin it: it's just not the kind of thing you need. I am always put off hearing canned laughter; people should be able to laugh where they want.

DB: Presumably you watch other shows for comparison and the one that's running now very strongly without a laugh-track is *The Larry Sanders Show*.
CAROLINE AHERNE: Oh, I love that. But it's not that kind of a feel. Because you're just in one room all the time, and they smoke all the time.

JMcG: How about working on film?
CAROLINE AHERNE: We had a brilliant director, Mark Mylod from *The Fast Show*, but we were changing stuff all the time. You see, me and Craig play boyfriend and girlfriend, and both wrote it and Henry. So we were thinking of better lines all the time and the poor actors were getting rewrites every five seconds, but it worked for the best. When we had the meetings with people at the BBC they would go: 'But there's no plot . . . there's really no plot. Couldn't they go to the pub or something like that?' But people don't: I don't think you need to have stuff happening. I hope I haven't built this up too much for when you watch it, and you say: 'Oh, it's a pile of shite.' But it *is* very different.

DB: What's your source: is it your family, or the folks next door or . . . ?
CAROLINE AHERNE: It's the three of us that wrote it – it's all our families. We've just strung together little things, or little things people have said that made us laugh, or characters . . . we've strung that together, rather than going: 'This is the beginning, middle and end.' People write best when they write what they know.

DB: **What part of Manchester are they in?**
CAROLINE AHERNE: We don't say, but it was set in Wythenshawe, where I'm from in south Manchester, in a big council estate. We filmed them all in Manchester – in a studio. It looks brilliant, though: it looks completely like a front room and a kitchen and everything.

DB: **Were the BBC receptive to the idea of a distinctively provincially-based comedy?**
CAROLINE AHERNE: I don't think that ever bothered them that it was so Northern: I mean, it really *is* Northern: I think there's a different way of living up there. There's not been a working-class sitcom for ages.

DB: **Do you think there's a source of comedy in the North?**
CAROLINE AHERNE: Yeah, I do, especially in Manchester, where everybody takes the piss out of each other, which I don't think London people do. It's a sort of dry sense of humour that's special in the North-West. In Manchester, it's a real thing amongst people of my age to take the mickey.

DB: **Will you go on with *The Royle Family*?**
CAROLINE AHERNE: They've already commissioned another one.

JMcG: **And would you like to write more?**
CAROLINE AHERNE: We're going to do a film next year. A comedy film. I play a hairdresser who's learning to drive, and she's a mobile hairdresser. Well, she's not, but she wants to go mobile. I've lost the plot! She wants to go mobile but she keeps failing her test. Me, Craig and Henry are writing it. I don't think we could work with anyone else now, because we don't mind if one of us tells another of us it's complete rubbish. Loads of the time you have to talk rubbish before something brilliant will come out, and we know each other so well that we can do it without feeling embarrassed or anything.

DB: **What brought you together?**
CAROLINE AHERNE: Me and Craig worked together on a radio station: I was on from two in the morning till seven in the morning and Craig was on in the day. We both got sacked on the same day, so I said: 'Oh, shall we write comedy?' and, because he was a painter and decorator before he went on the radio, he said: 'Yeah, but in case it don't work out, I'll keep me brush in turps!' I knew Henry because he was a stand-up and the Manchester comedy circuit was tiny. There was only me, Steve Coogan, John Thomson, Henry and

another lad called Bob. I started working on a regional programme, just doing Mrs Merton as an agony aunt in between, then they offered me a pilot. They said: 'What would you do if you had a half-hour?' I said: 'I'd do a Mrs Merton chat show.' Then we got Henry in because he had a computer, and we didn't. He was brilliant, and we did the pilot, and it was about a year later before the BBC said they would take it.

Now I've just moved up to London from Manchester. Craig still lives in Manchester – he comes up to London – and Henry lives in Brighton, so we all meet together. We wrote ads and things as well, and my characters in *The Fast Show,* I write them with Craig and Henry.

DB: **When you are writing for your *Fast Show* characters, do you meet the other writers and performers?**
CAROLINE AHERNE: Well, I am a bit different from the others in *The Fast Show*: I've been able to do only a few days with them, because it's always coincided with *Mrs Merton* or, this last time, *The Royle Family.* So we think up some things and ring up Charlie's house and if Paul answers he always laughs, but Charlie goes, 'No' – like that. So we always hope it's Paul that answers, and then for ages they ask us to write it down, and I say: 'Oh, it's in my head.' Anyway, we fax it to them. I usually do about three days on it and they do all my bits then. I don't do the studios because I hate performing in front of a live audience, so I just make all my characters somewhere on location. I get nervous performing in front of people. I'd rather do everything in a little room on my own.

DB: **But *Mrs Merton* is very much involved in the audience . . .**
CAROLINE AHERNE: Well, they're near enough the same audience every week – just the odd people who've come . . . We just started off asking our friends, and our friends' mums, and my doctor's receptionists and my hairdressers and that sort of a thing. The first few shows they put their coats on before it had finished! You could just see them behind me, getting their umbrellas and going! We had to say: 'Can you stop and take your coats off again?'

My mum's there, and my aunties and my best friend, and her mum and her two neighbours. But it is lovely that I know them all by name.

DB: **And what form do the *Mrs Merton* scripts take?**
CAROLINE AHERNE: We think of things that are funny to ask, but really the best questions always come off the top of your head. It's

about fifty per cent ad-lib and fifty per cent stuff we've written and made us laugh in the office. But the two of them are much ruder than me, and I have to stop them, because they get very, very rude. And you couldn't write things they think up, some of the things.

Horace is one of them I love to go to because he's just very funny, and then Ann, I always count on. I just go to the ones I know will always talk. But when I say: 'Any questions?' they all put their hands up. They're absolutely brilliant, they're really, really funny.

JMcG: **The appearance of Bernard Manning was amazing – he came on to open-minded applause, and he went off to hisses.**
CAROLINE AHERNE: I think people had thought: Oh, he doesn't really mean it; he's not really a racist. Richard Wilson was brilliant with him. I was so trying not to lose my temper with him because I knew if I lost my temper he'd have won. You could hear a pin drop in the audience. Usually they're eating, passing sweets round and everything, but they weren't that night. We'd thought up stuff to say to him, but I couldn't use any of it. One of the questions was going to be: 'So, have you got any advice for any young up-and-coming fat racist comedians?' But that would have gone over the heads of the audience, and they'd be thinking: Oh, look at her, wanting advice for young up-and-coming . . . ! There were so many agendas. The young part of the audience were shouting awful things to him, and there were the old biddies who had sort of always liked him but thought they shouldn't. The whole night was bizarre, really bizarre . . .

DB: **Everybody's ready for this, presumably? Richard Wilson is ready for Bernard – he knows what Bernard's like?**
CAROLINE AHERNE: Usually the guests don't know who's on with them, but we thought in this case we'd better ring Richard up, and there was no other date he could do. So in the end he said: 'Fine, but I'd rather not be sitting on the couch with him,' but anyway he did, and . . .

DB: **It looks like a piece of deliberate casting, knowing that Richard's a Labour Party supporter . . .**
CAROLINE AHERNE: It really wasn't. We're not that clever. We have such a struggle to get guests that whenever they can do it, we go, Yeah! It wasn't deliberate at all. But we couldn't have had a better guest with Bernard. Oh, yeah, we've had terrible trouble getting people on.

DB: **Do guests think the show's a trap of some kind?**

CAROLINE AHERNE: But it wasn't ever meant to be like that. People took it that way. We just wanted a warm, friendly show, with me dressed up as an old woman because you can ask much cheekier questions. I always hate it when they call it a spoof chat show: the guests don't know the questions, nothing's rehearsed, so it's not spoof.

JMcG: **When you put the stuff on, I mean, are you Mrs Merton?**
CAROLINE AHERNE: I'm not like that. I forget sometimes, and you can tell, I always do my own laugh. No, I only do Mrs Merton's voice as soon as the camera starts.

JMcG: **And you don't like having an audience.**
CAROLINE AHERNE: Oh, I hate it. I'd be quite happy if the shows never went out, if it was only me who watched them! I would, honest to God! If only me and me mum watched them! I don't mind if no one ever saw it . . .

DB: **Was the character written for the show or had you used her before?**
CAROLINE AHERNE: No, I already had it. I did her as an agony aunt on the radio, and I used to make up letters . . . I had loads of little characters. I used to do a nun, and I did a Country and Western singer.

DB: **Didn't you get used to performing in front of audiences when you worked as a stand-up comic?**
CAROLINE AHERNE: Oh, no, I've never liked it. I don't think I ever stayed on a full thirty minutes. I'd come off and say: 'How long was that?' 'Eleven minutes.' I won a competition the first time I did it, so I got a load of gigs from it – that was with the nun. But I never enjoyed it.

JMcG: **Has a Catholic background affected you in any way?**
CAROLINE AHERNE: I think it always affects everybody because you're just riddled with guilt. My two best friends went to a convent with me and we laugh more at dirty, rude things than anybody. All three of us are really good girls, but we've all got filthy mouths on us; we're always saying things, and really killing ourselves laughing. I suppose because we were brought up where it was so naughty to say rude things we just think it's dead funny to say them, even at our age.

JMcG: **Did you make them laugh in class?**
CAROLINE AHERNE: I could always make my mum laugh, by doing impressions of my aunties and things, and at one time she had a hysterectomy and I went to see her in the hospital, and then she used to love me to do an impression of her when she'd had the hysterectomy.

JMcG: **Why? Because she wasn't supposed to laugh because she'd had an operation?**
CAROLINE AHERNE: Yeah, that was what it was. Then I did drama at Poly, so I . . . I did want to go to . . . I did definitely want to do some sort of drama, not necessarily comedy. I think I just wanted to be an actress, but I didn't . . .

DB: **Didn't like audiences!**
CAROLINE AHERNE: Yeah.

John Morton

Less is more

The show that crept up on everyone who heard it on Radio 4 is *People Like Us*. Denis Norden and Barry Cryer were among those caught off guard by it, thinking that they were listening to a radio feature instead of a comedy. The insidious scripts were written by John Morton, who may well be the most courageous of all the writers we talked to. He told us his story at the Savile Club on his way between meetings about transferring *People Like Us* to television and work on *Kiss Me Kate,* a BBC sitcom co-written by Chris Langham, star of *People Like Us*. We complimented him on the way *People Like Us* had taken us by surprise.

JOHN MORTON: That's something you can do on radio. People are nearly always doing something else – driving, washing up – so you can sneak quite a lot of absurd stuff past them, and it only needs one of those things to finally register and you get that kind of: 'What? Did I really hear that?'

Radio's such a simple medium. I was amazed on the first recording day. I thought I'd be put in a box somewhere and fed sandwiches, but actually we did some read-throughs and then a rehearsal on tape and then the producer asked, 'What do you think?' I was able to talk to actors I'd only ever seen on the screen and I thought: This is fantastic. Radio's friendly in the sense that actors don't have to learn lines, and they're having a reasonably pleasant day, meeting people they've not seen for a while, nobody's fantastically egotistical – there's a real sense of good will. I've been amazed how I've been consulted on not just casting, but also rhythm of the scene, that kind of stuff. Of course on television, as I'm now beginning to realise, that's gone. The higher the stakes, the more marginalised you get as the writer.

The stuff I write, it's not topical, it's not fashionable, and it's not target-driven at all. I'm not out to have anybody in my sights. A lot of stuff, on television particularly, not so much in radio, I can see looked fantastic in proposal form, because the joke is the idea. You know, 'Let's deconstruct a sitcom and have a very large person and a very small person sharing a flat.' The idea is funnier than the working out of the idea. And you think: That's a really neat idea, and I can see why it was commissioned, but I've now got to sit through six half-hours of it. I saw that happening and I thought: I wonder whether I'll ever get in because I can't write that stuff.

JMcG: **Where did you start and how did you break in?**
JOHN MORTON: I was a teacher – English, the usual thing – in a sixth-form college in Winchester. It sounds crazy: I just stopped teaching and sold my house and started writing. People would say, 'God, that's really brave,' and they'd be thinking, That's really, my God, you are mad, completely. They'd say, 'So, are you working on a commission?' and I'd say, 'No, none.' And they'd go quieter and quieter. I'm not normally very confident generally, and I'm not very good at that many things: I'm a safe pair of hands in lots of areas, but only good enough to know what it would be like to be really good. But in scriptwriting in general, but certainly comedy, I'd often go to the theatre or listen to something on the radio and it would almost be like being dug in the ribs – I understood how it worked. Sometimes I'd get a feeling that they didn't do that quite right, that a line could have been tweaked. If I watch, say, professional crick-eters, I get the opposite feeling, which is: My God, I could never do that. What must it be like to do that?

DB: **You hadn't written anything?**
JOHN MORTON: No, but I also knew that I'd have to write an awful lot of stuff to chuck at the wall before anything would stick at all. It was almost wilfully naïve. If I'd thought about it – it was a bit like looking down when you're trying to climb up something – I would have stopped. Thank God for radio, because nobody else is going to risk hundreds of thousands of pounds on an unknown, but on radio they can throw a little bit of money at something and if it doesn't work, well, it doesn't work. Or if it does one pilot and nothing much happens, then they've wasted only a little bit of money. I don't think I'd ever have got going if it weren't for radio, so I feel very grateful for that.

JMcG: **How do you work with a director? Do you stand behind**

him the whole time?

JOHN MORTON: I'm very lucky, again, because in radio the producer is terribly collaborative. A lot of radio producers are fantastically busy anyway – they're juggling lots of projects – and they're
actually quite pleased if someone says: 'What about doing it this
way?' Also Chris Langham, who plays the main character, is very
collaborative, full of ideas, and his sense of timing is very similar to
mine. What tends to happen is that in the read-through everybody's
giving miles too much. At first it panicked me because the thing that
kills most comedy for me is that it's too obvious. I already know that
I am interested in directing, in that process of translating from page
to performance, because most actors in my tiny experience are quite
relieved when you say to them: 'That performance you just did in
the read-through was very funny and it's good that you can do that
stuff, like handstands and things, but . . . try not doing it.' Also they
tune in because Chris's timing is so Rolls-Royce, so less-is-more and
so understated, that eventually everybody comes down to a certain
level, and then the momentum starts to gather.

But it's a real bugbear of mine, a real bee in my bonnet, that most
of what I see in the TV comedy arena is overplayed and badly
directed. Just as a punter, not as any kind of person inside, I just see
stuff on in the sitcom slot and I think: Why didn't someone stop
them doing that? With the demarcation of jobs in the industry, there
doesn't seem to be anybody in television whose job it is to direct
performance. Because it's such a complex thing, compared with
radio; a director's got so much to think about.

We filmed a television pilot of the radio thing which is now going
to telly. You'd watch a scene being set up all morning and many specific and technical questions solved. Then finally we'd do a take and
the director would say: 'Yeah, that's it. We've finally got it right.'
But actually we hadn't got it *at all* right. It was technically perfect,
but nobody, because the director was so busy, there was no person
whose job it was. I found it very stressful because the classic cliché
is the writer who's a nightmare on the set, and won't go away. But
then I thought: Well, actually, I do care about this. So I had to kind
of sidle into a room saying, 'Yes, what about . . . ?' But again, so far
so good. People were very, very collaborative.

JMCG: **The longer you're in the business, the more you realise
that the actors save you. If you can get through to them and get
everybody away, they'll do it.**

JOHN MORTON: Chris Langham and I are just writing a sitcom
now for BBC 1 and I keep seeing new sitcoms coming out, trailed

and hyped, and I keep thinking: God, it didn't make me laugh. Is this what happens? Whatever you put in this end of the machine, does it always come out that way at the other end?

JMcG: **Are you doing it with an audience?**
JOHN MORTON: Yes, because the reason I've particularly enjoyed certain shows is partly to do with the fact there's a vicarious you there, people laughing in your stead, especially if you're watching on television just two of you or one of you. I enjoy the relationship between a studio audience and actors. And it also allows them to time jokes perfectly. One thing I never understand is why talented people make film comedies and then play the tape to an audience and then tape the laughter. It always goes wrong, because they're crashing the laughter all the time, and the laughter's crashing the timing.

I'm sure that the studio audience leads the wider audience because you can do lots of things when you've got an audience there. You can do jokes which they don't see coming, but you also get jokes where the pleasure is that they do see it coming, and an audience will set off before the line comes.

JMcG: **Is there a difference between British and American comedy?**
JOHN MORTON: The best of American humour is fantastic. But when you say 'the best of American humour' you're talking about Jewish humour, which is fantastically economical. I love the cadence and rhythm of Jewish comedy. I just wonder whether English English will do that. At the moment, writing this sitcom, I think: Can you do this with English English? You can't. There's no real English equivalent of 'I wish' which is two words: in English English you'd have to write about two sentences to get that across. Americans at their best seem to know how to underplay; they'll allow the audience to do more work.

As a punter, one of the things I like best is where you get a joke that's coming, or a routine that's coming, and they allow you to supply one of the beats in the comic argument. Rather than going, 'Look, here's a joke coming . . . here it comes . . . are you sure you're ready for this joke? Here it is . . . did you notice it?' which is like the British sitcom, I love it when you're given the credit of being able to share the joke. So I like it when Chris Langham, in *People Like Us* on radio, does this thing where he's talking, and he just kind of peters out and goes, 'What?' And nobody's said anything, but you allow the audience right in, and they're there in the kind of comic experience: 'Well, thank you. Thank you for letting me, for giving us the credit of being able to, do that bit of work,' and then of course you feel more attached to the show and the characters and the experience.

With prime-time shows on in England, there's a kind of paranoia that an audience won't get a joke. When we were recording *People Like Us*, someone was saying: 'I'm not sure. That line is so less-is-more that you may have to . . .' and I remember saying, 'It doesn't matter if they don't get that.' It would be nice to feel that you had enough jokes there that if one or two go past without people quite getting on board, well, that's OK.

JMcG: **How do you do it? Is it longhand or a word processor?**

JOHN MORTON: A processor. How on earth did people write scripts in the *Goon Show* days? Now, if you have an idea for moving something around when you're doing a rewrite, you do it in ten minutes, then look at it the other way again, and then you make a decision. Even if you want to change a character's name at the last minute for some silly reason, you can just do it, there and then, with a computer.

DB: **You've been working on your own, but now you're collaborating with Chris Langham. What are the differences?**

JOHN MORTON: I look forward to having a day in his company, but the best thing about it is that you don't get that blank screen or blank page. You don't get lonely and self-obsessed. It's an unhealthy thing to do, to sit on your own in a room for, whatever it is, five or six hours a day, thinking about a world you created. When I first started this, I thought I'd have lots of energy. I thought, compared with teaching, where you just have too much to do and you're run ragged by the end of the day, I thought, well, now I'm doing what I want, in my own time, so I'm going to have lots of excess energy. And I felt, of course, absolutely shattered. At the end of the first year I got shingles! The doctor said: 'That's quite unusual in a guy your age. Are you under a lot of stress? Are you working very hard?' and I said: 'No, I've never been under less stress.' It was a lesson, because there's a kind of energy which I didn't realise you used at all. You try explaining what you did today: 'I went to an office with another guy and we talked for five or six hours, then we had some coffee, and that was it.' I sometimes feel absolutely creased, but more so when I'm writing on my own.

DB: **Apart from fatigue, do you find any aspect of the work particularly difficult?**

JOHN MORTON: I find plotting the hardest, because I'm better at dialogue. If somebody said to me, 'Here's a situation: two people in a room. One wants this out of it; one wants that. OK, write the dialogue,' I wouldn't feel threatened by that. But actually the four or five or six weeks that you spend prior to that are absolutely essential, I now realise. Because if it's not set up correctly, and doesn't work as a story, if the audience doesn't want to know what happens next, there's no point in committing yourself to dialogue. I'm trying to learn not to rush into the dialogue. If you've got some ability, you ought to be able to make something funny. But it's the bit before that is really important, and that's the bit I find I have to make myself do.

I mentioned my bees in my bonnet, and they're mainly to do with less-is-more – that usually the more work you let the audience do, the funnier it is. So pratfalls are almost always funnier the other side of the door. In terms of television comedy and radio comedy, I like to see more jokes per minute. I'd like to think that people had packed the thing with jokes. I don't mean just obvious gags. But because of the way that adverts work in America, they used to have that thirty-second bit at the start of *Cheers* that was nothing to do with that week's plot, and there were often more, better-crafted jokes in that thirty seconds than in some entire British sitcoms.

Chris Evans, Danny Baker and Will Macdonald

The currency of seduction

The maelstrom which is *TFI Friday* was reproduced in miniature in the Ginger Television Productions office in central London. In Will Macdonald's room we sat as Danny Baker, unable to sit still, paced up and down, occasionally beating out the intro to the *EastEnders* title music on an electronic drum kit. When the gales of Baker blew themselves out for a few moments, Chris Evans took over with statements equally forceful but less wide-ranging. Will Macdonald waited judiciously for a break to place his comments.

Danny Baker, born in Deptford, south London, was a rock journalist before going into television, writing and appearing in such shows as *Win, Lose or Draw* and *Pets Win Prizes*. Chris Evans began his career sorting mail at a Manchester commercial radio station. He wrote scripts for Jonathan Ross before becoming a national figure on Channel 4's *The Big Breakfast*, followed by *Don't Forget Your Toothbrush*. Will Macdonald was educated at Eton and Brasenose College, Oxford. We left reeling, overwhelmed by such enthusiasm and energy.

JMcG: **How do you write it down?**
CHRIS EVANS: OK, this is how we put it down. Danny and I are very similar, I would say – wouldn't you, Danny? – in putting it down.

DANNY BAKER: In trying not to overcomplicate the process, let's say.

CHRIS EVANS: This is a radio show.

JMcG: **What, just a scrap of paper?**

CHRIS EVANS: That's it, yeah. The radio show has titles – memory pegs – that help us remember certain subjects when we're writing. *TFI Friday*, obviously, because it's telly, it's got to be planned out. We'll bring this list in and I'll give it to Danny. Danny'll have a similar list to this. Then Danny'll go and write the script, which is usually about eight pages long. Will, here, will get that script with Stephen John, the producer, and put it into a 75-page script which has got all the camera directions. But that's how it starts, and it's immediate.

DANNY BAKER: The only person I've ever found who it works for is Chris. It's kind of refreshing, it's almost the fear that drives you – I always say you can only write if there's a bike outside. For a long time I was intimidated by what I saw as the professional, laser-printed, way of doing it. But that meant nothing, because it wasn't actually very good . . . Chris doesn't find words that important. Chris is actions. Chris is big pictures, big strokes of the pen . . .

CHRIS EVANS: Pictures in my head . . .

DANNY BAKER: I was doing Angus Deayton's thing at the same time. That is every dot; that is analysed. That is a way of working that's suffocating for me, although I can do it, I like it. But *this* is the way I work: 'Whooosh!' – that's it, leave it alone, walk away from it. Even rehearsal is . . .

CHRIS EVANS: He rehearses as little as we need to . . .

DANNY BAKER: . . . it's a suffocating process.

CHRIS EVANS: . . . so that we can still enjoy the jokes.

JMcG: **And how do you feel in the middle of all this?**

WILL MACDONALD: Well, I stop them taking their clothes off and fighting naked in front of the fire, that's where I stop them! The interesting thing in what Danny was just saying is that television is quite restrictive, because these two of course do radio . . .

DANNY BAKER: And that is the underlying thing: we work as close to radio, which is where we both work best, as possible. And in fact some weeks we have said in rehearsal: 'Come on, everyone, it's radio.' Even down to the point, I don't know if it's subconscious or whatever, where the running joke we've got at the moment is drummers, playing under blankets, behind screens. That's radio.

CHRIS EVANS: The old cliché: the television we do is radio with pictures.

WILL MACDONALD: The unfortunate fact is that in radio you have a microphone and you have your thoughts and you can do it. Whereas in television, you have four days, you've got to tell the cameraman, the lighting man . . .

DANNY BAKER: I had been entirely intimidated by the television process: you have to rehearse it; it has to be done this way; you must stop the tape if something goes wrong, because the option of stopping tape is there. I never had half of the courage Chris has when he actually does the presenting. When we started this, we said: 'We don't stop. If there's a mistake, we'll get round it.' And we don't stop. A couple of times when it's been literally like the National Grid's gone down, that's the only thing that has ever stopped it. And all of this may seem just nuts and bolts, but the jokes we do on the show are 'found' humour. It is a soufflé: if you examine it, it'll fall down. We're saying: If you don't like that bit of the show, here's something else. A lot of the criticism that I've read about the programme is: 'They don't seem to take a lot of time,' as if we should be creating a new comedy, instead of just doing a joke for a joke's sake.

I do believe that – well, here we go. I knew we'd get round to this – because of the overwhelming, out-of-all-proportion, public-school influence on comedy, the working-class contribution to comedy has been lost. It's been lost in an insidious way but in a very real way, and it's almost a comedy pogrom.

It took this show to really open my eyes to it. People think it's a defence mechanism, or that it's what you put failure down to, saying: 'Oh, they're just a clique.' But they don't realise it really is like that and there is a total distrust of what working-class people find funny. The whole writer-performer thing is a bit of a curse; it's like Pandora's box. There's no reason why Ben Elton shouldn't do his own stuff, but Galton and Simpson didn't want to be Steptoe and Son; Johnny Speight wasn't Alf Garnett.

We call the shots, and if we find it funny we don't care about the chattering classes, or the whispering network, or the *Daily Mail* or the *Evening Standard* that want to say: 'Well, where do you fit in?

Oh, he was at Charterhouse . . . Oh, I know him.' We don't fit into that, we don't socialise with it, I'm a bleeding prat and we're almost militant about it, and that is why . . .

CHRIS EVANS: What do you mean, *almost*?

DANNY BAKER: The middle-class influence – I'm not talking from the point of view of hanging them from the lamp-posts – is now overwhelming: there is no other way. John Sullivan, who is – it's interesting – the best and the most productive, seems to be the last writer above it. But otherwise it's in their interests to make it a science. I'm not afeared of a middle-class, public-school, university-graduate influence, but the fact is it has dumbed television down, because as we know most of the people who spin out of these places are dizzy Roedean girls or thick grammar-school boys. And that's all there is to it: they are achieving those positions now without any worth.

WILL MACDONALD: That's not an attack on me, it's an attack on the system. I went to the same college as Michael Palin, although to be mentioned in the same sentence as him . . .

DANNY BAKER: I'm not talking about university, I'm talking about influence.

WILL MACDONALD: It's about influence and also about them feeding off each other, because that lot are always together, and public-school people and university people when they work together always feed off each other.

DANNY BAKER: We don't have anything to do with anyone else. We don't schmooze, we don't do drugs, we don't know the university system and we *do* go to pubs. Now, I've been doing telly twenty-two years, so it really isn't a chip on my shoulder, it's just a realisation after a long time of fucking around and wasting my time. I fucked around, I wasted my time, I never took anything seriously. I take this more seriously than any other show and yet it's less hassle than any other show. Finally you arrive in here, and you think: We can do this. For the first time, I know what you mean, and you know what we mean. It's that coming together.

CHRIS EVANS: Will is exactly the same. We are three so different characters. Danny and I have got more in common than me and

Will, for example, but Danny's a completely different animal from me. He's a book fiend, he's a film fiend, he's a knowledge fiend. I hate all that shit, right? I love the fact that Danny's got it and I learn so much off Danny, every week of my life, and I learn so much off Will, because he's got this unbelievable academic educated mind. And I'd like to think that we all learn something; it's a real stimulating atmosphere that we've got going. And we have to actually be careful when we see each other, because it's exhausting. I'm exhausted after I've been out with Danny, mentally and, usually, physically as well.

DANNY BAKER: The cynicism at meeting level and studio level towards comedy is almost like when comics get together. There's never a laugh, it's: 'What's that bit from? Where do I know that bit from? Oh, I know what that bit is.' Now, we don't do that.

The first record I ever knew was a 10-inch. *Max at the Met* – Max Miller at the Metropolitan, Edgware Road. I always had comedy albums, and I knew the words all the way through. Long before I knew *Sergeant Pepper*, I knew the 'Sunday Afternoon at Home' Hancock. I just absorbed it. And also I'm fucking proud of it! Only when I get to forty do I think: Jesus, I was reading Robert Benchley at *twelve*? It's no accident all these books are up there: I know them.

Consequently, when I arrive in media and people are writing jokes I'm clever enough to adapt the old jokes and present them as brand new. You can say that is getting away with something, or you can say that's how comedy has always been. You can go back as far as you want: Greek comedies, we're still dressing them up. When I came to telling and writing the stuff there was a cynicism towards it. I know loads of people who get the jokes, but they weren't 'clever' enough, they didn't pull the right levers for people who hadn't had the same background as me.

CHRIS EVANS: Danny is steeped in knowledge. There is not enough room in his body for what he knows.

DANNY BAKER: But isn't it interesting how you interpret it: *I* know it; *you* steal it. What's that about?

CHRIS EVANS: Because you put the work in to know it, and I didn't.

DANNY BAKER: It's not true.

CHRIS EVANS: Oh, it is completely true! You watch Sky Sports Live and after you've watched loads of football matches live I watch *Match of the Day* and *Match of the Day* is *you*! I get all the highlights! I do the same with Will! I get little bits of zoology. People think I know about zoology!

WILL MACDONALD: You are a song-thrush, because a song-thrush gets all its songs off other birds.

DANNY BAKER: Me and Chris met up, and we did think this stuff was funny. I believe there is a wonderful innocence about the *TFI* jokes – which are not allowed to breathe half the time because people think: They should be doing better. Yeah, we could put more time in it. We could hone it more, we could . . . but . . .

CHRIS EVANS: But the spontaneity and the energy are what wins, I think, and the naturalness of it. You'll never write a conversation as good as this one, ever. You'll never write a conversation as good as being in a pub. Nobody can write dialogue like dialogue writes itself. We try to re-create real life, which is very difficult. And you're starting from the third-place podium, and you're never going to get to the first place. So what we try and do is leave as much room there as possible, know where we're going, and, also, we don't write many punch lines. More funny things than jokes.

WILL MACDONALD: This is about expectation levels, as well, isn't it? You listen to Chris's radio show and that is, like he says, dialogue, that is conversation. You couldn't write that stuff. But as soon as you get to the television show, you take all of the dialogue that you've just said on the radio, but you then say: 'Well, actually, you can't do that,' and you go away and start analysing it . . .

CHRIS EVANS: You sanitise it; you want to cut down the risk because sometimes you have a dull conversation, but by cutting down the lows you cut down the potential for the highs.

DANNY BAKER: Here there's no constant, which is quite good. As we say, we'll have a meeting here on Tuesday. I usually write an eighty-per-cent-different show on the Wednesday sitting down, and then when I bring it on the Friday it'll again be re-invented by another fifty per cent when Chris sees it. So there are three versions we've come up with, and then the show goes on the air and it's yet more different.

CHRIS EVANS: We're not that bothered, because we know it's going to be all right anyway. It just will be all right. You know straight away when something's going to work. You just know.

DANNY BAKER: Television is all meetings, and you really don't need four days to get a show like ours together. You don't. It's the truth that dare not speak its name. One day. We could come in on a Friday and do it, we really could. Providing the physical things could be pulled.

CHRIS EVANS: That's why we said four-day production, because if we want a fork-lift truck they've got to go and get one. We come up with something like a toy and we just leave it there and say: 'That's it. Look at that.' Great questions are better than their answers. When you pose a great question, you don't really want to know the answer, because the answer's not going to be as good as the question, because it's probably a reasonable answer, which is dull. We want to be left with the funny thought . . .

DANNY BAKER: Why did Kamikaze pilots wear crash helmets?

CHRIS EVANS: Yeah, exactly.

DANNY BAKER: Somebody rang in and said, 'In fact it was for the radio.' I said: 'I don't want to know . . .'

CHRIS EVANS: I don't want to know the answer. I'm not interested in the answer.

DANNY BAKER: Exactly. All we try to do is get that soufflé up there and get it on the air before it all falls down. It really is just this hour of stuff that we don't think about one second after it's gone off the air and we trust nobody else does. Yeah, that was good, that was it, and there we go.

CHRIS EVANS: The nowness of now . . .

WILL MACDONALD: One of the most exciting things that happened was when half an hour, twenty minutes, before the show, Björk, who was going to do a ten-minute interview and a song, turned up, said: 'I'm in a bad mood. Don't want to be interviewed. I still want to do the song.' We said: 'Don't do it,' so we still had fifteen minutes of the show to fill . . .

CHRIS EVANS: We told her not to bother doing the song and sent her home . . .

WILL MACDONALD: It was genuinely exciting. Nobody was running around like people normally do in television, going: 'Oh, my God! We can't do this! We've got time to fill!' Everyone was going: 'This is brilliant. We've got fifteen minutes. Suddenly we've got this freedom that we don't normally have, to do things.'

CHRIS EVANS: There's no better time when you're doing your job than when you really start to earn your money. And you don't earn that between nine and five: you earn it from probably, one minute a week, at some point. And that was the bit we got paid for that week. I thought: Ooh, we're earning our money.
    The way we write the television show is different from the way we write the radio. We have to do the stuff that we don't like doing. Because we don't like the mechanics of putting it down. When you got the thought you had the fun in your head, and now you're going to put it on paper.

DANNY BAKER: You were asking earlier on: how do you get the thought down? I could do that. Chris can't. And I think his is a purer way of working. I actually can sit there at a screen and finish something. Whereas Chris is so impatient: 'I've got it now; that's in the bag. I'll come back to that.' And he won't. He's done stacks of stuff: 'I'm in the middle of this thing.' And I know he's not going to finish it, and *he* knows he's not going to finish it, but it's that capriciousness that started it in the first place.

CHRIS EVANS: I mean to finish it, but I know I can, and therefore I just won't, because I can't be arsed. I've done it. In my head, yeah.

DANNY BAKER: When we sit here and we've got to do *TFI Friday* we really will say, 'Let's just have a quick one,' and we really do shoot round the corner for a half. We are not, in the old-fashioned sense, professional like that. We will not sit here until the job is done. We will go out and trust something will turn up.

CHRIS EVANS: And it always does.

DANNY BAKER: We really want to do this show four times a week. *TFI Friday* should be a nightly show. It has that *Big Breakfast* feel: 'Look, don't lean on the jokes too much, they're just here, and here comes another one.' But the machinations of television and Chris's status see to it that it has to be this kind of show.

CHRIS EVANS: Recently Channel 4 said: 'We want you to come up with some new shows for us,' and I said: 'Well, to be honest, we're not a factory and we don't churn out cars that all look the same.' I said: 'You've got a thousand production companies in Britain: they can all do that for you. What we want to do is the next thing. Not the next show, the next *thing*.' I do think the future of telly is shows that are on five days a week. They're doing it in America, and their daily shows are better than our weekly shows. One reason they're better is because your expectation is lower, because it's a daily show. And the whole thing about Vic and Bob, for example. I love Vic and Bob. I think they're dead funny. And they'll work towards a new comedy series, a six-parter, and the expectation is so high, by the time it gets on the screen it's got no fucking chance, you know what I mean? Because your level of expectation is just too high.

If only you could get a TV show that people were willing to put up with for as long as they were willing to put up with a boring football match in the hope that in the last minute out of eighty-nine something might fucking happen . . . those European matches that get ten or eleven million viewers on ITV. Crap games, right? And you watch these things, and your girlfriend says, or your wife says: 'Is it good?' 'This is a crap game. This is just not good.' They must be thinking: Well, why are you fucking watching it? But it's the explosiveness of a goal as well.

DANNY BAKER: The people who just get on the mike in comedy clubs are the worst thing that's happened to comedy. 'Oh, it's easy. Anyone can do it.' No, they fucking can't. No, they can't. They really can't. The fact is that I should have been doing this twenty years ago instead of doing my own programmes. They should have said: 'You're one of the best writers around. We're going to put you with Chris. You go together.' But no, it had to be: you do your own material, he does his own material, I do . . . so consequently there will never be a—

CHRIS EVANS: Premier League of writers, you mean.

DANNY BAKER: Yeah, we'll never get there. In the States, of course, it's fairly respected and paid . . .

CHRIS EVANS: Because they know it works.

DANNY BAKER: Here nobody cares who writes jokes. People still say at *TFI*: 'Oh, what are you doing here?'

CHRIS EVANS: And they say that to me, occasionally, which is more—

DANNY BAKER: But that's it! Nobody cares . . . The preciousness of comedy, I find it fascinating. It's just behind the news department for being puffed up and a little too grand for itself. And, like I say, we do the longest run on television with *TFI Friday* and other people say: 'Oh, we're doing *six programmes* . . .'

JMcG: You've never written a sitcom?

DANNY BAKER: No, I'm going to and it will be extremely quick . . . The most complex script I've written, something like the *Comedy Awards*, I'll write in an hour and a half, from beginning to end, and there'll be some great jokes in there, but it has to be the right hour and a half. So it is the three weeks walking around, scratching your arse, thinking, I think I'll write the *Comedy Awards* in a minute, is probably part of that process. But the actual, physical sweat pours out from under my arms. I sit there – and I can have noise: I can do it in the middle of Oxford Street – and it will take an hour and a half. So a sitcom, when it happens, it'll be one of those things I can write . . .

I believe that British comedy is as strong as American comedy in totally different ways. Without exception I believe great British sitcoms have been grotesques, or class-based. I can't think of one that isn't. There just isn't one, because we don't like each other, class-wise. So you make an upper-class person or a working-class person a grotesque. They try these things like *Friends,* but they come across, still, like 'Anyone for tennis?' But if you put *Friends* with a cast from Surrey, or from Deptford, or from Edinburgh, it wouldn't be *Friends*; that's what people don't appreciate.

CHRIS EVANS: The most fun we have and the biggest laughs that we have are on the Tuesday in the meeting, right? After that, to be honest, it is downhill, because that is when you think of the joke. So what we try and do is get that moment on the air. So it's like a deconstruction kind of thing. So, under-written, everything is under-written.

DANNY BAKER: You've got to have pretty big boots on to change comedy. This century there's only been, like, ten . . . I do think all the good people, whether it's Ben Elton or whoever you want to mention . . . Stephen Fry . . . all the people know, 'Look, this stuff is like dynamite, and it's wet . . . That's wet dynamite, and we don't want to touch it. It's going to blow up on us.'

We always refer to the show as 'our little monkey show'. And we mean that we think it's really good, but we don't think it's come to change the world. The pure brief was to do something that's a laugh on Friday night. There's sniping: 'Oh: *TFI Friday*. Probably whatever Chris and Danny found funny in the pub on Thursday.' And I feel like saying: 'You're absolutely right. You know why? Because he's Chris Evans and I'm Danny Baker. We're not two blokes in the pub, going: "Haa, look at her over there!" No, you're talking about Chris Evans and Danny Baker. You're fucking straight it's what we find funny in the pub on Thursday. Slick, absolutely, yeah!'

DB: Does it ever happen that something does go wrong actually during the performance?
CHRIS EVANS: No, because nothing can . . . If something goes wrong it can only add to our show. It can never take away from it.

DANNY BAKER: Yeah, I think that's true. Well, God, we've had stuff that doesn't work before. That's all right. But so what?

CHRIS EVANS: We still think it's funny. I can't remember one thing out of two years that hasn't been funny, that hasn't worked.

DANNY BAKER: But there's loads of stuff that doesn't make it from second rehearsal. We say: 'Lose that.' Now, fortunately, we do have the clout and the budget to say 'Drop it', even though it's cost a lot of money.

DB: Do you learn from what you've done, as well? Do you watch the rerun?
DANNY BAKER: No. Never. Never, ever, ever.

CHRIS EVANS: I don't watch it.

DANNY BAKER: The only time ever I am overruled is by Chris and the only time he is overruled is by me.

CHRIS EVANS: Will's part of the whole equation.

DANNY BAKER: We are like this, and Will is not like this. That's why Will sits there.

CHRIS EVANS: Somebody's got to put all this down and it ain't going to be us two.

WILL MACDONALD: Yeah, I put it down, fuck it up, whatever you want.

DANNY BAKER: It must be real hard, because I wouldn't like to knock this kind of stuff that we have, this bombast that masks itself as being right all the time, but nevertheless have to pitch a corner. It would be murder!

CHRIS EVANS: Also, we cover for each other. If I'm having a bad day on a Friday (of which I've had a few), he ups the ante, and I do the same.

DANNY BAKER: That's exactly right, exactly right.

JMCG: **So you're equals?**
DANNY BAKER: Without a doubt. I've never known a relationship like it, working with anyone. Usually you sit there, and the script sits there, and you're out of the process. You're never, *ever* out of the process on this.

CHRIS EVANS: Come to the rehearsals . . . The first rehearsal's the best one, because if it goes well we don't do a dress rehearsal.

WILL MACDONALD: But then also, actually, during the show itself, we talk about rewriting on a Friday, but that rewriting happens in the second ad-break, after two parts of the show have already been done. If we find out we're three minutes overrunning and we have to basically rewrite a whole part, we do that in the ad-break before it goes out – and we're in the middle of a programme, so that process still goes on actually during the programme itself.

DB: **Real time, do you mean?**
WILL MACDONALD: Yeah, we do the show and record it, but it's 'as live'. Basically.

DANNY BAKER: One thing about this show more than any other programme around, it has very little romance about the craft of writing. I was a victim of it for a long time. I sat upstairs writing comedy; I tried it on my wife: 'When a writer looks out of the window, he's working . . .' Every writer tries that once, don't they? Oooh, you only try it once, because it doesn't work in real life. There is no romance about it because neither of us have any time . . . When someone says: 'I was in a writers' meeting,' a lot of people think: Oh, I'd love to be in that – a writer's meeting! Tossing ideas around. Here, there is no writers' meeting. There's a bit of shouting for forty-five minutes, and then we go away and make calls to each other. Writing is the wrong word for us – it's talking . . .

WILL MACDONALD: That's one of the first things I learned from Chris, because obviously, with the kind of upbringing I had, I was under a mountain of paper. So when I first sat down and came up with an idea for Chris, and he said, 'Come on, let's write,' I thought literally: pen, paper, typewriter, keyboard . . . But no, writing is about the germ of the idea.

DANNY BAKER: There is an arrogance that comes with working in comedy. It's puffed up; it's Masonic, almost . . .

CHRIS EVANS: But that's because it's the currency of seduction, isn't it, comedy?

DANNY BAKER: Yeah, yeah, there's all that side. Close-up magic, yeah.

CHRIS EVANS: It's the currency of seduction. If you can make people laugh, you can get women to bed, you can do business deals, you become popular. It is the best currency . . .

DANNY BAKER: My favourite newspaper headline: 'Laugh them into bed with Eddie Large' – that was it!

CHRIS EVANS: It's true, though, isn't it? It's true. If you can make people laugh, that is it, mate. The world is your fucking oyster.

DANNY BAKER: It is.